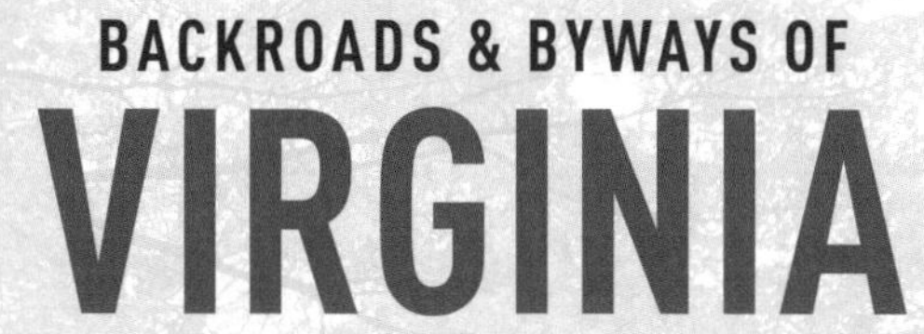

Drives, Day Trips & Weekend Excursions

THIRD EDITION

BILL LOHMANN

Countryman Press

An Imprint of W. W. Norton & Company
Independent Publishers Since 1923

Image page 158: iStock / lovingav

Printed in the United States of America

Manufacturing by Versa Press
Series book design by Chris Welch
Production manager: Devon Zahn

Countryman Press
www.countrymanpress.com

An imprint of W. W. Norton & Company, Inc.
500 Fifth Avenue, New York, NY 10110
www.wwnorton.com

978-1-68268-867-0

1 2 3 4 5 6 7 8 9 0

To my family

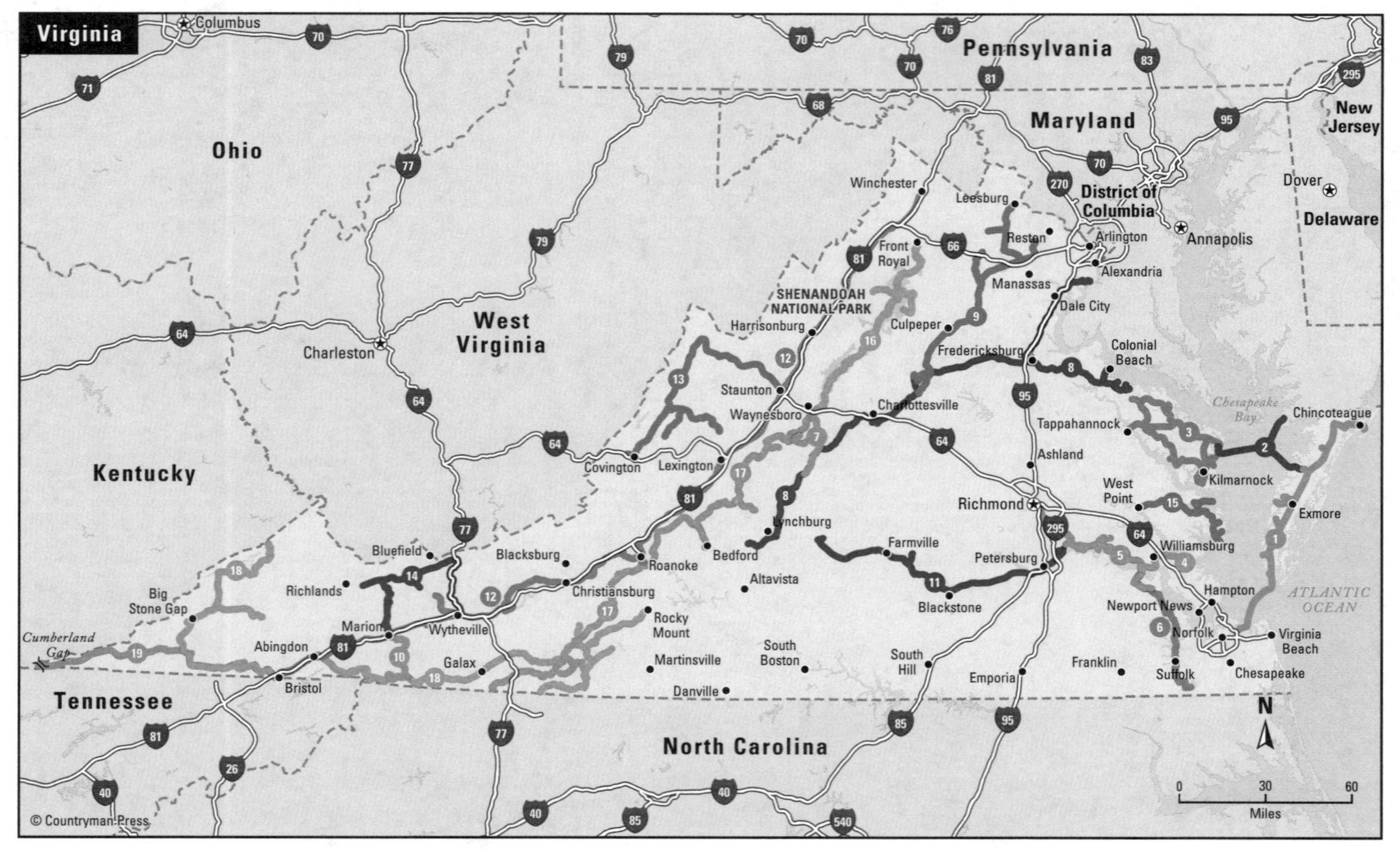
Virginia
Columbus
Pennsylvania
Maryland
New Jersey
Delaware
Ohio
West Virginia
Kentucky
Tennessee
North Carolina
District of Columbia
Dover
Annapolis
Winchester
Leesburg
Reston
Arlington
Alexandria
Front Royal
Manassas
Dale City
SHENANDOAH NATIONAL PARK
Harrisonburg
Culpeper
Fredericksburg
Colonial Beach
Charleston
Staunton
Waynesboro
Charlottesville
Chesapeake Bay
Chincoteague
Tappahannock
Ashland
Kilmarnock
Covington
Lexington
West Point
Richmond
Exmore
Lynchburg
Bluefield
Blacksburg
Bedford
Farmville
Williamsburg
Petersburg
Roanoke
Richlands
Altavista
Christiansburg
Hampton
ATLANTIC OCEAN
Big Stone Gap
Blackstone
Newport News
Rocky Mount
Marion
Wytheville
Norfolk
Virginia Beach
Cumberland Gap
Abingdon
South Boston
South Hill
Galax
Martinsville
Franklin
Emporia
Suffolk
Chesapeake
Bristol
Danville
N
0
30
60
Miles
© Countryman Press

Contents

Acknowledgments

Putting together this book was far from a solitary endeavor. There aren't enough pages to list everyone who lent a helping hand, but I'd like to thank a few people in particular: Tom Baker, Yvonne Thompson, Charlotte Whitted, Sharon and Don Compton, Skip Jones, Doug Rogers, Bob Wilson, and my good friend and former newspaper running mate Bob Brown.

And, of course, I offer special appreciation and love for my wife, Robin, who is well familiar with the occasionally strange and often wonderful roads my 40-plus years in journalism have led us down. For this edition of the book, she accompanied me on some of the trips, scribbled notes while I drove (so we didn't run off the road), and generally offered patience, support, and love, as she has all along. Thank you.

Introduction

This is how you really get to know Virginia: As you drive down US 13, the main thoroughfare for the length of the Eastern Shore, pull over at a farmers' market and buy a bag of sweet potatoes, tomatoes, or some other freshly harvested specialty. Linger and chat. Find out where you can get the best crab cakes or the tastiest clam fritters. Follow the advice.

Clear across the state, in the far southwestern corner, drive the Crooked Road—as the name suggests, a twisting ribbon of pavement that curls through the mountains—where old-time music comes alive at country stores, in cozy theaters, and on street corners outside music shops. Don't forget your guitar.

Interstate highways can carry you through Virginia, but only the back roads will bring the state to you. I know this from personal experience. I was born and raised in Virginia, and I've lived here for most of my adult life, but it wasn't until I started venturing into the hinterlands of the commonwealth that I truly started appreciating—and knowing—the state. I always knew, naturally, that from my home in the middle of the state I was no more than two hours from the beach and an hour from the mountains. But who knew what gems shined beyond my view off two-lane roads on the Eastern Shore or deep in the hills of the remote southwestern corner of the state?

My job as a columnist and feature writer for the *Richmond Times-Dispatch* took me all over Virginia, from the uninhabited barrier islands off the coast to deep into the western mountains. Everywhere I went, the people were hospitable and their stories rich, whether they were knee-deep in creek water digging clams, or they were sitting at the counter waiting on breakfast at the Hillsville Diner.

Over the years, I've traveled thousands of miles of roadways in Virginia—most of them paved—and I've filled who-knows-how-many reporters' notebooks, all of which has led me to conclude the state offers something for everyone.

LEFT: BURKE'S GARDEN IS A REMOTE AND PICTURESQUE VALLEY IN SOUTHWEST VIRGINIA

Virginia, of course, is steeped in history. You can cover almost 200 years of American history in a matter of a few hours and 23 miles. Start at Jamestown, the site of the first permanent English settlement in the New World, move on to Colonial Williamsburg, and then to Yorktown, where the British surrendered to end the Revolutionary War.

History reaches all over the state. Stroll through the place George Washington *really* slept at Mount Vernon, his estate and working farm on the Potomac River. Witness up close the genius of Thomas Jefferson—and learn of his loathsome personal flaws—at Monticello. Six other US presidents were born in Virginia, and most of their homes are open, too, including James Madison's Montpelier, James Monroe's Ash Lawn, William Henry Harrison's Berkeley Plantation, John Tyler's Sherwood Forest, and Woodrow Wilson's Manse. All, like Jefferson, were men of their times, meaning alongside their commendable qualities were character defects that made for complex histories.

Walk at dawn, as I have, through Manassas National Battlefield, site of two great Civil War battles—including the war's first major land battle—and stand at the muscular statue of Confederate General Thomas "Stonewall" Jackson. But don't stop at Manassas. Virginia brims with Civil War battlefields, stretching the width of the state and the length of the war, all the way to Appomattox, where Lee surrendered to Grant.

The Blue Ridge Parkway and Skyline Drive are two of the prettiest drives anywhere, particularly in the fall when the leaves start to turn and the mountains are awash in color. Follow the old Valley Turnpike, US 11, the route taken by immigrants streaming into the Shenandoah Valley in the seventeenth and eighteenth centuries. Or, if you have the time, take a trip on US 58, the state's longest road. Spread a blanket on the sand at Virginia Beach and watch the sun rise, then drive more than 500 miles westward and see the sun set at Cumberland Gap, the famed mountain passage that was young America's gateway to the West. The same feet that stood in the Atlantic surf can straddle the Virginia-Kentucky border at a stripe painted on the walkway at the Gap.

Wherever you go, don't be in a hurry. Linger over a second cup of coffee at a friendly diner or on the porch of a cabin tucked in the mist-covered hills near the Blue Ridge Parkway. Sip a glass of wine at one of the state's 300 wineries, or a pint of beer at one of the more than 200 craft breweries that have sprouted in cities and towns all over Virginia. If your taste runs to hard cider or distilled spirits, or even honest-to-goodness (legal) moonshine, Virginia has those, too.

Don't just drive. Get out, look around, breathe in the fresh air. Hike if you like. More than 500 miles of the Appalachian Trail—roughly a quarter of America's most famous walking path—unfurl through Virginia's mountains with easy access points for day or weekend expeditions. You can hike to the

RINGED BY MOUNTAINS, BURKE'S GARDEN OFFERS BREATHTAKING VIEWS WHEREVER YOU TURN

top of Mount Rogers, which is the highest peak in Virginia and just up a spur trail from the Appalachian Trail, or you can walk a couple of miles of the AT on more level terrain, enjoy a picnic, and get back in the car. But think how cool it will be to drop this line at your next cocktail party: "Well, yes, I've hiked the AT." Just don't mention how far.

Take your bicycle along. There are numerous rails-to-trails, multipurpose paths on converted rail beds, that are perfect for biking: Virginia Creeper Trail and New River Trail State Park, both in Southwest Virginia, are two. High Bridge Trail State Park, outside Farmville, is another, and the Virginia Capital Trail, which connects Richmond, Jamestown, and Williamsburg, is a popular path for cyclists and walkers.

There are festivals galore from spring through fall, celebrating all kinds of foods. How about the annual Ramp Festival on Whitetop Mountain in Grayson County? Ramps, if you don't know, are members of a species of wild onion that are tasty but also, ah, pungent.

You can pick apples, peaches, or berries in season at any number of pick-your-own orchards and farms, shop for antiques, lie on your back in an open field on a starry night and connect the dots of constellations, and, well, you get the idea. If you can think it, you can probably find it on the back roads of Virginia.

This book is representative of many years (and thousands of miles) of traveling around Virginia. Many of the places I'd visited before writing the book, some I hadn't. I certainly couldn't get to every place I wanted or that deserved to be included; this book is not meant to be exhaustive, but to include some places you might want to visit on a day or weekend drive. I made good use, as you might expect, of Google Maps—I'm sure other apps are fine, too—but it's also not a bad idea to keep a paper map handy for those times when modern technology fails you for one reason or another. I have a dog-eared copy of the Virginia State Road Atlas at the ready, and I've used it to venture into and out of some of Virginia's most remote areas. I call it "The Magic Map."

Other advice: Consider purchasing an annual pass from Virginia State Parks. The prices are modest and pay for themselves with visits to only a few parks. The state park system, by the way, is remarkable in its variety and quality, with 42 parks scattered across the commonwealth. (www.dcr.virginia.gov/state-parks) Make use of the terrific online resources of the various places you might want to visit around Virginia. A great starting place is the state's official tourism website: www.virginia.org.

My travels dramatically illustrate how close to the edge that family-run restaurants, shops, and other businesses in small towns and rural areas exist—particularly in a sour economy, such as during the pandemic, but even when times are good. I found restaurants that I remembered as thriving only a few years earlier sporting new names or new owners or, sadly, boarded up with no evidence of earlier success. This is another way of saying that information contained in any travel book can change in a hurry for any number of reasons.

Yet, I've also found the people who live far from the major thoroughfares are often, by necessity, a resilient bunch. They've battled for years against vanishing industries and dwindling populations, highway bypasses, and, in some cases, encroaching development, trying to maintain the way of life their families may have known for generations. Meeting people like that is enlightening and enriching and a lesson in perspective.

Working on a six-month series of stories about US 58 some years ago, *Times-Dispatch* photographer Bob Brown and I started at Virginia Beach and worked our way across the state, story by story and week by week, until we reached Cumberland Gap. We were proud of ourselves for the way we'd organized our journey until someone at the Gap, good-naturedly, told us: "You started at the wrong end."

Like everything else, it all depends on your point of view.

Every place has something to offer, but not every one has what might be considered a full-blown tourism industry with amusement parks or museums or bright, flashing lights. After touring a cave at Cumberland Gap National Historical Park many years ago, I was talking to Lucas Wilder, one of the young park rangers who led the delightful tour. He was born and raised down the road from the park, in a small community along US 58 called Ewing, and I could tell he loved the place. I asked him what there is for tourists to do around there. He was almost apologetic in saying, not much.

"That's a good thing," he said, "and a bad thing."

No, I said, thinking of the sheer beauty and tranquility of the valley along that stretch of road, that's a good thing.

COAST GUARD

1

A SHORE THING

The Eastern Shore

ESTIMATED LENGTH: 75 miles

ESTIMATED TIME: 2 days

HIGHLIGHTS: The wild ponies of **Chincoteague**—remember Misty?—made the **Eastern Shore** famous. However, a leisurely drive along US 13, the Shore's main artery, reveals this fertile agricultural peninsula wedged between the **Atlantic Ocean** and the **Chesapeake Bay** has much more to offer: charming small towns such as **Onancock**, its natural coastline, fresh seafood, and boutique wineries. Even motoring across the **Chesapeake Bay Bridge-Tunnel** is an event.

GETTING THERE: From Virginia Beach, head north on US 13 across the Chesapeake Bay Bridge-Tunnel.

Dubbed an "engineering wonder of the world," the Chesapeake Bay Bridge-Tunnel earns its praise, but it probably won't take your breath away—unless you have a phobia about driving over open water, or under it. The bridge-tunnel stretches more than 17 miles across the mouth of the Chesapeake Bay, from Virginia Beach to the southern tip of the Eastern Shore, and includes two mile-long tunnels that allow ships to sail in and out of the busy Port of Hampton Roads. As long as the weather's good and traffic is moving, driving across the bridge-tunnel takes less than a half-hour, a vast improvement over the ferry system that was in place before the bridge-tunnel opened in 1964.

We leave the mainland behind, exiting I-64 onto US 13, which carries us to the bridge-tunnel toll plaza. The one-way toll starts at $16 off-peak (and $21 during peak season, which includes Fridays through Sundays, from May 15 to September 15), but the return trip can cost as little as $1—depending on the time of year—if you make it within 24 hours of your original crossing and

LEFT: THE LIGHT OF ASSATEAGUE LIGHTHOUSE, ON THE EASTERN SHORE'S ASSATEAGUE ISLAND, CAN BE SEEN ALMOST 20 MILES OUT TO SEA ROBERT E. WILSON PHOTO

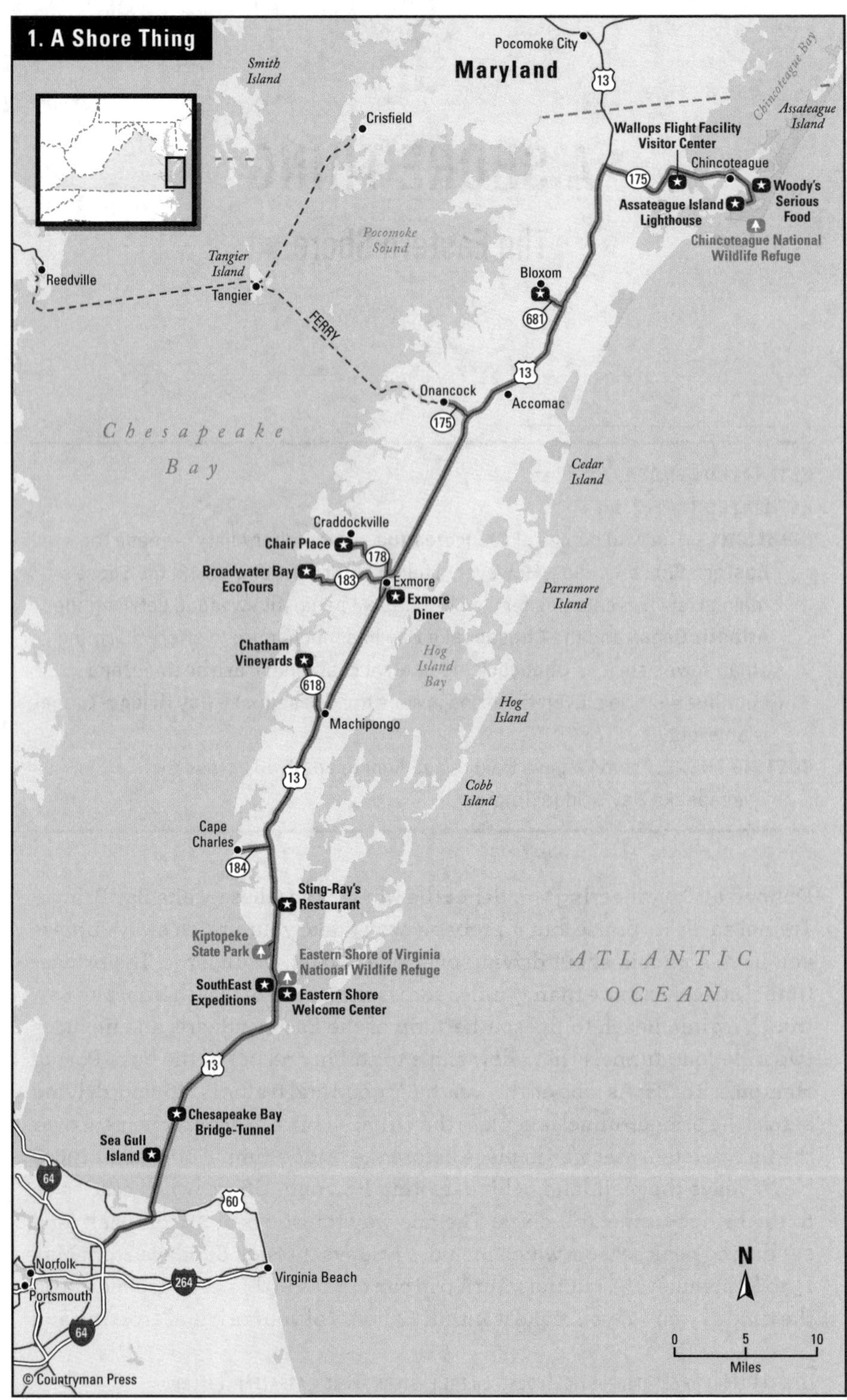

1. A Shore Thing
Smith Island
Maryland
Pocomoke City
13
Crisfield
Chincoteague Bay
Assateague Island
Wallops Flight Facility Visitor Center
Chincoteague
175
Woody's Serious Food
Assateague Island Lighthouse
Chincoteague National Wildlife Refuge
Pocomoke Sound
Tangier Island
Tangier
Reedville
FERRY
Bloxom
681
Onancock
Accomac
Chesapeake Bay
Cedar Island
Craddockville
Chair Place
178
Broadwater Bay EcoTours
183
Exmore
Exmore Diner
Parramore Island
Chatham Vineyards
618
Hog Island Bay
Hog Island
Machipongo
Cobb Island
Cape Charles
184
Sting-Ray's Restaurant
Kiptopeke State Park
Eastern Shore of Virginia National Wildlife Refuge
SouthEast Expeditions
Eastern Shore Welcome Center
ATLANTIC OCEAN
Chesapeake Bay Bridge-Tunnel
Sea Gull Island
64
60
Norfolk
Portsmouth
264
Virginia Beach
N
0 5 10
Miles
© Countryman Press

you use E-ZPass. In any case, it is recommended you consult cbbt.com for the most up-to-date toll information. A popular feature of the bridge-tunnel is a 625-foot fishing pier that extends from the southernmost of four man-made islands that anchor the tunnels (there are two 1-mile-long tunnels that run beneath shipping channels). The pier has long provided the rare opportunity for deep-sea fishing without a boat, given that the bay's depth runs 25 to 100 feet deep along the path of the bridge-tunnel, and has been a favorite destination for not only anglers fishing for bluefish, trout, croaker, flounder, and even sharks and stingrays, but also birdwatchers, photographers, and those who simply like to watch big ships pass through Thimble Shoal Channel.

However, construction of a parallel tunnel has led to the temporary closing of the pier and required the demolition of a restaurant and gift shop that once inhabited the island. Once the new tunnel is completed—anticipated to be in 2027—the fishing pier will be renovated and reopened to the public, though the restaurant and gift shop will not return.

"In many cases, we have folks who come to Virginia Beach or to the Hampton Roads area and actually take a morning or an afternoon just for the purpose of crossing, doing a U-turn . . . and going back across," says Jeffrey B. Holland, executive director of the bridge-tunnel. "It is a place to visit. But our primary mission is to provide the safest passage that we can for all traveling customers regardless of purpose."

Back in the car, we continue our ride across the bridge-tunnel. Once on the Shore, a new Eastern Shore Welcome Center on the east side of US 13 is a good place to load up on brochures and become acclimated to what's available on the Shore. Just beyond that is another visitor center, which is open on weekends, for the Eastern Shore of Virginia National Wildlife Refuge, that's tucked away and takes a little effort to find, but is worth the trouble. Just head east on Seaside Road and wend your way a short distance to the facility.

The refuge consists of more than 1,200 acres on the southern end of the Shore, set aside for protection largely because it's considered one of the most important migratory bird concentration points along the East Coast. In the fall, millions of birds and butterflies rest in the refuge until favorable winds help them cross the bay as they head south for the winter. The visitor center offers interactive exhibits, wildlife observation platforms, walking trails, and what might seem an unlikely addition—a 120-ton, 68-foot gun barrel that was on the USS *Missouri* when the Japanese surrendered, ending World War II—until you learn that, during World War II, the refuge was the site of Fort John Custis, where similarly big guns were stationed to protect the mouth of the Chesapeake Bay.

We return to US 13 and go north about 3 miles to VA 704, where we turn to the west and follow the signs to Kiptopeke State Park on the bay side of the Shore. Named for an American Indian who acted kindly toward early white settlers, Kiptopeke means "big water." The park, the former site of the

TOP: KIPTOPEKE STATE PARK, ON THE BAY SIDE OF THE EASTERN SHORE, IS A POPULAR PLACE FOR SWIMMING, FISHING, BOATING, AND BIKING
BOTTOM: THE LONG STRETCH OF BEACH AT ASSATEAGUE ISLAND NATIONAL SEASHORE BECKONS VISITORS TO THE OCEAN

old bay ferry landing, offers swimming, fishing, boating and walking trails, as well as a most unusual sight: the so-called Ghost Fleet of Kiptopeke, nine partially sunken concrete ships lined up just offshore to serve as a breakwater. We spend the late afternoon strolling on a woodland trail. We come to a steep wooden staircase, a substantial, low-hanging tree limb looming across it. Thump! I saw it coming but still managed to experience it headfirst. I highly recommend ducking.

Kiptopeke has a campground and cabins, but we already have a place for the night, just up the road in Cape Charles. First, though, we have dinner on our minds. We have a number of choices—none of them run-of-the-mill, roadside restaurants.

Sting-Ray's features fresh local seafood—and gas. Yes, it's situated at an Exxon Station on US 13, about 9 miles north of the bridge-tunnel. Order at the counter, take a seat, and your steamed crabs or soft-shell crab platter or whatever will be brought to you. The place has a good reputation and a nickname: Chez Exxon.

A couple of miles west of US 13 is Cape Charles, a bay town in the midst of a revival. Some of its fine old houses have been restored; others remain vacant and for sale. A few have been transformed into bed-and-breakfast inns. If you're hungry, Mason Avenue, the main business strip, offers a number of good options, including Kelly's Gingernut Pub, in a former bank building. The Shanty, featuring local seafood, is another good seasonal option. Another possibility is Rayfield's Pharmacy and its old-style soda fountain, where you can order breakfast, lunch, and ice cream.

SIDE TRACKS

Don't forget the homegrown wines at **Chatham Vineyards and Winery** in Machipongo, which has a retail tasting room open daily and hosts various events through the year.

I've visited Chatham Vineyards and Winery on a couple of occasions to sample the wines and talk to Jon Wehner, who operates the place with his wife, Mills, and their three children.

"The Eastern Shore is a wonderful climate for growing wine grapes," says Wehner. "It's a moderate maritime climate with a nice breeze from the bay or from the ocean, and nice, long Indian summers."

Lodging is available at a restored 1920 farmhouse on the property. In addition, if you like a little activity with your wine, Chatham Vineyards, in conjunction with SouthEast Expeditions, offers wine-kayak tours that feature paddling and sightseeing, as well as stops to enjoy the local wines.

"It's a great way to see some of the creeks off the bay," Wehner says. "You get a lot of eagles here. You see cranes, blue herons, snowy egrets. People are able to come here on a private farm, get a little exercise, and see the nature the Shore has to provide."

TOP: THE WATER TOWER BUILT TO RESEMBLE A LIGHTHOUSE WELCOMES VISITORS TO CAPE CHARLES, AT ONE TIME A BUSY RAILROAD TOWN
BOTTOM: MISTY, THE WILD PONY WHO MADE CHINCOTEAGUE FAMOUS, IS MEMORIALIZED ON THE TOWN'S MAIN STREET

SIDE TRACKS

If you have the time, rent, borrow, or buy a kayak or canoe and paddle around the creeks and inlets that help make the Shore such an intriguing place. Better yet, arrange a guided tour.

In fact, you'd be foolish to visit the undeveloped seaside barrier islands of the Shore without the assistance of a local guide such as Rick Kellam. The islands are not far offshore, but changing ocean tides make reaching them through the salt marshes and tidal mudflats tricky and even dangerous. Once there, though, you will be astounded by their untouched beauty.

"One of the last great places on Earth left in its natural form and not screwed up by man," Kellam tells me. "Yet."

The Nature Conservancy owns and protects many of the barrier islands, describing this stretch as "the longest expanse of coastal wilderness remaining on the East Coast."

Kellam, who's worked as a waterman and as an officer with the Virginia State Marine Police, operates **Broadwater Bay EcoTours**. On a previous trip, he took me to **Cedar Island**, steering his 24-foot skiff through 2 miles of marshes to reach the deserted island, inhabited by no other humans but covered with whelk shells.

Dave Burden of **SouthEast Expeditions** also leads tours, including kayaking excursions of favorite clamming spots in bayside creeks that probably don't look a whole lot different than when Captain John Smith explored here in 1608. Burden is not a Shore native, but he might as well be, having arrived in the 1990s, learning about and loving the place ever since. I once spent an afternoon with Burden, gathering and steaming a basket of littleneck clams. As we sat on a dock, dipping the clams in chardonnay from a local winery, Burden said, "Definitely, the best part of my job."

You can also find great food up the road in Exmore: the Exmore Diner is a converted railcar that first opened as a restaurant in 1954. The diner, 20 miles north of Cape Charles on US 13 Business, is one of the most popular restaurants on the Shore, and I quickly see why as we settle into a booth. The service is fast and friendly, and meals are reasonably priced. Just a cool place to eat.

Not far from Exmore, on the bay side, is a little town called Craddockville. There's not much there except on Thursday nights when music brings the Chair Place to life. The Chair Place is an old general store that Bill Aeschliman bought and turned into a chair-making shop. Aeschliman began holding rehearsals for his bluegrass band on Thursday evenings more than two decades ago and locals started showing up to listen. Next thing you know, people started bringing their instruments and joining in. The weekly jam was born. Everyone's invited.

"There's no telling who's going to show up and with what instruments," the Rev. Steve Jones, a guitarist and Presbyterian minister who jokingly

US 13 IS THE PRIMARY ARTERY ALONG THE EASTERN SHORE OF VIRGINIA, A SLENDER PENINSULA BETWEEN THE CHESAPEAKE BAY (ON THE LEFT) AND THE ATLANTIC OCEAN

called himself "the token preacher" of the bunch, told me when I visited a few years ago. "It's relaxed. It's comfortable. People can come here and listen to music and be entertained. The musicians don't worry about their skill level. We try to include everybody."

Chincoteague is our ultimate destination on the Shore so we can see the wild ponies made famous in *Misty of Chincoteague,* the 1947 classic by Marguerite Henry.

On the way, we visit Onancock, a picturesque town that's only 15 miles to the north of Exmore. On the bay side, Onancock has art galleries, the Roseland Theatre (an old-time movie house), a gourmet coffee shop, a wine bar, The Charlotte, a boutique hotel and restaurant, and Mallards at the Wharf, a fun restaurant.

Back to US 13, we point the car toward Chincoteague, just a few miles south of the Maryland border. An easy drive, US 13 is mostly four lanes with occasional traffic lights. Fields of corn, cotton, and tomatoes line the road. Vegetable stands sprout in warm weather, and it's not unusual to see farmers parked on the side of the road, their beds filled with watermelons or bushel baskets of Hayman sweet potatoes, the white-fleshed beauties that are a specialty on the Shore.

From Onancock, Chincoteague is another 20 miles north on US 13 and then 10 miles east on VA 175 toward the ocean. Before Chincoteague, though, we encounter the giant satellite dishes and tall fences that signal we are close to NASA's Wallops Flight Facility, where rockets have been launched since 1945, long before there was a NASA. We stop at the visitor center, which is on the right side of VA 175 as we drive toward Chincoteague. Admission is free to the center, which features exhibits related to Wallops' projects.

ROCKETS ARE ON DISPLAY AT NASA'S WALLOPS VISITOR CENTER

The most touristy of the Shore's towns, Chincoteague is actually an island that serves as a gateway to Assateague Island National Seashore. If dining or shopping is your wish, Chincoteague can fulfill that with a number of shops and restaurants. You also can play miniature golf to your heart's content, and catch a film at the renovated Island Theatre movie house. Traffic can be congested on busy summer days, but it's not impossible to navigate. The town has plenty of lodging, too.

Our mission, though, is the national seashore and, within it, the

MUSIC JAMS HAVE BECOME A TRADITION AT THE CHAIR PLACE IN CRADDOCKVILLE

WOODY'S SERIOUS FOOD IS A POPULAR OUTDOOR DINING SPOT IN CHINCOTEAGUE

Chincoteague National Wildlife Refuge. That's where the ponies live. From the main road, we see the ponies—from a distance—roaming through the vast expanses of wild grasses. We also spy them from an observation deck we reach following an easy mile-long walk through a pine forest. Less easy are the 198 steps up to the top of the red-and-white-striped Assateague Island Lighthouse. Hoof it up and enjoy the magnificent view of the surrounding islands and salt marshes.

Hike and bike your way around the park, or simply drive as we do to the end of the road, which brings us to one of the prettiest beaches you'll ever want to see. The park contains miles and miles of pristine beach. On summer weekends, the crowds are thick and parking is a challenge, but it's worth dipping your toes—or more—in the Atlantic.

For a late lunch, we leave the park, cross the causeway, return to the traffic circle re-entering the town of Chincoteague, and park at Woody's Serious Food, a seriously good barbecue place with a beach motif and clothes drying on a line. I favor the barbecue trailer from a previous trip, being fond of The Memphis, a pulled pork sandwich smothered with cole slaw and red barbecue sauce. The proprietor cooks the meat in a smoker behind the trailer. The rest of the food is homemade, too.

After a quick stop for an ice cream cone, we head for home, back down US 13 and a return trip across the Chesapeake Bay Bridge-Tunnel.

TOP: THE 17.6-MILE-LONG CHESAPEAKE BAY BRIDGE-TUNNEL CONNECTS THE MAINLAND OF VIRGINIA WITH THE EASTERN SHORE CHESAPEAKE BAY BRIDGE-TUNNEL
BOTTOM: AN AERIAL VIEW OF THE MARSHES THAT SEPARATE THE OCEANSIDE BARRIER ISLANDS FROM THE REST OF THE EASTERN SHORE

IN THE AREA

Accommodations

BAYVIEW WATERFRONT, 35350 Copes Drive, Belle Haven. Call 757-442-6963. Website: www.bayviewwaterfrontbedandbreakfast.com. Bed-and-breakfast inn overlooking Occohannock Creek and the Chesapeake Bay beyond.

CHARLOTTE HOTEL & RESTAURANT, 7 North Street, Onancock. Call 757-787-7400. Website: www.thecharlottehotel.com. In a building that was an early 1900s hotel, the Charlotte is a boutique hotel and gourmet restaurant that features a full-service bar, intimate dining room, and art gallery.

HOTEL CAPE CHARLES, 235 Mason Avenue, Cape Charles. Call 757-695-3854. Website: www.hotelcapecharles.com. Boutique hotel in the heart of Cape Charles.

THE INN AT ONANCOCK, 30 North Street, Onancock. Call 757-789-7711. Website: www.innatonancock.com. Gourmet bed-and-breakfast within three blocks of the town wharf.

WATERSIDE INN, Chincoteague Island, 3761 S. Main Street, Chincoteague Island. Call 757-336-3434. Website: www.watersideinn.biz. Waterfront rooms with private balconies.

Attractions and Recreation

BARRIER ISLANDS CENTER, 7295 Young Street, Machipongo. Call 757-678-5550. Website: www.barrierislandscenter.org. At historic Almshouse Farm, the center celebrates the way of life of people who lived on Virginia's barrier islands.

BETWEEN THE WATERS BIKE TOUR. Call 757-678-7157. Website: www.cbes.org. A cycling event on the fourth Saturday in October featuring routes of 25, 40, 60, and 100 miles around the Shore, benefits the nonprofit Citizens for a Better Eastern Shore.

BROADWATER BAY ECOTOURS, 6035 Killmon Point Road, Exmore. Call 757-442-4363 or 757-710-0568. Website: www.broadwaterbayecotour.com. Guided tours of the Shore's barrier islands.

A BOAT HEADS OFF FROM CHINCOTEAGUE'S WATERFRONT PARK

CHAIR PLACE, 33638 Craddockville Road, Craddockville. Website: www.facebook.com/profile.php?id=100066756217408.

CHATHAM VINEYARDS AND WINERY, 9232 Chatham Road, Machipongo. Call 757-678-5588. Website: www.chathamvineyards.com. Winery is open to the public. Tours and tasting.

CHESAPEAKE BAY BRIDGE-TUNNEL. Call 757-331-2960. Website: www.cbbt.com. Spans 17 miles across the mouth of the Chesapeake Bay.

CHINCOTEAGUE NATIONAL WILDLIFE REFUGE, 8231 Beach Road, Chincoteague. Call 757-336-6122. Website: www.fws.gov/refuge/chincoteague. Highlights include Assateague Lighthouse, Assateague Island National Seashore, Herbert H. Bateman Educational and Administrative Center.

EASTERN SHORE OF VIRGINIA NATIONAL WILDLIFE REFUGE, 32205 Seaside Road, Cape Charles. Call 757-331-3425. Website: www.fws.gov /refuge/eastern-shore-virginia. Visitor center, wildlife observation decks, walking trails.

EASTERN SHORE RAILWAY MUSEUM, 18468 Dunne Avenue, Parksley. Call 757-665-7245. Website: www.facebook.com/p/Eastern-Shore-Railway -Museum-100078380284412. Historic rail cars open to the public.

KIPTOPEKE STATE PARK, 3540 Kiptopeke Drive, Cape Charles. Call 757-331-2267. Website: www.dcr.virginia.gov/state-parks/kiptopeke. Birding, boating, fishing, swimming, hiking, camping.

NASA WALLOPS FLIGHT FACILITY VISITOR CENTER, Wallops Island. Call 757-824-1404. Website: www.nasa.gov/wallops/visitor-center. Rockets, exhibits.

SOUTHEAST EXPEDITIONS, Cape Charles. Call 757-802-5210. Website: www.southeastexpeditions.com. Kayak tours and rentals.

Dining

BILL'S PRIME SEAFOOD & STEAKS, 4040 Main Street, Chincoteague Island. Call 757-336-5831. Website: www.billsprime.com. Fresh seafood, hand-cut steaks, chops, pasta.

BIZZOTTO'S GALLERY AND CAFFÉ, 41 Market Street, Onancock. Call 757-787-3103. Website: www.onancock.org/bizzottos-gallery-cafe. Gallery and restaurant, featuring international cuisine and local favorites such as crab cakes.

CAPE CHARLES COFFEE HOUSE, 241 Mason Avenue, Cape Charles. Call 757-331-1880. Website: www.capecharlescoffeehouse.com.

DON'S SEAFOOD MARKET & RESTAURANT, 4113 Main Street, Chincoteague. Call 757-336-5715. Website: www.donsseafoodrestaurant.com.

KELLY'S GINGERNUT PUB, 133 Mason Avenue, Cape Charles. Call 757-331-3222. Website: www.kellysgingernut.com. Watering hole and fine restaurant in an old bank building.

MALLARDS AT THE WHARF, 2 Market Street, Onancock. Call 757-787-8558. Website: www.eatatmallards.com. Wide-ranging menu that changes seasonally. Great atmosphere on the water.

THE SHANTY, 33 Marina Village Road, Cape Charles. Call 757-695-3853. Website: www.shantyseafood.com.

STING-RAY'S RESTAURANT, 26507 Lankford Highway, Cape Charles. Call 757-331-1541. Website: stingrays1950.wixsite.com/stingrays. Popular, sit-down seafood restaurant in the back of a gas station.

WOODY'S SERIOUS FOOD, 6700 Maddox Boulevard, Chincoteague. Website: www.woodysseriousfood.com. Outdoor, beach-themed food truck with outstanding barbecue and smoked chicken with homemade sides and desserts. Open seasonally.

YUK-YUK AND JOE'S RESTAURANT AND BAR, 15617 Courthouse Road, Eastville. Call 757-678-7870. Website: www.facebook.com/yukyukandjoes. Popular local spot off the beaten path that won't wow you with ambience but does serve good food.

Other Contacts

EASTERN SHORE OF VIRGINIA TOURISM. Call 757-331-1660. Website: www.visitesva.com.

2

ISLAND GETAWAY

Tangier Island

ESTIMATED LENGTH: 18 miles (by water) from Reedville

ESTIMATED TIME: 2 days

HIGHLIGHTS: The ferry ride across the **Chesapeake Bay**, strolling or riding a bicycle or golf cart along the island's narrow lanes (you will see only an occasional small car or pickup truck), the **Tangier History Museum and Interpretive Cultural Center**, the crab cakes, soft-shell crabs and other seafood, hearing the islanders' distinctive English dialect, and, in general, an up-close view of life on **Tangier**.

GETTING THERE: The easiest way is by passenger ferry. Seasonal ferries operate daily from Reedville, at the eastern end of US 360 on the mainland (or "western shore," as islanders refer to it) and from Onancock, just off US 13, on the Eastern Shore, and from Crisfield, Maryland. A daily mail boat that carries passengers operates between Tangier and Crisfield, Maryland. The island also has an airstrip for private planes and helicopters.

It's late morning and as Captain Linwood Bowis deftly nestles the *Chesapeake Breeze* alongside the dock at Tangier Island, he reminds ferry passengers about to disembark of the day's schedule.

"Departure time this afternoon is 2:15," he says over the boat's public-address system. "If you miss it, no problem. I'll be back tomorrow."

The line always gets a laugh, but it's no joke. Unless you own or charter a boat or aircraft, a passenger ferry is your only way on or off the island. For those of us planning to stay the night, the pressure is off, and we can focus on finding the island's best crab cake or some other seafood delight for lunch. Everyone else checks their watches.

I didn't ride 90 minutes on a ferry for a burger, so I go in search of a crab

LEFT: SUNRISE ARRIVES AT THE HARBOR OF TANGIER ISLAND

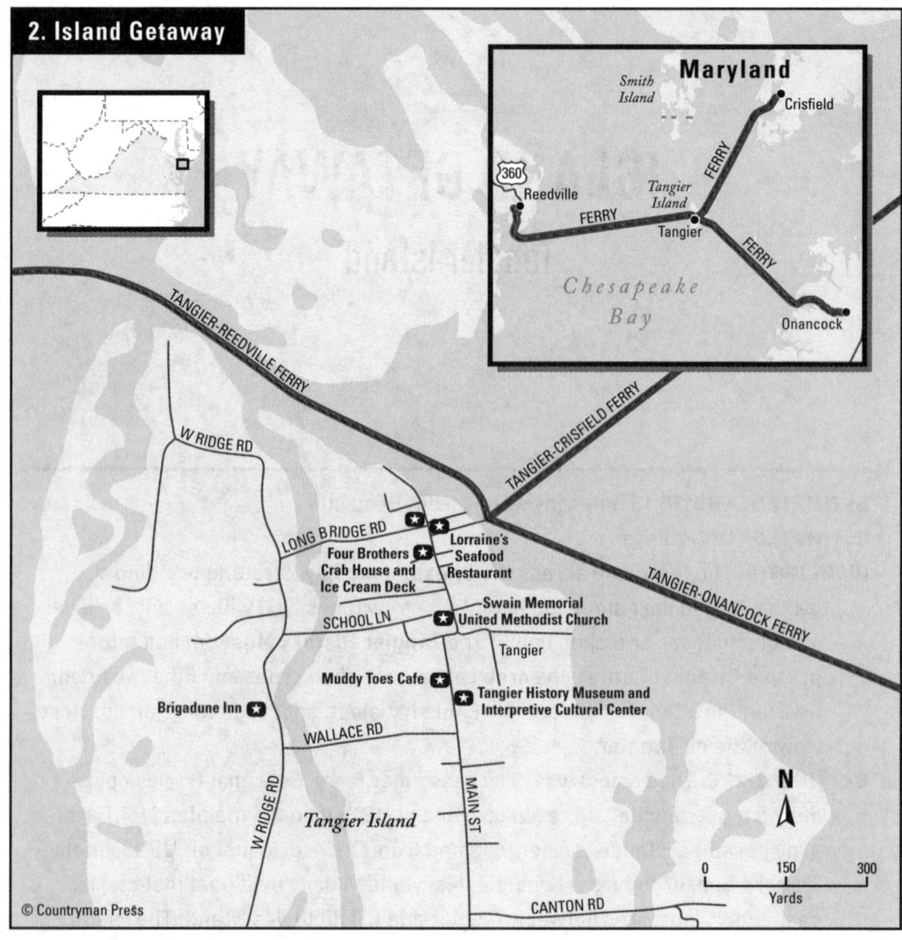

cake, a Tangier specialty since crabbing has long been one of the main occupations on the island. You can always count on Lorraine's Seafood Restaurant, which is open year-round, for crab cakes or whatever else you need food-wise. You can reach Lorraine's by walking from the dock to Main Ridge Road and turning right. It's not far, but then nothing is on Tangier.

After lunch, it's time to think about getting around the island. You can rent a golf cart or a bicycle at Four Brothers Crab House and Ice Cream Deck, or, if you like guided tours you can catch a ride in one of several stretch golf carts waiting near the dock and be chauffeured around the island by a resident offering an expert description of the place.

Unhindered by time and knowing where I'm going, I choose to walk.

I stop first at the Tangier History Museum and Interpretive Cultural Center, a converted gift shop that tells the island's story in a charmingly downhome way. It also provides Tangier's only public restrooms, aside from those in the handful of restaurants on the island.

TANGIER IS A WISP OF AN ISLAND IN THE MIDDLE OF THE CHESAPEAKE BAY

Locals and visitors gather on the inviting front porch for chitchat or games of checkers with colored seashells as game pieces. Inside the museum, photographs, newspaper and magazine clippings, and an extensive timeline tell the history of the island that for centuries, the story goes, was a hunting ground for Native Americans. The English didn't show up until 1608, when Captain John Smith came upon the island while exploring the bay.

Many of the island's residents speak with a thick accent. High tide is *hoi toid*.

You also can keep track of the last-name sweepstakes. About half of island residents have one of three last names: Parks, Pruitt, or Crockett. Thomas, Marshall, and Dise are other common surnames on the island.

Besides name games, you can touch a crab pot and other tools of the watermen's trade, or watch a video featuring interviews with residents. Better yet, talk to an actual resident.

"Most of us are friendly and nice and love to see new faces on the island," said Gayle Laird, a native of Tangier, who was volunteering at the museum on the day I visited. "I love it here. I wouldn't ever want to leave."

It's said once you get the marsh mud of Tangier between your toes, you'll always return. Part of Tangier's appeal is what it is not. It is not a resort, and

I've made numerous trips to **Tangier** over the years, and I've come to know my way around the place, although considering the size of the shrinking island—a mile wide, 3 miles long, and mostly marshland—that's hardly a claim to fame. I've also come to develop an appreciation for the islanders, their heritage, and their warm hospitality.

Theirs is not an easy life. Depending on whom you believe, erosion, rising seas or sinking land, or some combination, are taking their land—at the current rate of land loss, some scientists believe the island could be uninhabitable within a few decades—and modern realities are doing the same to their livelihoods. For generations, the people of Tangier made their livings crabbing in the waters around the island. But reduced crab populations and government regulations have forced watermen to find work elsewhere, as only a few dozen still crab for a living. Many leave the island, at least temporarily, to work on tugboats. Young islanders, seeking a more secure future, increasingly move to the mainland for other kinds of jobs and come back only to visit. The result: Tangier's population is down to around 400, far from its peak of 1,200 in the 1930s.

So, what you see as you walk around Tangier is not only a quaint little island, as it's often described by visitors, but, if circumstances don't change, a vanishing one.

A DWINDLING NUMBER OF TANGIERMEN MAKE THEIR LIVINGS WORKING THE WATERS OF THE CHESAPEAKE BAY

THE TANGIER HISTORY MUSEUM SERVES AS A REPOSITORY OF THE ISLAND'S HISTORY AND A VISITOR CENTER FOR TOURISTS

it is not Disney World. It is real. A little rough around the edges in spots, but very real, and quite beautiful.

Lodging is limited on the island. The only hotel is the Brigadune Inn, which has been renovated in recent years and is open year-round. A few short-term rentals, à la Airbnb, have popped up.

"We call it our 'happy place,' and we are endlessly amazed by the fantastic people from all over the world that we get to meet," says Barb Baechtel, who, along with her husband, Rob, owns and manages the Brigadune. The Baechtels "retired" to Tangier after living in Washington, DC. "We never intended to be innkeepers, but here we are—and it's the best thing ever. We are having so much fun. Exhausted fun, but fun, nonetheless."

She adds, "The people of Tangier are our family. We are dedicated servants of this community and will never live anywhere else, if we can help it."

A few other notes about the island:

- Reservations are highly recommended.
- The pandemic proved to be particularly brutal for the remote island's economy. A couple of hotels and several restaurants didn't make it out the other side. Plans were in the works to reopen some of the closed restaurants, and there are high hopes for a new coffee shop, Muddy Toes Cafe.

- The island has a single market, a typical, small-town grocery that sells a little bit of everything. For serious shopping, islanders take the year-round ferry to **Crisfield**, where some keep cars, and then drive to **Salisbury**, the closest thing to a big city, which is one of the reasons many Tangiermen, as they're traditionally known, identify more with Maryland than Virginia.
- There are no banks on the island, but there is one ATM. Most businesses accept credit cards.
- Cell phone service is unreliable.
- You won't find alcohol for sale on the island, but no one objects if you bring it with you and enjoy it discreetly and responsibly.

THE NARROW LANES OF THE ISLAND ARE PERFECT FOR STROLLING, OR TOURING THE ISLAND BY BICYCLE

I resume my stroll on the streets that are surprisingly busy, but not in the way most of us have come to think of busy streets. A young mother pushes her small child in a stroller. A father pedals a bicycle, his little girl in the basket. Golf carts putter past. A cat ambles beside me for a short distance before ducking through a gate. Cats are everywhere on Tangier, reportedly numbering in the hundreds. You can't travel far without seeing one sprawled lazily on a sidewalk or stealthily pursuing a seafood dinner.

I stop and read trail markers, some tacked to telephone poles, which offer nuggets about the island: the story behind certain homes, the account of long-gone wharves, the descriptions of wading birds such as great blue herons and snowy egrets that high-step gingerly through the marshes.

Tangiermen live in three distinct sections on the island, separated by marshes and connected by footbridges. Their homes seem crowded together because they are: of the island's estimated 700 acres, all but about 80 are marshland, and even those 80 go under water when exceptionally high tides periodically wash over the island. With land at a premium, it's not unusual to find family cemeteries in front yards or wedged between homes.

Like any small town, Tangier's hodgepodge of houses includes a few structures that are rundown and boarded up. Others, though, are as pretty as pictures, surrounded by neatly trimmed yards and white picket fences, precisely what you would expect to find in an island paradise.

Swain Memorial United Methodist, constructed in the 1890s, is the island's centerpiece, a handsome white frame church whose steeple, along with the island's water tower, defines the Tangier skyline. The island's other church, New Testament Church, a non-denominational congregation that splintered from Swain in the 1940s, is just down the lane.

Faith and religion play vital roles in the island's history. When British troops occupied Tangier during the War of 1812, it was, as the story goes, a Methodist preacher, Joshua Thomas, the "parson of the islands," who was asked to deliver a sermon to the troops before their attack on Baltimore. Thomas preached that the British would be defeated, as they were. More recently, in the 1990s, island leaders turned down a Hollywood offer to have scenes of a Paul Newman-Kevin Costner movie, *Message in a Bottle*, filmed here because the script contained sex and swearing.

The island's schoolhouse sits behind Swain. Tangier Combined School is the last public school in Virginia housing K–12 under one roof. Enrollment is typically less than 100. They don't have many snow days here, but on occasion, the school opens late or lets out early when high tides threaten to lap at the front steps.

It takes me a couple of hours to cover the island by foot, stopping along the way to enjoy the view and speak to passersby or those sitting, only a few feet away, on their front porches. By bicycle, you can ride everywhere in less than an hour.

THE ISLAND GETS CROWDED WHEN THE DAILY FERRIES ARRIVE WITH THEIR DAY-TRIPPING TOURISTS

For a truly different glimpse of the island, tag along with a waterman, who will show tourists where he pulls crab pots and point out ospreys, eagles, and other wildlife along the way. Or take in a sunset from Tangier's wisp of a beach that curls around the southern end of the island. On a late summer evening, the pinks and oranges of the setting sun fill the sky, offering not only beauty but novelty: there are few places in Virginia, other than the Eastern Shore, where you can watch the sun sink into the sea.

The next day, I take a bike ride around the island, pedaling:

- Past the airstrip that a few years ago lost a few feet because of encroaching waters of the bay,
- Past the site of the medical center (mainland doctors fly in periodically to care for islanders, although a physician assistant and nurses live on the island),

TANGIER ISLAND, FIGHTING EROSION AND RISING WATER LEVELS, IS LOSING GROUND TO THE BAY

THE MORNING SUN PEEKS OVER THE CRAB HOUSES OF TANGIER ISLAND

- Past the dock, where retired watermen sit on benches and solve the world's problems; the daily arrival of the mail boat from Crisfield is a happily anticipated event,
- Past the volunteer fire department, a critical component on an island of wooden homes,
- Over a bridge to the small section known as Canton,
- Past the occasional soft-drink vending machine, stationed randomly alongside the roadway.

It's a kick to ride on 4-foot-wide strips of asphalt with official state route numbers and to see golf carts halt at the occasional stop sign. Watch your lead foot: The posted speed limit is 15 mph.

For my last lunch before departing, I stop at Lorraine's. Lorraine Marshall runs the place, as she has since the 1980s. It's the only restaurant on the island open year-round.

I order the day's special: a crab cake sandwich on a bun with cole slaw. Marshall's daughter, Jamie, who's helped her mom at the restaurant since she was a teenager, fries the crab cake while I take a seat. The sandwich is, as I anticipate, terrific, and I polish it off quickly.

"Hope you enjoyed it!" Jamie says as I stand to go. "Come back again."

I head to the dock where the tourists returning to Reedville wait patiently

to board the *Chesapeake Breeze*, which, as Linwood Bowis promised, returned. Departure time, as we well know, is 2:15 pm.

Bowis, the second-generation boat captain and husband of a Tangier native, says not everyone who makes the trip to Tangier knows exactly what to expect. But in general, he says, ferry-goers enjoy traveling there on a boat and "seem to enjoy seeing something different."

The island's history attracts some visitors; the out-of-the-way nature of the place appeals to others.

"But some," Bowis said with a smile, "just want to eat a crab cake."

IN THE AREA

Accommodations

THE BRIGADUNE INN, 16650 Hog Ridge Road, Tangier Island. Call 757-891-2580. Website: www.brigaduneinn.com. Open year-round.

Attractions

TANGIER HISTORY MUSEUM AND INTERPRETATIVE CULTURAL CENTER, 16215 Main Ridge Road. Call 757-891-2374. Website: www.virginia.org/listing/tangier-history-museum/15746/.

Dining

FOUR BROTHERS CRAB HOUSE AND ICE CREAM DECK, 16128 Main Ridge Road. Call 757-891-2999. Website: www.fourbrotherscrabhouse.com.

LORRAINE'S SEAFOOD RESTAURANT, 4409 Chambers Lane. Call 757-891-2225. Open year-round.

MUDDY TOES CAFE, 16200 Main Ridge Road, Tangier Island. Call 757-993-0891. Website: www.facebook.com/muddytoescafe. Cafe and coffee shop.

Transportation

TANGIER ISLAND CRUISE FROM REEDVILLE, 468 Buzzard Point Road, Reedville. Call 804-453-2628. Website: www.tangiercruise.com. May through October.

TANGIER ONANCOCK FERRY. Call 757-891-2505. Website: www.tangierferry.com. May through October.

TANGIER ISLAND CRUISES FROM CRISFIELD, MARYLAND, 1001 W. Main Street, Crisfield. Call 410-968-2338. Website: www.tangierislandcruises.com. May through October.

M&S CHARTERS, TANGIER. Call 757 891 2440. Website: www.tangierisland-va.com/tangiercharters. Daily cruises from Crisfield to Tangier, year-round.

ON TANGIER: Bicycles and golf carts may be rented at Four Brothers Crab House and Ice Cream Deck. Call 757-891-2999. Website: www.fourbrotherscrabhouse.com.

3

LAID-BACK RETREAT

The Northern Neck

ESTIMATED LENGTH: 100 miles

ESTIMATED TIME: Weekend

HIGHLIGHTS: Leave the worries of the world behind with a drive through farms, forests, and small towns such as **Warsaw, Montross, Reedville, Kilmarnock,** and **Irvington**. Dip your toes or a fishing line in the **Rappahannock** or **Potomac** rivers or the **Chesapeake Bay**. Look for bald eagles or osprey at **Belle Isle State Park** or colonial architecture at **Historic Christ Church**. Enjoy a meal at one of the Northern Neck's fine restaurants, be it on the waterfront or in a converted convenience store. Or take a journey on the **Virginia Oyster Trail**.

GETTING THERE: From Richmond, go east on US 360 to cross the Rappahannock River at **Tappahannock**, or, alternatively, follow VA 33 east through **West Point** and **Saluda** to cross the Rappahannock at **White Stone**, on the eastern end of the Northern Neck. From Washington and points north, use I-95 or US 301 to reach VA 3 or US 17, either of which will lead you to the Northern Neck.

The true, laid-back spirit of the Northern Neck is amply displayed all over this watery retreat, but nowhere more affectionately than in a cemetery behind Wicomico Parish Church in the village of Wicomico Church. There, on the gravestone of John Carr Clarke Byrne, a longtime Neck resident who died at age 80 in 1995, are these words: I'd rather be on Mill Creek.

Mill Creek is only one of many preferred destinations on the Northern Neck—or simply the Neck, as locals know it—a lush peninsula bounded by the Potomac River to the north, the Rappahannock River to the south, and the Chesapeake Bay to the east. George Washington, who was born here, called this place "the garden of Virginia." The term "neck" comes from the

LEFT: DITCHLEY, AN ESTATE DATING TO THE 1600s JUST OUTSIDE KILMARNOCK, IS NOW A WORKING FARM, AS WELL AS HOME TO DITCHLEY CIDER WORKS TOM BAKER

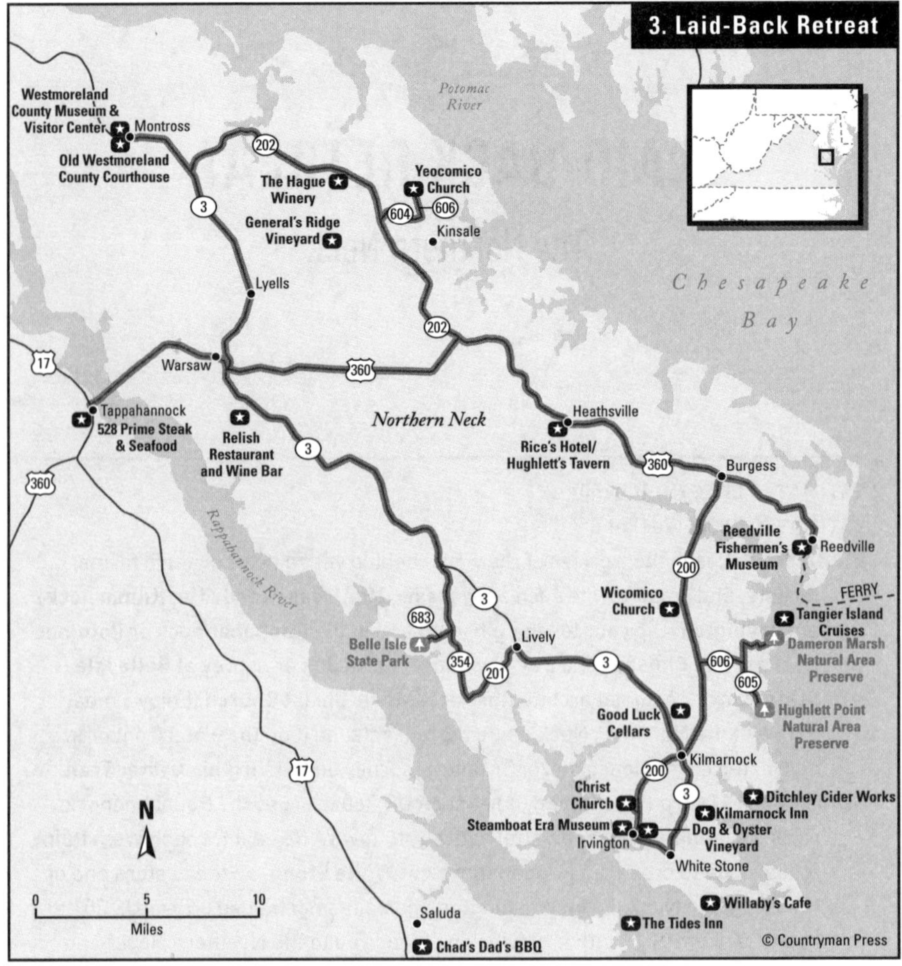

shape of the peninsula, and it's the northernmost of Virginia's peninsulas along the Chesapeake Bay.

Since bridges replaced ferries in the twentieth century and made this area more accessible to outlying areas, the Neck has become a popular weekend and summer getaway for city folk, who covet its easygoing pace. Indeed, those who come here regularly to unwind report a great weight lifting from their shoulders as soon as they cross one of the bridges onto the Neck. Your biggest worry here should be where to find a good crab cake. The vibe? "The vibe," says my friend Tom Baker, who has been visiting the Neck since he was a child and has now retired there, "is low blood pressure."

Years ago, not wanting to appear underdressed when arranging to meet a friend on a weekday at his office in Kilmarnock, one of the Neck's more

REEDVILLE MARKS THE EASTERN END OF THE ROAD FOR US 360

picturesque little towns, I asked if I should wear a tie. "No neckties," he said, "on the Neck."

As appearances go, the Neck hasn't changed much over the years. It has avoided the explosive growth that often plagues rural areas revealed as little slices of paradise. The Neck remains largely farms and forests, interrupted by small towns such as Warsaw, Montross, and Reedville. Homes of all types—from massive mansions to tiny weekend cottages—pepper the shoreline. Its proportion of the 65-and-over population is significantly higher than the rest of Virginia.

Naturally, water is the area's greatest distinction. With more than 1,100 miles of shoreline counting the bay, rivers, creeks, and inlets, the Neck has been home to generations of watermen, recreational sailors and anglers, and explorers. Captain John Smith left Jamestown to sail the Potomac and Rappahannock rivers in the early 1600s. Today, bird-watchers do most of the discovering on the Neck, with eagles and ospreys among the residents, but there are plenty of other prizes—history, nature, and wineries—to find, too. Not many traffic lights, either.

With a variety of entry points onto the Neck, you can make a driving tour of the area going in almost any direction. Be assured, you can turn off any little side road and find something worthy of exploration. You likely won't get lost; you'll run into water eventually. For general touring, you probably will want to use some combination of US 360 and VA 3, the primary roads in the region.

One way to access the Neck is by crossing the bridge over the Rappahannock from Tappahannock on US 360. The stretch of road through Tappahannock offers all manner of food options (and fuel and lodging). Aside from the standard chains, there are places such as To-Do Cafe (comfort food), 528 Prime Steak and Seafood (occupying the space that for decades housed the popular Lowery's Seafood Restaurant), and Northern Neck Burger. Ice cream? A couple of good options within a mile of each other: Better Than A Great Day and Acme Ice Cream Parlor—an old-style soda fountain in a former gas station.

Once across the river, it's decision time: Warsaw, 6 miles beyond the bridge, marks the intersection of US 360 and VA 3. Warsaw, by the way, is indeed named for the city in Poland. The town was called Richmond County Courthouse until 1830, when residents renamed it Warsaw in sympathy with the Polish struggle for independence. If you take VA 3 to the north, you go to Montross. If you take VA 3 south, it heads toward Kilmarnock. If you continue to head east on US 360, Reedville is the ultimate destination, as the road dead-ends just before splashing into Cockrell Creek.

Drive north on VA 3, and you will come upon Montross in 12 miles. On the way to Montross—and, really, most anyplace on the Neck, you'll probably come upon a roadside produce stand. Stop and pick up a couple of quarts of

The Northern Neck is one of the access points for the **Virginia Oyster Trail**, which celebrates the state's oyster industry. The trail isn't an actual trail so much as it's a collection of oyster-related endeavors—from waterman tours to raw bars, from wineries to bed-and-breakfasts—that help visitors discover the pleasures of the bivalve that grows along the state's Eastern and Western shores.

"The oyster is to Virginia what the lobster is to Maine," said former Virginia governor Terry McAuliffe, announcing the launching of the trail. "When it comes to oysters, Virginia is all in."

The earliest English settlers marveled at the abundance and size of the oysters they found upon arrival in the New World, but the industry fell on lean times in the 1990s due to overfishing and disease. The oyster industry has staged a remarkable comeback in recent years.

The upshot? Virginia has become the largest producer of fresh, farm-raised oysters on the East Coast.

The state's oysters come from no fewer than eight regions around the Chesapeake Bay and Atlantic Ocean, meaning the oysters have that many distinctive flavors, from sweet to salty.

YEOCOMICO CHURCH, WELL OFF THE WELL-TRAVELED PATH, IS THE FINAL RESTING PLACE OF AUTHOR JOHN DOS PASSOS

strawberries in springtime or other fresh, just-picked fruits and vegetables at other times of the year.

The seat of Westmoreland County, Montross boasts a courthouse that dates to 1707 and, on its grounds, the nation's first sculptured Vietnam War Memorial. If you've never seen a lock of George Washington's hair, step into the nearby Westmoreland County Museum and Visitor Center. Washington's birthplace is not 10 miles away, on the Potomac.

If you're in an exploring mood, venture over to VA 606, between Kinsale and Tucker Hill, and search out the oldest church in Westmoreland County, Yeocomico Church. The Neck, besides having a number of eateries occupying former filling stations, is full of churches. George Washington attended the church, first built in 1655 and rebuilt in 1706. Author John Dos Passos is buried in the cemetery.

To reach Reedville, go east on US 360, through Callao and Heathsville, where you might want to stop at Rice's Hotel/Hughlett's Tavern, a restored 1700s structure that now houses a blacksmith shop, restaurant, and gift shop. Then, it's on to Reedville, reputed to have been the wealthiest community in the nation in the early 1900s because of the menhaden fishing industry. The industry is much reduced, but the stately Victorian mansions built by those early boat captains and factory owners remain along the last stretch of US 360. Millionaires Row, some of the locals call it.

The Reedville Fishermen's Museum tells the story of the area's watermen and their reliance on the bay and its tributaries for their livelihoods. A restored skipjack and a replica of the boat John Smith built to explore the bay more than 400 years ago are among the displays. If you're hungry, Crazy Crab and Reedville Market—both on Main Street—are good dinner options. Otherwise, Chitterchats Ice Cream Parlor, also on Main, is always a worthy stop; I highly recommend a double scoop of cookie dough ice cream. All, though, have limited operating hours.

The daily ferry to Tangier Island, mid-May until mid-October, leaves from Buzzard's Point Marina, just up the creek from the town itself and accessible by way of Fairport Road, just west of Reedville off US 360.

Driving on the Neck requires patience and planning, since everything seems to be about 20 minutes from everything else—like driving from Reedville to Kilmarnock. From Reedville head back west on US 360 to Burgess, then turn south on VA 200 (aka Jessie Ball Dupont Memorial Highway). Before you get to Kilmarnock, though, turn left on VA 606 (Shiloh School Road) to VA 605 (Balls Neck Road). Head left to the Dameron Marsh Natural Area Preserve or right to Hughlett Point Natural Area Preserve. Both state-protected wisps of land jut into the bay. At Dameron, flanked by Mill

REEDVILLE GREW UP AROUND THE FISHING INDUSTRY, AND THE REEDVILLE FISHERMEN'S MUSEUM TELLS THAT STORY

SIDE TRACKS

Tappahannock, a historic waterfront town on the Rappahannock, is a gateway to the Northern Neck when traveling on US 360 from Richmond.

It is the oldest town in Essex County and has an American Indian history that goes back long before Captain John Smith visited in 1608. The historic section of town, along the river and not far from the Downing Bridge that crosses over to the Neck, features several centuries-old structures, as well as St. Margaret's School, an independent, Episcopal, all-girls boarding school that's been in operation for more than a century.

The town has weathered its share of tragedy in recent years, including a tornado that cut a swath through town in 2016 and a massive 2022 fire that caused millions of dollars in damages, destroying a stretch of Prince Street. Firefighters from more than a dozen jurisdictions responded to the call, pumping water from the river to extinguish the blaze.

Efforts were already underway to revitalize Tapahannock's downtown, which is worth a stop and a leisurely stroll before heading over to the Neck.

Creek, walk in solitude on a gravel road through the marsh, a haven for birds and other critters. It's lovely, but take along bug spray.

Back to VA 200, continue to Kilmarnock, a tidy little town, excellent for walking, with numerous interesting shops. When you need a bite to eat, try any number of casual, reasonably priced dining spots, which include Northern Neck Burger or Car Wash Cafe, a wonderful little restaurant in a former convenience store. Another good place is Filibusters, the restaurant at the Kilmarnock Inn, where a crab-cake sandwich was my choice.

From Kilmarnock, go south on either VA 3 to White Stone or VA 200 to Irvington. Both roads eventually meet anyway. White Stone, like every other town on the Neck, offers good food possibilities: Willaby's on the Rappahannock (at the foot of the Robert O. Norris Bridge) is always a good bet.

Just outside of Kilmarnock, you will find Ditchley Cider Works, a relatively new operation in a historic setting. The property known as Ditchley, developed by the Lee family, dates to the 1600s, and the central portion of the main manor house was constructed in the 1750s. The estate was purchased in 1929 by Alfred I. and Jessie Ball Dupont and eventually passed to the Dupont Foundation before Cathy Calhoun and her husband, Paul Grosklags, came along and purchased the property in 2014. Calhoun and Grosklags have completed extensive renovations of the manor house and caretaker's house, established a large apple orchard for the purpose of producing hard cider, and are raising grass-fed beef and heritage hogs. Ditchley Cider Works is open on weekends—and for weddings and other special events—for purchase of its ciders and meat products.

For a completely different experience, between Kilmarnock and Irvington, is Compass Entertainment Complex, a multipurpose family entertainment center that features, among other activities, an arcade, batting cages, a climbing wall, Go-Karts, the area's only multiscreen movie theater, a restaurant, and, when the weather turns cold, the Northern Neck's only public outdoor ice-skating rink.

Irvington is a great little community best known, perhaps, for Christ Church, a restored Colonial-era church built by Robert "King" Carter, a powerful and wealthy landowner at the turn of the eighteenth century, and The Tides, a renowned resort (with golf course). But Irvington also offers the Steamboat Era Museum—which, as you might expect, celebrates the steamboat history of the region, the 1800s and early 1900s—eclectic shops, and The Hope & Glory Inn, a romantic bed-and-breakfast in a nineteenth-century, butter yellow schoolhouse. One of its amenities: a secluded, outdoor, claw-foot garden tub for bathing under the stars.

To complete a driving loop of the Neck, head north on VA 3, back toward Warsaw, but for a change of pace turn off on VA 201 at Lively and go 3 miles, then right on VA 354 for another 3 miles, and then left on VA 683 to the

THE KILMARNOCK INN IS A FINE PLACE TO FIND LOCAL SEAFOOD; LODGING IS ALSO AVAILABLE

entrance to Belle Isle State Park, one of Virginia's newest state parks. Trails for hiking, biking, and horseback riding follow old farm roads through fields and marshes. Bikes and canoes are available for rent. Walking might be best, though, for stopping and watching in quiet awe through binoculars at, say, a trio of bald eagles, perched in a treetop a few hundred yards in the distance. Ospreys are everywhere. Same for great blue herons. The place is a wonderland for bird-watchers.

It's like what my friend, Jann Steele, a longtime, part-time resident of the Neck, tells me when we stop on an empty road to admire a picture-perfect view of a gently moving creek.

"One of the things I love about the Northern Neck," says Steele, who lives in the tiny community of Sharps, a former steamship town, "is you can go around a curve and feel like you're in the middle of a wilderness where no one has ever been."

IN THE AREA

Accommodations

BACK INN TIME, 445 Irvington Road, Kilmarnock. Call 804-435-2318. Website: www.backinntime.biz. Early 1900s Southern manor turned into a bed-and-breakfast.

THE HOPE AND GLORY INN, 65 Tavern Road, Irvington. Call 804-438-6053. Website: www.hopeandglory.com. Old schoolhouse converted into a bed-and-breakfast inn.

KILMARNOCK INN AND RESTAURANT, 34 E. Church Street, Kilmarnock. Call 804-435-0034. Website: www.kilmarnockinn.com. Seven cottages, named for Virginia-born presidents, steps from downtown Kilmarnock.

THE TIDES INN, 480 King Carter Drive, Irvington. Call 804-438-5000. Website: www.tidesinn.com. Luxury resort on its own peninsula.

Attractions and Recreation

DITCHLEY CIDER WORKS, 1571 Ditchley Road, Kilmarnock. Call 804-435-3851. Website: www.ditchleyciderworks.com. Working farm and cidery on a historic site. Ciders and meat products available through online store. Open on weekends and for special events.

RICE'S HOTEL/HUGHLETT'S TAVERN, 73 Monument Place, Heathsville. Call 804-580-3377. Website: www.rhhtfoundationinc.org. Restored 1700s building with blacksmith forge, quilt guild, tavern restaurant, and gift shop.

BELLE ISLE STATE PARK, 1632 Belle Isle Road, Lancaster. Call 804-462-5030. Website: www.dcr.virginia.gov/state-parks/belle-isle. Hiking trails, canoeing, birding.

COMPASS ENTERTAINMENT COMPLEX, 100 Entertainment Drive, Irvington. Call 804-884-4386. Website: www.compassentertainment complex.com. Multipurpose family entertainment.

HISTORIC CHRIST CHURCH, 420 Christ Church Road, Weems. Call 804-438-6855. Website: www.christchurch1735.org. Completed in 1735, Christ Church is a well-preserved example of Colonial Virginia's parish churches. Open for tours.

KILMARNOCK MUSEUM, 76 N. Main Street, Kilmarnock. Website: www .kilmarnockva.com/places/kilmarnock-museum. Repository of local artifacts and historic displays in one of the oldest buildings in Kilmarnock.

OLD FARM TRUCK MARKET, 435 Rappahannock Drive, White Stone. Website: www.oldfarmtruckmarket.com. Market and kitchen featuring locally raised produce and meats.

REEDVILLE FISHERMEN'S MUSEUM, 504 Main Street, Reedville. Call 804-453-6529. Website: www.rfmuseum.org. Preserves heritage of maritime history of lower Chesapeake Bay.

YEOCOMICO CHURCH, 1219 Old Yeocomico Road, Kinsale. Website: cople parish.com. The oldest church in Westmoreland County.

Dining

CAR WASH CAFE, 481 N. Main Street, Kilmarnock. Call 804-435-0405. Website: www.facebook.com/profile.php?id=61552956216386. Homemade favorites served in a former convenience store.

CHAD'S DAD'S BBQ, 1051 General Puller Highway, Saluda. Website: www .facebook.com/Chadsdadsbbq. Small place, good food.

528 PRIME STEAK & SEAFOOD, 528 S. Church Lane, Tappahannock. Call 804-925-6009. Website: www.528primesteakseafood.com. Family-friendly dining, featuring steaks and locally sourced seafood. In the same space as Lowery's, a venerable local favorite that dates back almost a century.

NORTHERN NECK BURGER CO., 62 Irvington Road, Kilmarnock, and 303 Queen Street, Tappahannock. Call 804-577-4400 or 804-925-6100. Website: www.nnburger.com. Some of the best burgers in Virginia.

RELISH RESTAURANT AND WINE BAR, 115 Main Street,Warsaw. Call 804-761-6727. Website: www.relishnnk.com. Contemporary, farm-to-table Southern cuisine.

THE CORNER RESTAURANT, 5360 Mary Ball Road, Lively. Call 804-462-0110. Small town bar and grill.

THE OAKS, 5434 Mary Ball Road, Lively. Call 804-462-7050. Down-home place.

WILLABY'S CAFE, 327 Old Ferry Road, White Stone. Call 804-435-0000. Website: www.willabys.com.

Other Contacts

NORTHERN NECK TOURISM COMMISSION, P.O. Box 1707, Warsaw. Call 804-333-1919. Website: www.northernneck.org.

THE VIRGINIA OYSTER TRAIL. Call 757-829-0500. Website: www.virginiaoystertrail.com. Tours, markets, more.

4

HISTORIC TRIANGLE

Jamestown, Williamsburg, and Yorktown

ESTIMATED LENGTH: 23 miles

ESTIMATED TIME: Day trip

HIGHLIGHTS: Visiting **Jamestown**, **Colonial Williamsburg**, and **Yorktown**, historic sites that represent, one could argue, the birthplace of the United States, all connected by the scenic, 23-mile **Colonial Parkway**. Jamestown is where America was born, Williamsburg is where its system of government was nurtured, and Yorktown is where the young nation won its independence.

GETTING THERE: To reach **Jamestown** from I-64, take Exit 242A and take VA 199 west to either the Colonial Parkway or VA 31, and follow the signs. Or for an altogether different approach, come from the south side of the **James River**, taking VA 10 to VA 31 north to the free **Jamestown-Scotland Ferry**. Coming across the water to Jamestown will afford you a modern-day view of what the first colonists saw upon arriving there.

You can't very well make a serious tour of Virginia without hitting a site or two of where it all started: the historic triangle of Jamestown, Williamsburg, and Yorktown. It can be an enlightening and moving experience.

Stand on the deck of the *Discovery,* the 66-foot-long, full-size replica of the tiny ship that sailed from London in 1606, and gaze out over the bow. Imagine the placid waters of the James River with heaving swells in the Atlantic, and, if your imagination is vivid enough, you get some sense of what it must have been like for the passengers and crew aboard, heading into the great unknown. Four months they were on that ship. Only slightly less amazing than the fact they reached the New World intact is that they didn't kill each other in the process. Their boat was small and cramped, their provisions limited, their anxiety must have been high and their patience thin.

LEFT: VISITORS CAN BOARD RE-CREATIONS OF THE *SUSAN CONSTANT, GODSPEED,* AND *DISCOVERY* AT JAMESTOWN SETTLEMENT JAMESTOWN-YORKTOWN FOUNDATION

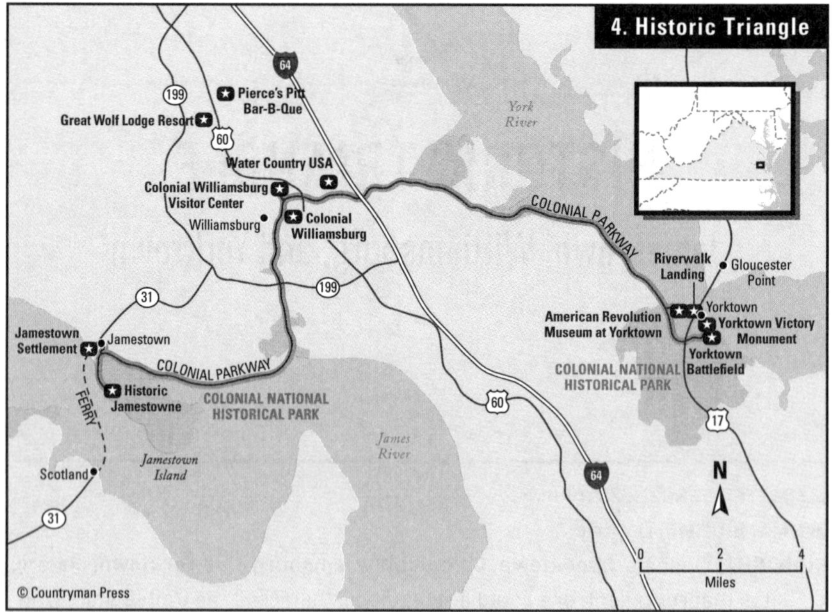

Many of the English settlers, in fact, did not survive long-term in the place they called Jamestown—named for their king, James I—but the settlement did, and America was born.

The *Discovery,* along with replicas of its larger sister ships, *Susan Constant* and *Godspeed,* are usually moored and available for boarding at Jamestown Settlement, a sprawling indoor and outdoor museum that tells the story of America's first permanent English settlement through gallery exhibits, film, and living history. Hanging around Jamestown Settlement and the adjacent Historic Jamestowne, the original site of the colony that's now jointly administered by the National Park Service and Preservation Virginia, is at once an instructive and humbling experience. What must it have been like to try to build a life here, so far from all they knew and in the face of terrible hardships such as illness and famine, not to mention fear and loneliness?

Our plan is to start at Jamestown, then drive 10 miles east along the Colonial Parkway to Colonial Williamsburg, grab some lunch and see some sights, then drive another 13 miles to the eastern end of the parkway at Yorktown. It will be a full day.

First, a note about admission. Jamestown Settlement and the American Revolution Museum at Yorktown are operated by the Jamestown-Yorktown Foundation, an educational agency of the commonwealth of Virginia. Tickets may be purchased for each or in combination with the other nearby sites—Historic Jamestowne, Yorktown Battlefield, and Colonial Williamsburg—through the America's Historic Triangle seven-day ticket.

A STATUE OF CAPTAIN JOHN SMITH KEEPS WATCH AT HISTORIC JAMESTOWNE, THE SITE OF THE FIRST PERMANENT ENGLISH SETTLEMENT

At Jamestown Settlement, we come first to the theater and galleries, so we watch a film that provides context for what we're about to see outside, and we browse exhibits arranged in a helpful timeline that covers the convergence of English, Native American, and African American cultures. Outdoors, we explore the Powhatan Indian way of life at a re-creation of Paspahegh Town. The Paspahegh were one of more than 30 Algonquian-speaking tribal groups that belonged to the Powhatan chiefdom. The re-creation is based on archaeological findings near the river, oral tradition from Virginia tribes, and descriptions and illustrations recorded by the earliest English colonists. Costumed historical interpreters demonstrate traditional Powhatan activities, including growing and preparing food, making pottery, and weaving natural fibers, as well as how a dugout canoe was made using Powhatan techniques. A walkway leads to James Fort, a re-creation of the triangular-shaped fort constructed by the colonists that includes wattle-and-daub houses with thatched roofs, a church, and a blacksmith

THE COLONIAL PARKWAY, A PLEASANT 23-MILE DRIVE THAT CONNECTS JAMESTOWN, COLONIAL WILLIAMSBURG, AND YORKTOWN

shop, where a demonstration is taking place. Then, it's down to the dock, and a few minutes exploring the ships.

Jamestown Settlement has long been incorporating Indigenous, English, and West Central African cultures in its exhibits and presentations, but constantly leans on new research to more accurately—and respectfully—tell their stories, a museum spokeswoman tells me. "We're wanting to get it right," she says.

If all of this history leaves you hungry, Jamestown Settlement Café, back in the museum's main building just down the hall from the ticket counter, offers the requisite burgers and sandwiches, but also Brunswick stew, vegetarian chili, and even homemade bread pudding with apple-raisin sauce for dessert, on the day we were there.

To reach Historic Jamestowne, about a mile away, get on the Colonial Parkway at Jamestown Settlement and head east along the river. The visitor center is, of course, a good place to start. We walk past the statue of Pocahontas where children are posing for family snapshots, and then past the nearby church tower, the only seventeenth-century building still standing at Jamestown. The church itself was built in 1906, on the site of several previous churches that either burned or fell into disrepair.

You reach the site of the original fort by crossing a footbridge over a pitch and tar swamp. A guide tells me the fort wasn't as close to the water as it appears; in the early 1600s, the shoreline was maybe the distance of a football field out into where the river is now. Erosion is the culprit. As we stand on the seawall, I notice the river lapping gently, but persistently, at the bank.

Since 1994, the Jamestown Rediscovery archaeological project at Historic Jamestowne has been bringing to life the stories of early James Fort, and ongoing archaeological work is always turning up something new (or old).

No doubt those first colonists had a tough time, and it wasn't all their doing. Studies indicate they showed up in Jamestown during the worst drought in 800 years. We stroll along the shore and peek into an ongoing archaeological dig site. We see some of the discovered items at the Voorhees Archaearium, Historic Jamestowne's archaeology museum, which masterfully uses scientific research and artifacts such as shards of pottery, surgical tools, and a human skeleton to tell the settlement's story.

Off to Colonial Williamsburg we head, but before we get away from Jamestown, we stop at the Jamestown glasshouse near the entrance to the park and watch artisans demonstrating the techniques of seventeenth-century glassblowing, which happened to be one of the first industries at Jamestown.

Colonial Williamsburg, the reconstructed colonial capital, is a 10-mile ride along the Colonial Parkway, the limited-access, three-lane road—the middle lane is for passing—with no commercial development to detract

VISITORS ARE TREATED TO AN ARTILLERY DEMONSTRATION AT THE AMERICAN REVOLUTION MUSEUM AT YORKTOWN JAMESTOWN-YORKTOWN FOUNDATION

from its natural setting. The maximum speed limit is 45 miles per hour. The parkway, a unit of the National Park Service, traverses the peninsula from the James River to the York River, connecting the two NPS properties: Historic Jamestowne and Yorktown Battlefield. Colonial Williamsburg is in the middle.

Williamsburg thrived as Virginia's capital for most of the 1700s, before it was moved to Richmond. By the early 1900s, however, much of the historic town had fallen into disrepair. Philanthropist John D. Rockefeller Jr. spearheaded an effort to restore the town, and now it thrives as a major tourist attraction.

We arrive and park at the Colonial Williamsburg visitor center, just off the parkway and US 60. The parking lot is huge, and the center itself, where tickets are purchased and information gathered, has the feel of an airline terminal. Shuttles are available to the historic area—free with admission tickets or available for a fee if you don't wish to buy a ticket—but we opt to walk on a footbridge that carries us first through Great Hopes Plantation, a living history site that's representative of rural Virginia in the 1700s, and then over and under roadways into the town itself.

There is much to do and see in Colonial Williamsburg, from demonstrations by shoemakers and chocolate-makers to tours of the Governor's Palace and Bruton Parish Church. One thing to remember: You can visit Colonial

VISITORS CAN ROAM THE YORKTOWN BATTLEFIELD ON A BLUFF ABOVE THE YORK RIVER

STATUES OF GEORGE WASHINGTON, COMMANDER OF THE AMERICAN FORCES, AND ADM. FRANÇOIS DE GRASSE, COMMANDER OF THE FRENCH FLEET, MEET ON THE YORKTOWN WATERFRONT

Williamsburg and walk up and down the streets to your heart's content, but you must purchase an admission ticket to enter many of the buildings or take advantage of guided tours and that sort of thing.

We roam along Duke of Gloucester Street—the central avenue in the historic district—and stick our noses in the apothecary, the blacksmith's, and a tavern or two. We watch and listen as a fife-and-drum corps marches past. No cars here, just horse-drawn carriages. We walk around the old capitol and over to the Governor's Palace, where we go around back to the formal gardens where we get lost, briefly, in the tall boxwood maze. I remember the maze as a kid, coming here on school field trips, and I still think it's one of the neatest things in town.

We stop at the bakery behind the Raleigh Tavern and purchase gingerbread and peanut butter cookies, apple cider and root beer, and enjoy them at a picnic table in the shade behind the shop. Now that we've had dessert, we head for lunch at the other end of Duke of Gloucester, at the Cheese Shop in Merchants Square (near an entrance to the College of William and Mary). The gourmet food shop, a favorite of locals and tourists, which often makes for long lines, sells all kinds of cheeses, naturally, but also great sandwiches. I go with the Virginia ham salad on rye, while my son settles on a small tub of freshly made mixed-bean salad. We are both pleased with our choices, as we enjoy lunch at tables on the front patio, a great vantage point for people-watching. Numerous shops and restaurants in the Merchants Square area make this an easy place to spend a considerable amount of time.

Increasingly, there is more to Williamsburg than the familiar story schoolchildren have long learned about the colonial period. One such focal point is First Baptist Church of Williamsburg, one of America's earliest African American congregations, which was founded by enslaved and free Black worshipers. Colonial Williamsburg has partnered with the church and the Let Freedom Ring Foundation in an archaeological project to locate the first site of the church and to learn more about the people who worshiped there.

A short drive from Williamsburg, you will find Jolly's Mill Pond, a 200-year-old tree farm and pond with a rich, though still emerging, history. In the late 1700s or early 1800s, enslaved African Americans carved earth from a steep hillside by hand and with that dirt built a ⅛-mile-long dam to create a 50-acre lake that powered a grist mill for a century and made the place a vital hub of the community. But there's more—much more—to the story. The property is not far from Freedom Park, one of the first free Black settlements in America, and throughout its history, Jolly's Mill Pond was home to different socioeconomic tiers of Blacks: enslaved, free, and those who farmed the land. It represents a different sort of history than what is typically found a few miles away, along the cobblestone streets of Colonial Williamsburg.

"We are peeling back the layers of Black history on the property, which is multifaceted and goes beyond the flat narrative that most of us have grown up learning about Black history," Angi Kane tells me. She owns the property with her husband, Bill, and the Kanes' background adds another angle to the property's story: Angi, an Emmy-winning filmmaker who grew up in Brooklyn, is Black, and Bill, whose family acquired the property in the 1950s as a weekend getaway, is white. He spent his childhood exploring the woods and fishing the pond without being aware of the full history of the property.

Their goal is to preserve the legacy of Jolly's Mill Pond and to share the history and wonder of the place through educational tours and other public outreach. You can arrange a tour and learn more by contacting the Kanes at www.jollysmillpond.com.

Yorktown, site of the climactic battle of the American Revolution, is another 13 miles east on the parkway, and, like Jamestown, it has two major attractions: the American Revolution Museum (formerly Yorktown Victory Center) and Yorktown Battlefield, both of which chronicle the colonial experience to the end of the war, which culminated in the surrender of British General Charles Lord Cornwallis at Yorktown in 1781.

The American Revolution Museum, which replaced Yorktown Victory Center in 2016, features innovative indoor exhibits—including the thunder

YOUR SENSE OF ADVENTURE AND NAVIGATION WILL COME IN HANDY AT THE GARDEN MAZE BEHIND THE GOVERNOR'S PALACE IN COLONIAL WILLIAMSBURG

of cannon fire—and outdoor living history to tell the dramatic story of the Revolution. Re-creations of a Continental Army encampment and an eighteenth-century farm based on a real family who lived nearby lend a take-you-there element to the visit.

Yorktown Battlefield, a unit of the National Park Service, offers a visitor center with artifacts such as General George Washington's military tents, and ranger-led programs or self-guided driving and walking tours of the battlefield. We walk on trails among the earthworks and cannon and admire the view of sailboats on the river. We cross a long pedestrian bridge over a ravine to reach the Yorktown Victory Monument. Nearly 100 feet tall, the monument to commemorate the victory over the British was authorized by the Continental Congress in October 1781. Construction began—a century later. The monument was finally completed in 1884.

Yorktown, which sits on a bluff high above the river, looks like a colonial town with narrow streets and grand old houses, one of which belonged to Thomas Nelson Jr., who signed the Declaration of Independence. Daylight fading, we negotiate a narrow footpath down the hill to the waterfront where we find, beneath the bluff, Cornwallis' Cave, its small opening blocked by a gate and marked by a sign. As the story goes, Cornwallis moved his headquarters to the cave to escape the assault by American and French troops. More likely, the cave was used by a British gun crew to defend against the French fleet. As the story also goes, the cave is haunted, though we decide not to hang around to find out.

While the streets above are fairly quiet, the waterfront is far busier, even on a weeknight. We stroll past Yorktown Pub, its doors open to the warm evening and music spilling out. Just a few feet from the beach and something of a landmark, the popular pub attracts locals and tourists with fresh seafood, homemade desserts, and a convivial atmosphere. Farther down the bricked-over, waterfront path, we come to Riverwalk Landing, a multi-million-dollar retail development trying to capture a little waterfront magic with shopping and dining in this once-thriving seaport with terrific views of the river and the George P. Coleman Bridge, a 3,750-foot-long double-swing-span bridge over the river that connects Yorktown to Gloucester County.

As we look up, we see the headlights of cars and trucks heading into the dusk. In less than 25 miles, we have traveled more than 400 years through American history. Not a bad day's work.

IN THE AREA

Accommodations

GREAT WOLF LODGE RESORT, 549 East Rochambeau Drive, Williamsburg. Call 800-551-9653. Website: www.greatwolf.com. Indoor water park, lodging, dining, and spa.

COLONIAL WILLIAMSBURG RESORTS, Williamsburg. Call 800-231-7240. Website: www.colonialwilliamsburghotels.com. Variety of lodging types, from motel to premium hotel.

Attractions and Recreation

AMERICAN REVOLUTION MUSEUM, 200 Water Street, Yorktown. Call 757-253-4838. Website: www.jyfmuseums.org.

BUSCH GARDENS, One Busch Gardens Boulevard, Williamsburg. Call 757-229-4386. Website: www.buschgardens.com/williamsburg. Theme Park. Seasonal.

COLONIAL NATIONAL HISTORICAL PARK, including **Historic Jamestowne**, **Yorktown Battlefield**, and **Colonial Parkway**, P.O. Box 210, Yorktown. Call 757-898-2410. Website: www.nps.gov/colo.

COLONIAL WILLIAMSBURG, 101 Visitor Center Drive, Williamsburg. Call 888-965-7254. Website: www.colonialwilliamsburg.org. Billed as the "world's largest US history museum."

JAMESTOWN SETTLEMENT, 2110 Jamestown Road, Route 31 S., Williamsburg. Call 757-253-4838. Website: www.jyfmuseums.org

WATER COUNTRY USA, 176 Water Country Parkway, Williamsburg. Call 757-229-4386. Website: www.watercountryusa.com. Outdoor water park. Seasonal.

Dining

THE CHEESE SHOP, 410 W. Duke of Gloucester Street, Williamsburg. Call 757-220-0298. Website: www.cheeseshopwilliamsburg.com. Sandwiches, cheese, freshly baked breads, specialty foods, wine cellar.

PIERCE'S PITT BAR-B-QUE, 447 East Rochambeau, Williamsburg. Call 757-565-2955. Website: www.pierces.com. A local tradition with barbecue, burgers, hot dogs, and chicken.

WATER STREET GRILLE, 323 Water Street, Yorktown. Call 757-369-5644. Website: www.waterstreetgrille.net. Casual dining featuring seafood, salad, sandwiches, and pizza.

Other Contacts

JAMESTOWN-SCOTLAND FERRY, 16289 Rolfe Highway, Surry, or 2110 Jamestown Road, Williamsburg, on the Jamestown side. Call 1-800-823-3779. Website: www.vdot.virginia.gov/travel/ferry-jamestown.asp.

5

OLD HOUSES, NEW STORIES

The Former Plantations of VA 5

ESTIMATED LENGTH: 40 miles

ESTIMATED TIME: Day trip or weekend

HIGHLIGHTS: A drive along VA 5, also known as John Tyler Memorial Highway, is the old river road between Richmond and Jamestown. Tours of several of the grand **James River** plantations—**Berkeley, Sherwood Forest, Shirley,** and **Westover**—represent the first westward expansion of English-speaking America and almost 400 years of the nation's history. For lunch or dinner, **Ronnie's Ribs, Wings & Other Things, Cul's Courthouse Grille,** and **Indian Fields Tavern** are good spots. Alongside the road most of the way runs the **Virginia Capital Trail**, a 52-mile-long, fully paved, bicycle and pedestrian trail between downtown Richmond and Jamestown Settlement.

GETTING THERE: From downtown Richmond, take Main Street east to where it meets VA 5 and follow road to Jamestown. By way of I-295, go to Exit 22A and then east on VA 5.

Historical markers, sometimes clumped like spring flowers, are common sights along VA 5, a mostly pleasant two-lane road that rambles through forests and farmland along the north shore of the James River, between Richmond and Jamestown. This stretch of road is home to the James River plantations, large estates east of Richmond, where the fledgling American colonies developed their first successful commerce (i.e., cultivating tobacco). So, history along the road has long been within easy reach. The complete history, however, is more elusive and still evolving.

Growing up in the Richmond area, in the middle of where so much of America took shape, we were fed a steady diet of Virginia history, and rightly so. We just didn't get the full story. That situation is still being remedied as

LEFT: THE LANE TO HISTORIC WESTOVER, A FORMER COLONIAL PLANTATION, WHERE A MORE COMPLETE STORY IS EMERGING

Before beginning the drive, you should know that one of the best things about this route isn't the road at all, but a paved path that runs alongside VA 5 much of the way. The **Virginia Capital Trail**, a 52-mile-long bicycle and pedestrian trail, connects Richmond to Jamestown and Williamsburg.

The trail offers a slower-paced perspective of this historic route. Convenient parking is available in downtown Richmond at Great Shiplock Park, at Four Mile Creek trailhead at I-295 and VA 5, in the town of Charles City, at Chickahominy Riverfront Park on the Chickahominy River, and, of course, in Jamestown and Williamsburg.

Soon after the trail was completed, we parked at Four Mile Creek Park trailhead and pedaled 20 miles to Charles City, stopping for lunch at **Cul's Courthouse Grille**, near the county's courthouse complex and just off the trail. Housed in a former general store that dates to the 1800s, Cul's offers a good selection of sandwiches and salads and even serious entrées (though its menu is thin on vegetarian offerings), and is a popular stop for cyclists, as evidenced by the logjam of bikes parked outside on the Saturday afternoon of our ride. **Indian Fields Tavern**, a couple of miles west of the courthouse, is right on VA 5. Closer to Richmond—between I-295 and downtown—is the **Original Ronnie's BBQ**, right on the trail on New Market Road. Pitmaster Ronnie Logan has decades of experience and ran a popular food truck and catering business before opening his stand-alone shop. His food is outstanding.

THE VIRGINIA CAPITAL TRAIL IS A 52-MILE-LONG PAVED TRAIL FOR PEDESTRIANS AND CYCLISTS THAT PARALLELS VA 5 BETWEEN RICHMOND AND JAMESTOWN

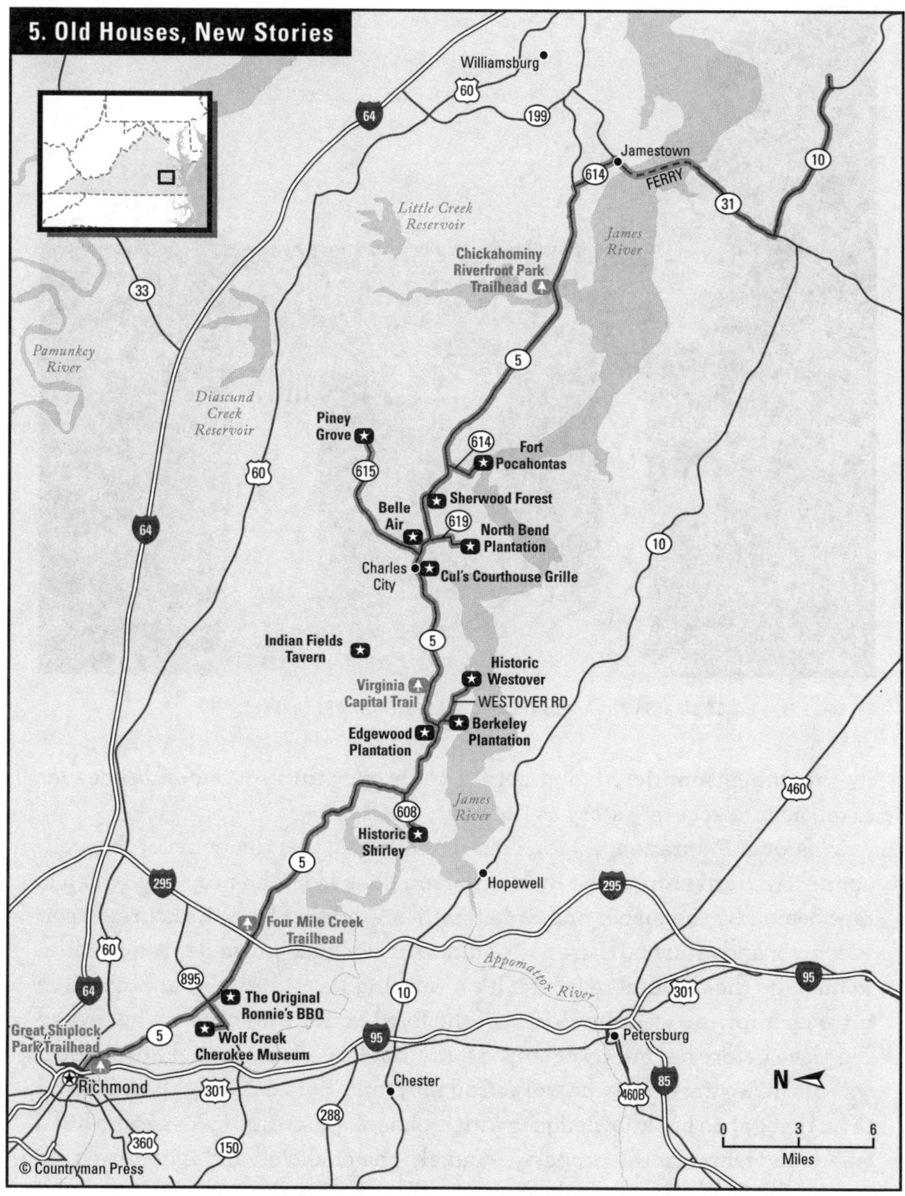

we try to come to grips with the not-so-rosy past, working, in particular, to better incorporate the role of enslaved people—their contributions, their sufferings, their lives. Organizations operating large, more-celebrated historic places have made significant headway in recent decades in that regard, but the situation is more challenging for individuals connected to historic sites who want to do the right thing but lack the resources to root out the truth.

The James River plantations are a case in point. None of them are owned

BERKELEY PLANTATION STAKES ITS CLAIM AS THE SITE OF AMERICA'S FIRST THANKSGIVING

by government entities, though some remain open to the public and endeavor to tell a more accurate story as they go.

Westover Plantation, established in the 1700s, was the home of the well-connected Byrd family. The Byrds are long gone from the property, which is now owned by the Fisher and Erda families. Andrea Fisher Erda grew up at Westover and returned there as an adult with her husband and three children to manage the 1,000-acre estate. It's a working farm, and it's her home. She grew up knowing well the stories of the Byrd family and others who owned the place before her family acquired it in 1921. Less clear, she acknowledged, was the history of those who worked on the plantation. One way she is hoping to fix that gap in her knowledge is with archaeological digs to learn who lived where and when on the property—namely, the enslaved and indentured, as well as the Indigenous people who were there before the European settlers.

"These are extraordinary places with so much history attached to them, and the problem is that only one side of that history has been told," Erda tells me of the James River plantations in general and Westover in particular. "Now, that is not an active whitewash, which some people accuse plantation owners of, but it's what is in the public record. As a family home, I don't have the staff, and I don't have the resources, to comb the records for stories that probably weren't even written down. It's super-important to tell those stories, but it's not as if they're right there: do I want to talk about the rich white man, or do I want to talk about the person who was enslaved? I'd love to talk about them both."

Westover's grounds and gardens are open daily, and interior tours of the house are by appointment. I visit in spring 2023 to walk through the gardens and along the riverfront in what is the front yard of the magnificent house. My visit coincides with an archaeological dig, a search for evidence of enslaved living quarters on a bluff above the James River, about a quarter-mile from the main house. The dig is conducted by a team from the Virginia Department of Historic Resources, invited in by Erda. They are following up on the discovery from a dig a year earlier of nineteenth-century artifacts, such as machine-cut nails and ceramic and bottle glass that seemed to confirm the location indicated by historical maps. They also found stones fashioned into projectile points and scraping tools dating back possibly thousands of years, according to state archaeologist Michael Clem.

"I'm determined to tell the story of these folks whose story is every bit as important as that of the owners of the property," says Clem.

Archaeology is perhaps the best way to tell this side of the story. There are no records about the hundreds of enslaved who lived and worked at Westover and no structures remaining from that era. Records and maps also indicate a courthouse and an ordinary (a resting place or tavern) for travelers visiting the courthouse were nearby in what amounted to downtown Charles City in those days. Clem hopes to keep returning to Westover to search for those sites. Erda hopes he does, too, though, as she says, her family receives no public funding and has "no onus whatsoever on us" to open their home to state archaeologists or even to the public. "But we think it's important," she says, noting Westover "is a piece of American history." She also hopes Westover will become the "restorative, peaceful place" that she knows for all people. "History cannot be undone," a statement says on the Westover website, "but we hope that in its truthful telling, there are opportunities for reconciliation and healing for people of all skin colors."

The situation is similar at other historic homes along VA 5—Berkeley, Shirley, and Sherwood Forest, among them—that are private residences open to the public. The current owners are working to shed light on the grim episodes of their history and make a point of acknowledging the under-told history. In a statement on Berkeley's website, the Jamieson family that resides there says, "We believe that Black Americans, Indigenous People, and their descendants deserve justice, respect, and support as they have suffered unimaginable tragedies and losses through enslavement and genocide at the foundation of America. We are working with researchers and historians to uncover all aspects of this site's past, and there is much work and responsibility ahead to make this site a place for healing and awareness."

The first official Thanksgiving in America—at least, to Virginians' way of thinking—was held at Berkeley in 1619, two years before the Pilgrims at Plim-

CUL'S COURTHOUSE GRILLE IN CHARLES CITY IS A POPULAR DESTINATION FOR CYLISTS ALONG THE VIRGINIA CAPITAL TRAIL

oth Plantation. Benjamin Harrison V, a signer of the Declaration of Independence, and William Henry Harrison, ninth president of the United States, were born here. (The 23rd president, Benjamin Harrison, was a grandson of William Henry Harrison, but he was born in Ohio.) During the Civil War, US General George B. McClellan set up his headquarters at Berkeley, which is where one of his soldiers composed "Taps" and played it for the first time. President Lincoln came here twice to confer with McClellan.

On a visit a few years ago, I arrive a few minutes before the house tour begins, so I stroll through the terraced boxwood gardens, past the magnolias and crape myrtles, then walk down a long, tree-sheltered lane to the river, gently lapping at the shore. I return to the house and notice a cannonball lodged in an upper wall of an outbuilding next door. The tour begins in the basement museum of the great house, a 1726 Georgian mansion that is said to be the oldest three-story brick home in Virginia. We watch a video about the plantation and then head up to the main floor to learn more about the place.

The first bourbon whiskey was distilled here in 1621, and each of the first ten US presidents visited here. After the Civil War, the Harrisons never regained the house, and it fell into disrepair. A former drummer boy among McClelland's troops, John Jamieson, returned in 1907 and purchased the plantation, and he set about restoring the home. His descendants still own Berkeley, and it remains a working farm.

On the same day we visit Berkeley, we venture 3 miles to Shirley Plantation. Shirley's grounds, gardens, and outbuildings are open for self-guided tours; guided house tours are offered several days each week. At Shirley, twelve generations of the Hill-Carter family have lived and worked here. The 800-acre plantation, established in 1613, only six years after the colonists arrived at Jamestown, is considered the oldest family-owned business in North America. Tobacco was the early ticket to prosperity; the plantation has diversified since. The brick mansion was completed in 1738. A guide rings a bell to signal the beginning of the house tour.

We learn the name Shirley comes from the British couple who were given the royal land grant for the property in 1613—the wife's maiden name was Shirley. They never set foot on the land, but the name stuck. We admire the exquisite "flying staircase" that rises three stories without any visible means of support; the guide says hidden wrought-iron straps secure the stairs to the walls. We see a baby bed where Robert E. Lee slept; his mother, Anne Hill Carter, was born here, and she was married to Henry "Light Horse Harry" Lee in the parlor. Despite that connection, Union soldiers spared the home during the Civil War because of kindnesses shown by the family toward the

SHERWOOD FOREST, THE HOME OF PRESIDENT JOHN TYLER, STRETCHES FOR 300 FEET IN LENGTH

A LONG WALKING PATH AT BERKELEY PLANTATION, NEAR THE BANKS OF THE JAMES RIVER

troops; McClellan issued an order protecting the house from looting.

Fifteen miles east of Shirley is Sherwood Forest, the home of John Tyler, the tenth US president. The length of the house immediately stands out; it's as long as a football field. The main portion of the house was constructed about 1720, but has been added onto over the years, including a narrow ballroom, a caretaker once told me, that John Tyler had built so he and his friends could dance the Virginia Reel at home.

Tyler was the first vice president to ascend to the presidency due to the death of a president. He succeeded President William Henry Harrison, who died only a month after his inauguration. Harrison, of course, lived just up the river at Berkeley, but Tyler wasn't a neighbor at the time. He didn't purchase the plantation until 1842, when he was already in the White House, and he renamed it Sherwood Forest because of his reputation as a political outlaw. An amazing fact: Tyler served as president from 1841 to 1845, yet his grandson Harrison Tyler was still alive when this book was revised in 2023. How? John Tyler fathered a son at age sixty-three. That child fathered a son at age seventy-five, in 1928. That son is Harrison Tyler, who resided part-time at Sherwood Forest until recent years.

The grounds are open daily and house tours are given by appointment at Sherwood Forest, which is still maintained by the Tyler family, some of whom have begun more closely examining its history. Frances Tyler, the president's great-great-granddaughter, began looking into the history of the enslaved while she was in college. Research led her to the names of those enslaved by John Tyler and meetings with descendants of the enslaved in Charles City County. She read letters written by her ancestors and was "disgusted" by the way her great-great-grandparents referred to Black people and "overwhelmingly sad" to learn details of that part of Sherwood Forest history she had never been told. She grew up in Richmond but visited Sherwood Forest for holidays and other family gatherings. It's a place she loves, she says, but she aims to "acknowledge this history that has been silenced and omitted. It's definitely a work in progress." She is busy with law school when we speak, but she has created a website that addresses the history of the enslaved at Sherwood Forest and developed training for those who give tours there to incorporate the stories of enslaved people they know about. "I'd love to see it continue to expand as we find out more," she says.

Down by the river, about a 3-mile drive from Sherwood Forest, is the site of Fort Pocahontas, an earthen Civil War fort notable because it was built and maintained by Black Union troops. The fort lay forgotten and overgrown for more than a century until a military historian discovered it. Harrison Tyler, Frances' grandfather, purchased the land to preserve it for historical and archaeological research. Guided tours for groups of 10 or more are available by appointment through a private foundation of the Tyler family.

Other former plantations along the north bank of the James include Edgewood and North Bend (both now bed-and-breakfasts), Belle Air and Kittiewan (which are occasionally open for house tours) and Burlington, a wedding and event venue.

HISTORIC WESTOVER IS AMONG A NUMBER OF COLONIAL PLANTATIONS BUILT ALONG THE JAMES RIVER EAST OF RICHMOND

IN THE AREA

Accommodations

EDGEWOOD PLANTATION BED AND BREAKFAST, 4800 John Tyler Memorial Highway, Charles City. Call 804-829-2962. Website: www.edgewoodplantation.com.

NORTH BEND PLANTATION BED AND BREAKFAST, 12200 Weyanoke Road, Charles City. Call 804-829-5176. Website: www.northbendplantation.com.

PINEY GROVE BED AND BREAKFAST AT SOUTHALL'S PLANTATION, 16920 Southall Plantation Lane, Charles City. Call 804-829-2480. Website: www.pineygrove.com.

RIVER'S REST MARINA & RESORT, 9100 Willcox Neck Road, Charles City. Call 804-829-2753. Website: www.riversrest.com. A twenty-one room motel overlooking the marina and the Chickahominy River.

Attractions and Recreation

BERKELEY PLANTATION, 12602 Harrison Landing Road, Charles City. Call 804-829-6018. Website: www.berkeleyplantation.com.

FORT POCAHONTAS, 14501 John Tyler Memorial Highway, Charles City. Call 804-829-9722. Website: www.fortpocahontas.org. Earthen Civil War fort.

HISTORIC SHIRLEY, 501 Shirley Plantation Road, Charles City. Call 804-829-5121. Website: www.historicshirley.com.

HISTORIC WESTOVER, 7000 Westover Road, Charles City. Call 804-829-2882. Website: www.historicwestover.com.

SHERWOOD FOREST PLANTATION, 14501 John Tyler Memorial Highway, Charles City. Call 804-829-5377. Websites: www.sherwoodforest.org and www.presidentjohntylersenslavedhouseholds.com.

VIRGINIA CAPITAL TRAIL. Website: www.virginiacapitaltrail.org. A 52-mile-long biking and walking trail connecting Richmond, Jamestown, and Williamsburg.

WOLF CREEK CHEROKEE MUSEUM, 7400 Osborne Turnpike, Richmond. Website: wolfcreekcherokee.com.

Dining

CUL'S COURTHOUSE GRILLE, 10801 Courthouse Road, Charles City. Call 804-829-2205. Website: www.culscourthousegrille.com.

EDWARDS VIRGINIA HAM SHOPPE, 11381 Rolfe Highway, Surry. Call 757-294-3688. (There is also a location at 5541C Richmond Road, Williamsburg.) Website: www.edwardsvaham.com.

INDIAN FIELDS TAVERN, 9220 John Tyler Memorial Highway, Charles City. Call 804-829-2200. Website: www.facebook.com/indianfieldstavern. Restaurant in an old farmhouse.

RONNIE'S RIBS, WINGS & OTHER THINGS, 2097 New Market Road, Richmond. Call 804-507-1917. Website: www.theoriginalronnies.com.

Other Contacts

CHARLES CITY VISITOR CENTER, 10760 Courthouse Road. Website: www.charlescity.org.

RICHMOND NATIONAL BATTLEFIELD PARK, Richmond. Call 804-226-1981. Website: www.nps.gov/rich. Battlefields and forts along VA 5.

REFLECTION
PIER
This plaque recognizes the contributions of Indigenous people,
Moses Grandy, the Underground Railroad Freedom Seekers,
Maroons and supporters for their sacrifice
and contributions to American history.
Let this pier and lake forever be enjoyed by all people as
a place of healing, reflection and hope, as it was for
others seeking refuge before us.
Dedicated on this Day of Remembrance - August 6, 2022

6

SWAMPED

A Pleasant Visit to the Great Dismal Swamp

ESTIMATED LENGTH: 50 miles

ESTIMATED TIME: Day or weekend

HIGHLIGHTS: The centerpiece of the trip is the **Great Dismal Swamp National Wildlife Refuge**, a wonderful place to enjoy nature and to find quiet and solitude. Hike or bike or simply drive; the easiest thing to do is drive the **Lake Drummond Wildlife Drive**, a 6-mile ride to Lake Drummond. Just be aware of your surroundings and know where you're going. You really don't want to become lost. Other possible stops include **Suffolk**, **Smithfield**, and **Surry**, where you'll find **Bacon's Castle**, built in 1665 and considered one of the most important colonial buildings in America.

GETTING THERE: From Richmond, drive south on I-95 then east on US 460 toward the Great Dismal Swamp National Wildlife Refuge. From Virginia Beach, drive west on US 58 to Suffolk then south to the swamp.

For the longest time, it never occurred to me to *want* to visit a swamp. Not even if it was deemed "great."

But there the Great Dismal Swamp sat on every state map in every school classroom that had one, large and looming, on the border with North Carolina—and not the least bit enticing to me. I mean, I knew what lived in swamps—or thought I knew—and I was perfectly fine with leaving well enough alone.

Until 2002, when photographer Bob Brown and I embarked on a six-month-long series to write about life along Virginia's longest road, US 58. Guess what highway borders the swamp? So, we made arrangements to visit Great Dismal Swamp National Wildlife Refuge and meet the refuge's manager, Lloyd Culp, who gave us a tour and a pep talk about the swamp, which, it turns out, is an incredibly interesting place. It's a wonderfully rich habitat for all kinds

LEFT: LAKE DRUMMOND, REACHABLE BY DRIVING OR HIKING, IS THE CENTERPIECE OF THE GREAT DISMAL SWAMP NATIONAL WILDLIFE REFUGE

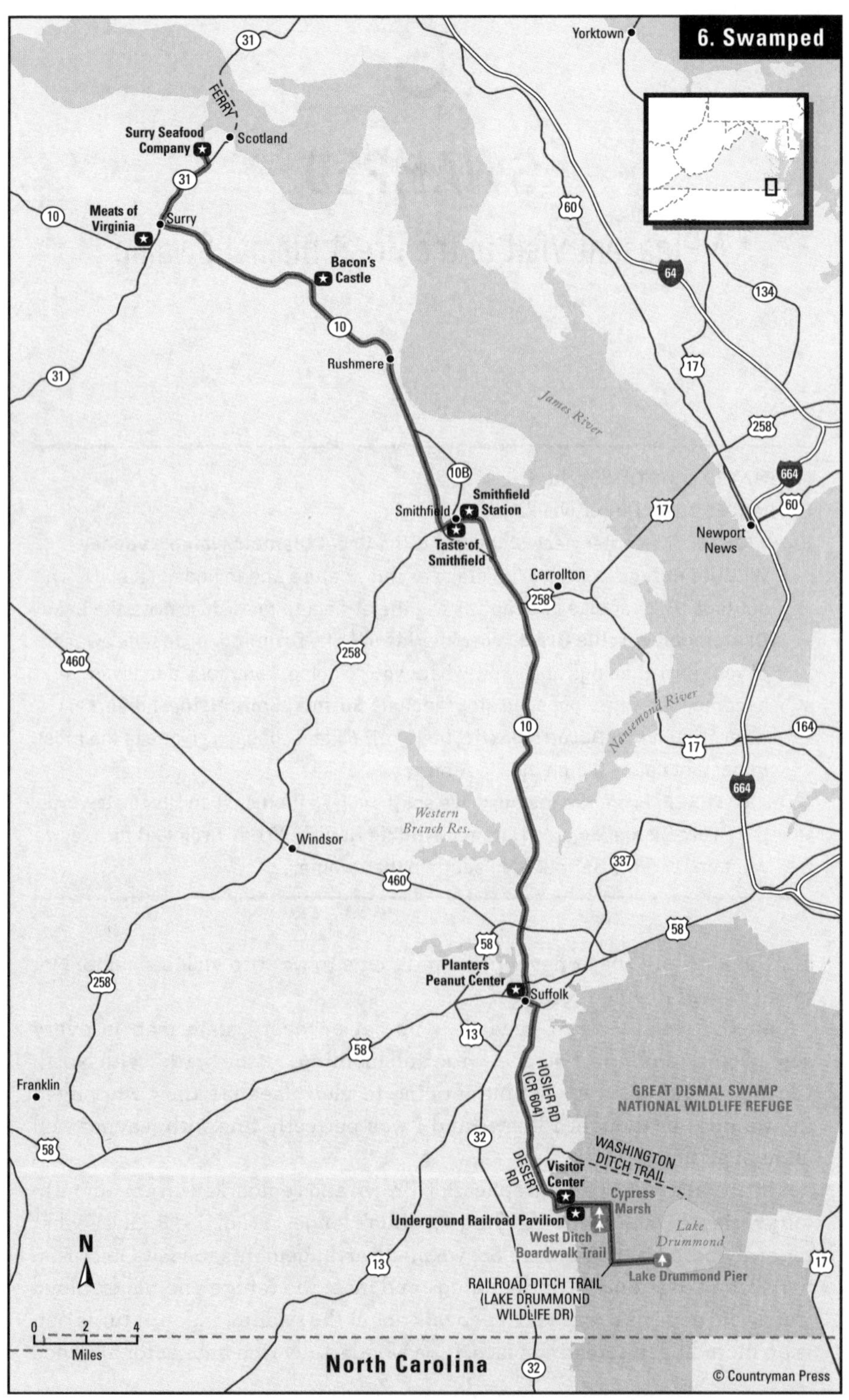

6. Swamped
Yorktown
Scotland
Surry Seafood Company
Meats of Virginia
Surry
Bacon's Castle
Rushmere
James River
Smithfield
Smithfield Station
Taste of Smithfield
Carrollton
Newport News
Nansemond River
Western Branch Res.
Windsor
Planters Peanut Center
Suffolk
Franklin
HOSIER RD (CR 604)
DESERT RD
GREAT DISMAL SWAMP NATIONAL WILDLIFE REFUGE
WASHINGTON DITCH TRAIL
Visitor Center
Cypress Marsh
Underground Railroad Pavilion
West Ditch Boardwalk Trail
Lake Drummond
Lake Drummond Pier
RAILROAD DITCH TRAIL (LAKE DRUMMOND WILDLIFE DR)
FERRY
North Carolina
Miles
© Countryman Press

VISITORS CAN STROLL THROUGH THE SWAMP ON SEVERAL ELEVATED BOARDWALK TRAILS THROUGHOUT THE REFUGE

of critters—birds, butterflies, and black bears, among forty-seven species of mammals, though no alligators—and the setting for a fascinating history.

The refuge consists of 112,000 acres of forested wetland with 3,100-acre Lake Drummond, one of only two natural lakes in Virginia, at its center. As big as it is, the refuge is merely what's left of a vast swamp that once covered more than a million acres. As you drive into the refuge along the old logging road that networks through the swamp, you immediately get the feeling of being in another world—but it's a world not far from the real one: as the crow flies, it's only about 30 miles from the middle of Lake Drummond to the bustling oceanfront at Virginia Beach, and more than 1.5 million people live within an hour's drive of the swamp.

The refuge offers opportunities for hiking and biking, nature photography, hunting (at specified times), fishing and boating, strolling along accessible wooden boardwalks, or simply driving around to see the sights. No matter what activity you engage in, you should keep in mind what Culp told me on my first visit: if you're not careful, the thick forest of the swamp is an easy place to get lost.

"You get 50 yards off these roads, and it all looks the same," he said. "And at night, this place is spooky. We've had a few folks get lost and spend one or two nights in the swamp, and they do find religion."

We didn't get lost on that first trip, though we did have to wait a few minutes for a large turtle to cross the road before we could pass. Buoyed by that success, I returned two decades later with my wife to spend a very pleasant late fall Saturday, the autumn being an optimal time to visit the swamp and get out and walk around, says Chris Lowe, the refuge's current manager. Spring, too. Summer can be hot and buggy, and winter is the refuge's wettest season, though you should be fine if you stay on the boardwalks or roads.

"We get a lot of people that come into the headquarters . . . and say, 'I was in the area, looking for things to do, and I heard about this place, and I HAD to see it,'" Lowe says. "We have a little something for everybody. It has significant natural resource amenities, significant for the flora and fauna and habitat protection, and it's also significant for the cultural history of the United States and the formation of this country. It's quiet and serene, and it is an escape."

The swamp got its name—"dismal"—from the surveyor William Byrd II, who wasn't impressed by the place when he went there in 1728 to determine the Virginia colony's southern boundary. He described it as "a horrible desert" where "the foul damps ascend without ceasing, corrupt the air and render it unfit for respiration." He also wrote, "Never was rum . . . found more necessary than in this dirty place." Well, then.

Others have felt more generous about the place. Indigenous people apparently lived there, beginning thousands of years ago, as archaeological digs have unearthed tools, weapons, and projectile points. From the 1600s through the Civil War, the swamp proved to be truly a refuge for tens of thousands of enslaved people seeking freedom, as they created settlements deep in the swamp. Some used the swamp as a way station as they headed North; others, remarkably, made it their home.

Like many other places in Virginia, George Washington left his stamp here. As a young man, he and other investors created the Dismal Swamp Company with a plan to drain the swamp, which, they thought, would result in the creation of profitable land. They used enslaved workers to build draining ditches and roads, and though the original plan ultimately failed, the company found commercial success in cutting down trees for lumber, which launched two centuries of tree-harvesting that forever changed the face of the swamp. By the mid-twentieth century, most of the swamp's virgin timber was gone. The Great Dismal Swamp National Refuge was established in 1974 with a mission to protect and preserve what was left of the swamp.

"What honestly excites me is the challenge of managing and trying to restore the swamp to something that will be more resilient and healthier going into the future," Lowe says. And also welcoming visitors. "We definitely want to get people to come out here and enjoy it," he says.

A good place to start is the visitor center, which is just off Desert Road, on the western edge of the refuge. Turn on Headquarters Access Road. You can gather all sorts of information there, but you can also download maps and other info on the refuge's website.

The most popular destination in the swamp, Lowe says, is Lake Drummond. You can easily get there, as we did, on a self-guided drive accessed from the Railroad Ditch trailhead on Desert Road, just south of the turnoff for the visitor center. The drive is a 6-mile (one-way) route along one of those old logging roads, a narrow, gravel road with those ditches dug all those years ago to drain the swamp alongside. The route takes you past three boardwalks along the way, the first of which is a short walk to the Underground Railroad Pavilion, where interpretive signage provides a history of the swamp as a home for "maroons"—as those who inhabited the place were called.

Next up is the Cypress Marsh and Boardwalk, a 10-acre marsh created by a series of controlled burns, conducted to mimic the effect of wildfires that allow a different habitat to take hold. Keep your eyes open: you might see beavers, otters, wood ducks, or great blue herons. The third boardwalk is the West Ditch Boardwalk Trail, a short trail that leads to a bald cypress tree that is approximately 800 years old, one of the few old-growth trees remaining in the swamp, though its top was broken off by a lightning strike, leaving it at only about half of its original height.

ONE OF THE PEDESTRIAN TRAILS, ALONG A DITCH CONSTRUCTED TO DRAIN THE SWAMP CENTURIES AGO, IS IN AN AREA SURVEYED BY GEORGE WASHINGTON

SMITHFIELD, FAMOUS FOR ITS HAMS, IS AN HOUR'S DRIVE NORTH OF THE GREAT DISMAL SWAMP

At the end of the route, you will reach Lake Drummond, where you will find a small parking area and a pier offering a good vantage point. The lake is more than 2 miles across—a massive, though shallow, body of water where, on windy days, whitecaps several feet high can make Drummond look like a roiling sea. Bald cypress trees stand tall in the water.

The refuge offers more than 40 miles of earthen road trails for hiking and biking, through four entrances: Portsmouth Ditch Entrance, Jericho Lane Entrance, Washington Ditch entrance, or the aforementioned Railroad Ditch Entrance. The Washington Ditch Trail is perhaps the best for hiking and biking. It's named for George Washington, who directed the surveying and digging of the ditch, and is a 4.5-mile dirt road that leads to Lake Drummond. We walked along it for a while but didn't go as far as the lake.

Trails are open from sunrise to sunset, but you probably don't want to be in there after dark anyway. Also note that cell service is limited throughout the refuge.

Another potential stop is **Bacon's Castle** in Surry, about an hour's drive north of the Great Dismal Swamp Refuge. Bacon's Castle isn't much of a castle but is a stately and historically significant home: the oldest brick dwelling in North America. The original part of the house was constructed in 1665 and is a rare example of high-style Jacobean architecture.

It also boasts the oldest English formal garden in North America, which was reconstructed by the Garden Club of Virginia. The house is named for Nathaniel Bacon, who led an uprising against colonial governor Sir William Berkeley in 1676, during which some of his followers temporarily took over the house that was owned by a friend of the governor and used it as a fort to protect themselves. Bacon himself never set foot on the one-time plantation, as far as anyone knows.

"It was the first rebellion against the English crown," said Jennifer Hurst-Wender, who at the time of my first visit was director of museum operations for Preservation Virginia, which acquired Bacon's Castle in the 1970s, saved it from falling in on itself, and has opened it to the public since the 1980s. "This is the only place you're going to hear that story, except for Jamestown."

The rebellion ultimately failed: Bacon died of disease and some of the rebels who took over the house were executed. The name "Bacon's Castle" began to show up in court documents in the early nineteenth century, when it was popular to dub large houses "castles," according to Hurst-Wender.

BACON'S CASTLE IS THE OLDEST BRICK DWELLING OF ITS KIND IN NORTH AMERICA
PRESERVATION VIRGINIA

IN THE AREA

Accommodations

SMITHFIELD STATION, 415 South Church Street, Smithfield. Call 877-703-7701. Website: www.smithfieldstation.com. Waterfront inn, restaurant, marina, and conference center.

Attractions and Recreation

GREAT DISMAL SWAMP NATIONAL WIDLIFE REFUGE, 3100 Desert Road, Suffolk. Call 757-986-3705. Website: www.fws.gov/refuge/great-dismal-swamp.

BACON'S CASTLE, 465 Bacon's Castle Trail, Surry. Call 757-357-5976. Website: www.preservationvirginia.org/historic-sites/bacons-castle.

Dining

MEATS OF VIRGINIA, 11381 Rolfe Highway, Elberon. Call 757-294-3688. Website: www.meatsofvirginia.com. Butcher shop and deli.

SURRY SEAFOOD COMPANY, 633 Marina Drive, Surry. Call 757-294-3700. Website: www.surryseafoodco.com. Waterfront dining with inside and outside dining area with terrific seafood, burgers, salads, and more.

TASTE OF SMITHFIELD, 217 Main Street, Smithfield. Call 757-357-8950. Website: www.tasteofsmithfield.com. Fresh, authentic Southern food.

Other Contacts

GENUINE SMITHFIELD, 319 Main Street, Smithfield. Call 757-357-5182. Website: www.genuinesmithfieldva.com. Smithfield Isle of Wight Convention and Visitor Bureau.

SURRY COUNTY TOURISM, 267 Church Street, Surry. Call 757-758-0146. Website: www.surrycountytourism.com.

THE SALTY SOUTHERN ROUTE. Website: www.saltysouthernroute.com. Connecting the dots of Virginia's pork and peanuts.

VISIT SUFFOLK, 524 N. Main Street, Suffolk. Call 757-514-4130. Website: www.visitsuffolkva.com. Suffolk tourism.

afton
mountain
VINEYARDS
2013
PINOT NOIR

7

QUENCHING A THIRST

Nelson's Wineries, Breweries, Distilleries, and Cideries

ESTIMATED LENGTH: 30 miles

ESTIMATED TIME: Day trip (or take your time and make a weekend of it)

HIGHLIGHTS: **Wintergreen Resort**, a year-round mountain retreat known for its snow-skiing in the winter and golf and other activities in warmer weather, is a short drive from **Nellysford**. Drive east on VA 6 to US 29 and head toward **Lovingston** and visit the Nelson County Historical Society's **Oakland Museum** and the **Virginia Distillery**. If you're a fan of "The Waltons" you might consider a side trip to **Walton's Mountain Museum in Schuyler**, the boyhood home of Earl Hamner Jr., creator of the television series. You can hike a section of the **Appalachian Trail** or visit **Crabtree Falls**, the highest cascading waterfall east of the Mississippi River, or take a stroll in the dark through the **Blue Ridge Tunnel**, a former railroad tunnel under I-64. Accommodations primarily include inns and bed-and-breakfasts.

GETTING THERE: A good place to start is near **Afton**, not far from **Waynesboro**, where US 250 (Rockfish Gap Turnpike) meets VA 151 (Critzers Shop Road), and head south through Nelson County at the foot of the Blue Ridge Mountains on VA 151, a scenic byway that is marketed as **Nelson 151** with five vineyards, three breweries, a distillery, and two cideries in a 14-mile stretch.

The scenery alone is worth the drive through Nelson County. This is one pretty place and always has been, though it has developed slowly but surely in recent years, becoming a refined draw for tourists, particularly those seeking recreation or a glass of locally made wine, beer, or spirits. The county has come a long way from the dark days of August 1969 when Hurricane Camille, a category 5 storm, swept through the region with such ferocity and so much rain—it dumped at least 27 inches in just a few hours overnight—

LEFT: AFTON MOUNTAIN VINEYARDS OFFERS AWARD-WINNING WINES AND TASTINGS IN AN EXQUISITE SETTING

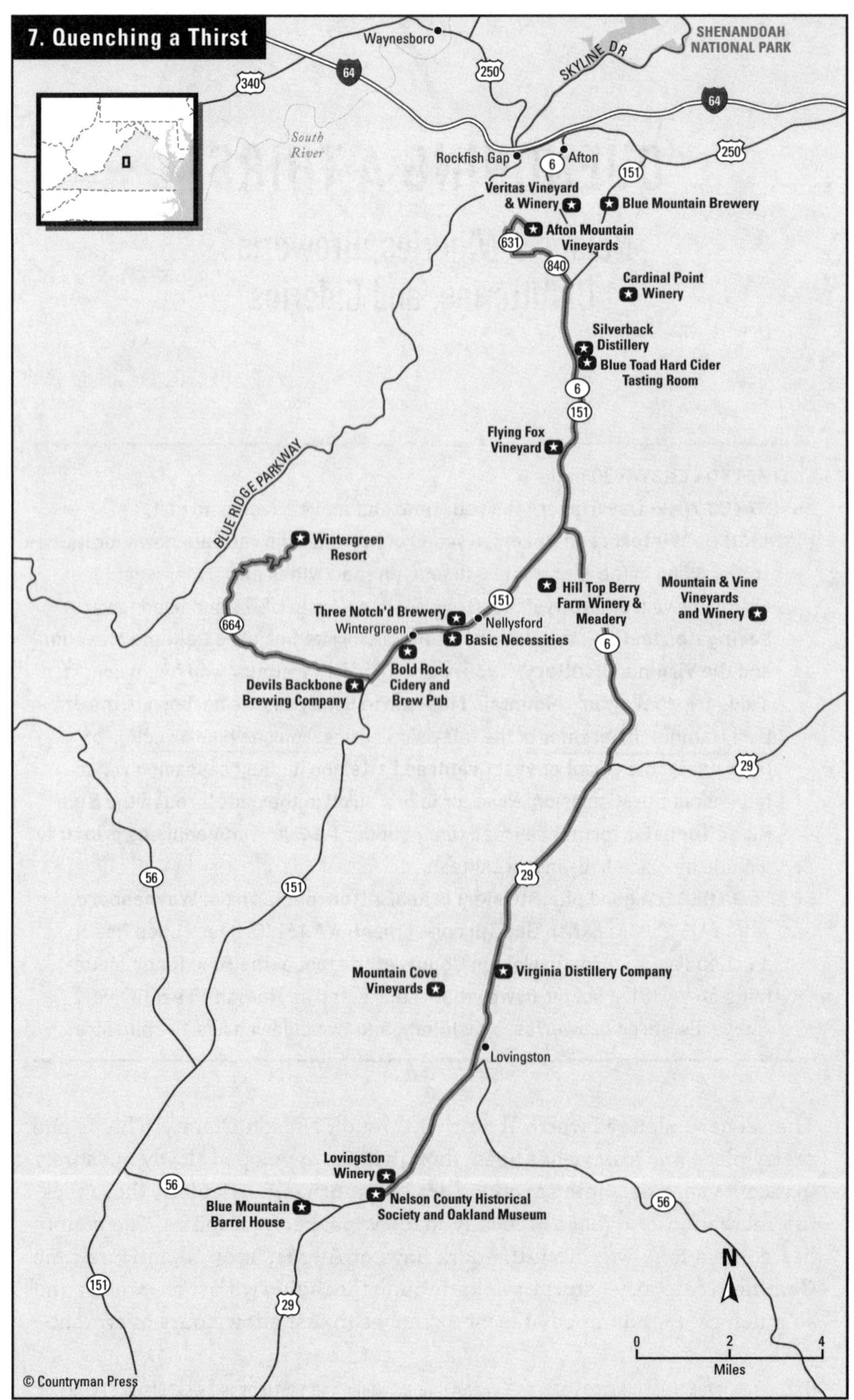
7. Quenching a Thirst
Waynesboro
SHENANDOAH NATIONAL PARK
SKYLINE DR
South River
Rockfish Gap
Afton
Veritas Vineyard & Winery
Blue Mountain Brewery
Afton Mountain Vineyards
Cardinal Point Winery
Silverback Distillery
Blue Toad Hard Cider Tasting Room
Flying Fox Vineyard
BLUE RIDGE PARKWAY
Wintergreen Resort
Hill Top Berry Farm Winery & Meadery
Mountain & Vine Vineyards and Winery
Three Notch'd Brewery
Nellysford
Wintergreen
Basic Necessities
Bold Rock Cidery and Brew Pub
Devils Backbone Brewing Company
Mountain Cove Vineyards
Virginia Distillery Company
Lovingston
Lovingston Winery
Blue Mountain Barrel House
Nelson County Historical Society and Oakland Museum
Miles
© Countryman Press

THE PAVILION AT AFTON MOUNTAIN VINEYARDS OFFERS A PICTURE-POSTCARD VIEW OF THE VINEYARDS AND THE BLUE RIDGE MOUNTAINS BEYOND

that the National Weather Service said it was "the probable maximum rainfall which meteorologists computed to be theoretically possible," according to Encyclopedia Virginia. Mountain streams flooded, causing flash floods and landslides as residents slept. More than 150 were killed. In such a small, quiet county, it was a catastrophe beyond imagination. You can learn about Hurricane Camille and the flood, among other county history, at the Nelson County Historical Society's Oakland Museum, housed in an old tavern, on US 29 north in Lovingston.

The face of Nelson began to change in 1975 with the opening of ski slopes at Wintergreen Resort. Since then, it has become a four-season resort with golf, tennis, a spa, and other outdoor recreation such as hiking, fly fishing, and swimming. There are condos and vacation homes along with a variety of dining options and a conference center. In the summer, Wintergreen Music, a nonprofit organization, presents its well-regarded month-long Music Festival in the summer, bringing high-quality performances to various venues around the area.

These days, the arrival of wineries, breweries, and distilleries has made Nelson even more of a destination.

Elizabeth Smith, who co-owns Afton Mountain Vineyards with her husband, Tony, came up with a phrase that perfectly captures the essence of the marriage between Nelson and its vineyards: "Grapes don't grow in ugly places." You don't have to look far to find the inspiration for the slogan. Standing on the patio of the Afton Mountain Vineyards tasting room, there is nothing but beauty all around, the gently rolling countryside extending far into the distance. Nelson has become a "hot ticket," as Smith describes it, for visitors wanting a weekend of wine-tasting, farm-to-table dining—or even getting married in as pretty a setting as you can imagine.

Smith grew up in Albemarle County, the next county over, near Charlottesville. She laughs and recalls that Nelson was "boondocks" to her and her friends. There wasn't much to do in Nelson back then except to ski at Wintergreen, and it seemed so far away—even though it was the next door. "It was the back of beyond," she said. She doesn't feel that way anymore.

"It's such a stellar place to be," she says when I drop by the vineyard.

Why? Well, in the grape-growing and wine-making business, she says, there are certain things you really like to have: the right climate, suitable elevation, and nearby mountains offering protection from westward-approaching storms. Nelson offers all of that plus this: good, clean water.

"The water around here is plentiful and delicious," Smith says. "Just naturally great water."

Everyone I talk to in Nelson seems to mention this: the water.

One brewmaster tells me the high-quality water makes good brewers—and their beer—even better.

At Silverback Distillery, CEO, owner, and distiller Christine Riggle-

BOLD ROCK HARD CIDER IS A POPULAR STOP ALONG NELSON 151

TOP: OUTDOOR DINING IS AN OPTION AT BLUE MOUNTAIN BREWERY
BOTTOM: A SCULPTURE CUTS A DRAMATIC FIGURE AGAINST A MOUNTAIN BACKDROP AT VERITAS VINEYARD NEAR AFTON ALEXANDRA LOHMANN

SIDE TRACKS

Afton Mountain Vineyards, 234 Vineyard Lane, Afton. Call 540-546-8667. Website: www.aftonmountainvineyards.com.

Blue Mountain Barrel House, 495 Cooperative Way, Arrington. Call 434-263-4002. Website: www.bluemountainbarrel.com.

Blue Mountain Brewery, 9519 Critzer's Shop Road, Afton. Call 540-456-8020. Website: www.bluemountainbrewery.com.

Blue Toad Hard Cider Tasting Room, 462 Winery Lane, Roseland. Call 434-996-6992. Website: www.bluetoadhardcider.com.

Bold Rock Cidery and Brew Pub, 1020 Rockfish Valley Highway, Nellysford. Call 434-361-1030. Website: boldrock.com.

Bryant's Brewing, 3224 E. Branch Loop, Roseland. Call 434-818-1215. Website: bryantscider.com.

Cardinal Point Winery, 9423 Batesville Road, Afton. Call 540-456-8400. Website: www.cardinalpointwinery.com.

DelFosse Vineyards and Winery, 500 DelFosse Winery Lane, Faber. Call 434-263-6100. Website: www.delfossewine.com.

Devils Backbone Brewing Company, 200 Crandall Run, Roseland. Call 434-361-1001. Website: dbbrewingcompany.com.

Flying Fox Vineyard, 10368 Critzer Shop Road, Afton. Call 434-361-1692. Website: www.flyingfoxvineyard.com.

Hazy Mountain Vineyards and Brewery, 240 Hazy Mountain Lane, Afton. Call 540-302-2529. Website: www.hazy-mountain.com.

Hill Top Berry Farm & Winery, 2800 Berry Hill Road, Nellysford. Call 434-361-1266. Website: www.hilltopberrywine.com.

Lovingston Winery, 885 Freshwater Cove Lane, Lovingston. Call 434-263-8467. Website: lovingstonwinery.com.

Mountain Cove Vineyards, 1362 Fortunes Cove Lane, Lovingston. Call 434-263-5392. Website: www.mountaincovevineyards.com.

Silverback Distillery, 9374 Rockfish Valley Highway, Afton. Call 540-456-7070. Website: www.sbdistillery.com.

Three Notch'd, 151, 2461 Rockfish Valley Highway, Nellysford. Call 434-226-0020. Website: www.threenotchdbrewing.com.

Valley Road Vineyards, 9264 Crtizers Shop Road, Afton. Call 540-456-6350. Website: www.valleyroadwines.com.

Veritas Vineyard & Winery, 151 Veritas Lane, Afton. Call 540-456-8000. Website: www.veritaswines.com.

Virginia Distillery Co., 299 Eades Lane, Lovingston. Call 434-285-2900. Website: www.vadistillery.com.

Wild Man Dan Brewery, 279 Avon Road, Afton. Call 540-798-1781. Website: www.wmdb3.com.

man says the water quality is "absolutely amazing." The folks at Bold Rock Cidery said the same, as did Gareth Moore, CEO of Virginia Distillery Co., who says the area's "culture of hard work and craftsmanship" played into his firm's decision to come to Nelson, but it was also the natural resources, including "the abundant supply of clean, iron-free water necessary for making whiskey."

So, you get the idea. Feel free to drink the water—or anything else you might find at the wineries, breweries, distilleries, or cideries.

VA 151 is a state-designated scenic highway and also a primary artery for that sort of development with seven wineries, six breweries, four distilleries, and three cideries along a 14-mile stretch of the road roughly from near Afton to Nellysford and a little beyond. There are even more in other parts of the county. That's a lot of beer, wine, and liquor, as well as hard cider, for a county with a population of about 15,000, and a far cry from 2002 when there were just two wineries in the county before it started recruiting wineries. Word spread, success begat success, and here we are.

To really appreciate what Nelson has become, you need to make a few stops.

Afton Mountain Vineyards, off VA 6, a short distance from VA 151, is one of the county's oldest vineyards, dating back to the 1970s. The Smiths acquired it in 2009, more than doubled the acreage planted in grape vines, and now produce a variety of wines. They welcome visitors for tastings—the patio with its panoramic views of the countryside is a great place to sit and sip—but large groups need reservations.

Any of the wineries, breweries, distilleries, or cideries welcome visitors, though it's not a bad idea to call ahead and check their hours.

Devils Backbone, which also has a second location in Lexington, has an outdoor stage at its Nelson site for musical acts. Food is available at all of the breweries. Three Notch'd also produces bourbon.

You can't miss Silverback Distillery, between Afton and Nellysford: it's the place with the large, carved gorilla out front. The family-run distillery produces a variety of liquors. Samples are available.

Riggleman, the CEO, tells me it was a visit to Scotland that inspired her desire to open a distillery, though

DEVILS BACKBONE BREWING COMPANY HAS ITS MAIN OPERATION, INCLUDING A RESTAURANT, IN NELSON COUNTY

A CARVED GORILLA IS THE MASCOT OF SILVERBACK DISTILLERY

she also acknowledged liquor production runs in her family. "My great-grandmother and her sister used to make bathtub gin," she says, "and my husband's family used to be (whisky) runners." She and husband, Denver, looked around for a suitable location and loved Nelson. "We know what it's like to be in a city, which is great, but we were ready to take a deep breath and enjoy the fresh air and enjoy the scenery. There are no city lights to interfere with the night sky, and we just love the people."

Bold Rock Cidery was a long time in the making. John Washburn acquired 50 acres on the Rockfish River two decades before he knew what he wanted to do with the land. The answer? Produce craft cider, using apples from nearby orchards. A key to the whole plan proved to be persuading New Zealand cider-maker Brian Shakes to join him and guide the operation. Their first bottle of cider was produced in 2012, and Bold Rock has grown quickly, tripling its capacity with the opening of its Cider Barn, a production facility and taproom, where you have a marvelous view of the countryside through its huge windows or outside on the deck. If you go, notice the nice touches throughout the building, which was constructed with native oak beams, salvaged handmade bricks, fireplace mantels from cherry trees from an orchard on the property, and the real conversation piece: a 150-year-

TOP: THE PUBLIC CAN WATCH THE BOTTLING PROCESS AT BOLD ROCK HARD CIDER ALEXANDRA LOHMANN
BOTTOM: THE CIDER BARN AT BOLD ROCK HARD CIDER FEATURES NOT ONLY A TAPROOM BUT A LOVELY SPACE FOR MUSICAL EVENTS

BASIC NECESSITIES IS A FINE A PLACE TO STOP FOR WINE, CHEESE, OR A GOOD MEAL IN NELLYSFORD ALEXANDRA LOHMANN

old, 6,000-pound beam engraved with the Bold Rock motto: "Be Bold. Tread Lightly. Make It Happen."

Restaurants in the area include an interesting place in Nellysford called Basic Necessities, a cozy wine and cheese shop with a café, which features good food, and a terrific atmosphere.

If you head over to the Lovingston area on US 29, check out the Virginia Distillery and its visitor center. You can enjoy tastings and handcrafted cocktails made with local ingredients. "Our museum and video experience, which is part of the tour, will give visitors to the distillery a chance to learn firsthand about the history of whisky-making in Nelson County," says CEO Moore.

IN THE AREA

Accommodations

For a list of inns, bed-and-breakfasts, and campgrounds, visit www.nelsoncounty.com.

Attractions and Recreation

BLUE RIDGE TUNNEL, East Trailhead, 215 Afton Depot Lane, Afton; West Trailhead, 483 Three Notched Mountain Highway, Waynesboro. Call 434-263-7015. Website: blueridgetunnel.org. A former railroad tunnel that, at 4,237 feet in length, was the longest tunnel in the United States when it was completed in the 1850s. Total hike is just over 2 miles on a crushed-stone path. Bring a flashlight.

NELSON COUNTY HISTORICAL SOCIETY'S OAKLAND MUSEUM, 5365 Thomas Nelson Highway, Arrington. Call 434-263-8400. Website: nelson-historical.org.

WALTON'S MOUNTAIN MUSEUM, 6484 Rockfish River Road, Schuyler. Call 434-831-2000. Website: walton-mountain.org.

WINTERGREEN RESORT, Route 664, Wintergreen. Call 434-325-2200. Website: www.wintergreenresort.com.

Dining

BASIC NECESSITIES, 2226 Rockfish Valley Highway, Nellysford. Call 434-361-1766. Website: www.basicnecessities.us.

BLUE RIDGE PIG, 2198 Rockfish Valley Highway, Nellysford. Call 434-361-1170. Website: www.theblueridgepig.com.

GIUSEPPE'S ITALIAN RESTAURANT, 2842 Rockfish Valley Highway, Nellysford. Call 434-361-9170. Website: www.nelsoncounty.com/giuseppes-italian-restaurant.

Other Contacts

NELSON 151. Website: nelson151.com.

8

HAIL TO THE CHIEFS

Virginia, Mother of Presidents

ESTIMATED LENGTH: About 200 miles (at least)

ESTIMATED TIME: Multiday

HIGHLIGHTS: History, of course, and scenery, given that navigating to any of the presidential homes will take you through some of the loveliest parts of Virginia. **George Washington's Mount Vernon** and **Thomas Jefferson's Monticello** headline the presidential homes and are major attractions. Along the way, you might take the opportunity to find lodging or dinner or just poke around the old riverfront resort town of **Colonial Beach** (not far from Mount Vernon) and **Charlottesville** (near Monticello). Frozen custard at **Carl's** is a good reason to stop in Fredericksburg.

GETTING THERE: You can hit the homes of four of the first five US presidents—**Mount Vernon** (Washington), **Montpelier** (James Madison), **Monticello** (Jefferson), and **Highland** (James Monroe) in a relatively tidy, 120-mile line between Alexandria and Charlottesville, largely via US 15, through rolling countryside, though it would be nearly impossible to do all four in a day. A long weekend, maybe. Better yet, add some days and miles, starting at **Washington's Birthplace National Monument** and include going to Staunton to see Woodrow Wilson's birthplace. (For more about Staunton, see the chapter on Valley Pike.) Then, if you are so inclined, head to Richmond and visit the homes of John Tyler and William Henry Harrison along the James River, east of the capital. (For more on Tyler and Harrison's homes, see the chapter on Old Houses, New Stories.) If you really want to cover your presidential bases, you might also make plans to visit **Jefferson's Poplar Forest**, his private retreat in Bedford County—about a 90-minute drive from Monticello—that is considered by many as his architectural masterpiece, which, considering Monticello, is saying something.

LEFT: GEORGE WASHINGTON'S MOUNT VERNON IS ON THE BANKS OF THE POTOMAC RIVER
MOUNT VERNON LADIES' ASSOCIATION

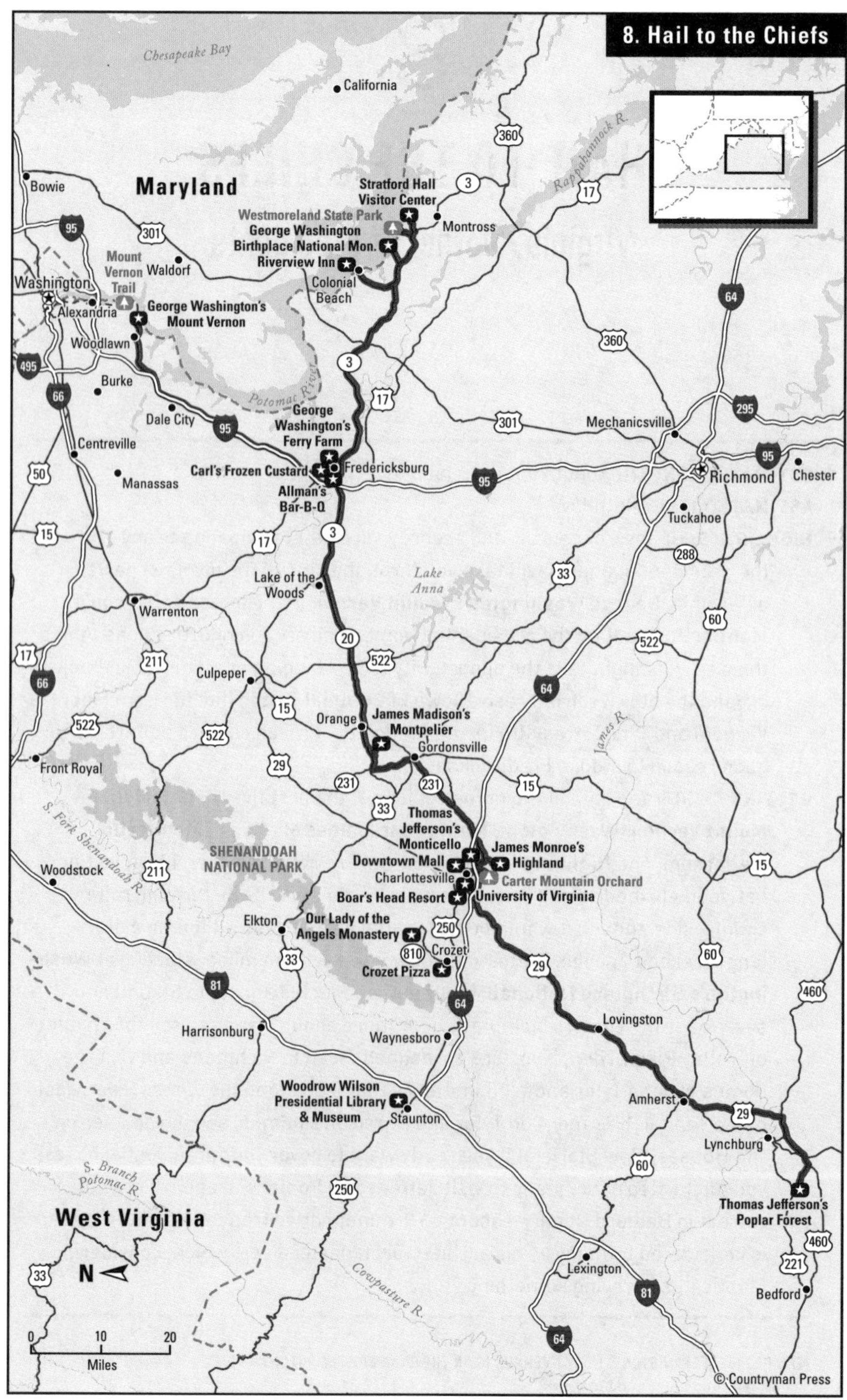
8. Hail to the Chiefs
Chesapeake Bay
California
Maryland
Bowie
Stratford Hall Visitor Center
Westmoreland State Park
George Washington Birthplace National Mon.
Montross
Riverview Inn
Colonial Beach
Mount Vernon Trail
Waldorf
Washington
Alexandria
George Washington's Mount Vernon
Woodlawn
Burke
Potomac River
Dale City
George Washington's Ferry Farm
Centreville
Carl's Frozen Custard
Fredericksburg
Manassas
Allman's Bar-B-Q
Mechanicsville
Richmond
Chester
Tuckahoe
Rappahannock R.
Lake of the Woods
Lake Anna
Warrenton
Culpeper
Orange
James Madison's Montpelier
Gordonsville
James R.
Front Royal
S. Fork Shenandoah R.
SHENANDOAH NATIONAL PARK
Woodstock
Thomas Jefferson's Monticello
Downtown Mall
Charlottesville
Boar's Head Resort
James Monroe's Highland
Carter Mountain Orchard
University of Virginia
Elkton
Our Lady of the Angels Monastery
Crozet
Crozet Pizza
Harrisonburg
Waynesboro
Lovingston
Woodrow Wilson Presidential Library & Museum
Staunton
Amherst
Lynchburg
Thomas Jefferson's Poplar Forest
S. Branch Potomac R.
West Virginia
Cowpasture R.
Lexington
Bedford
N
0 10 20
Miles
© Countryman Press

One of Virginia's claims to fame is being the birthplace of four of the first five US presidents, eight in all—more than any other state. As a result, there are numerous presidential homes around Virginia open to the public, as well as other historic places connected with the presidents.

(As an FYI: one of those eight presidents from Virginia is hardly commemorated at all. Zachary Taylor was born in 1784 in Orange County—in the same general area as Jefferson, Monroe, and Madison, who was a cousin of Taylor's—though it is noted with little more than a historical marker, because his family moved to Kentucky soon after his birth.)

Though these sites date back hundreds of years, the history being told is still evolving. New research is constantly discovering new truths about the presidents—not always in the best light—and the places they dwelled and the times in which they lived.

"I would say the diversification of the story writ large started in the later 1980s and early 1990s, when historic sites started to catch up with what academic historians were doing in looking beyond the activities of elite white men," Elizabeth Chew tells me in 2023. "To look at women. To look at people of color. It's taken thirty years to become as commonplace and widespread as it is now."

At the time of our conversation, Chew was senior director and chief

JAMES MADISON'S MONTPELIER IS IN THE LUSH COUNTRYSIDE OF CENTRAL VIRGINIA
JAMES MADISON'S MONTPELIER

curator of museum programs at James Madison's Montpelier, where the story of Madison is told, of course, but increasingly also the story of enslaved people who lived and worked there.

"I want people to hear the entire story of our country—the good, the bad, and the ugly," says Chew, who previously worked for the Thomas Jefferson Foundation, which owns and operates Monticello, Jefferson's mountaintop home. "I want them to understand that James Madison was the father of the US Constitution; it would not exist without him. He was a brilliant political theorist, he was the fourth president of the United States, he was the Secretary of State—and he enslaved hundreds of people over the course of his life and never freed a single person. Those facts exist side-by-side. They don't cancel each other out. People need to keep the whole story in their heads."

A lot of us grew up with an oversimplified, mythologized view of the founders, which was neither accurate nor fair to them or us. They were remarkable men but also real people with real shortcomings. No one is surrounded by greater legend than Washington, which is why a visit to Mount Vernon can be an illuminating experience.

"Often people know he's the guy on the dollar bill or he's a marble statue on a pedestal, and they know he was the first president," says Matt Briney,

THE VIEW FROM JAMES MADISON'S OFFICE PROVIDES AN EXQUISITE VIEW OF THE ESTATE
JAMES MADISON'S MONTPELIER

vice president of media and communications at George Washington's Mount Vernon. "But they really don't know who he was, and this has created this kind of otherworldly individual that doesn't make him very relatable. I think Mount Vernon is really his autobiography. You can learn about his successes and his failures and get to know him more deeply as a person . . . and explore the past through the eyes of Washington the man, not the marble statue."

Similarly, at Monticello, "telling a more complete story" is the goal, says Brandon Dillard, director of historic interpretation and audience engagement for the Thomas Jefferson Foundation, which has incorporated stories of the enslaved into the narrative at Monticello: where they worked, where they lived, who they were. Decades of archaeological, documentary, and oral research helped uncover those histories that had been previously unknown or ignored.

"I think Monticello is an incredibly important place because . . . it is a symbol of democracy, through and through, of government built on the ideals of freedom and equality and Jefferson's radical vision of what that world might look like—and it is also a symbol of these gross inequalities that existed in the founding era of our nation. There's a real challenge when people try to discuss history as an either-or—all good or all bad—and that's not very human. The reality is that in order for us to understand it, it's both. I would argue there is perhaps no better place in America to understand the depth of that complexity than Monticello."

GEORGE WASHINGTON

George Washington was first in war, first in peace, and so he might as well be first in this chapter. Before Mount Vernon, though, let's start at a less well-known Washington site: his birthplace, a pretty piece of land on the Northern Neck of Virginia, wedged between Popes Creek and the Potomac River, preserved now as the George Washington Birthplace National Monument. It covers more than 500 acres of land where seven generations of the Washington family lived and where George was born in 1732 and is a good 90-minute drive from Mount Vernon.

"George Washington Birthplace is a little-known gem among National Park Service sites," said Melissa Cobern, the park's longtime superintendent. "It's also one of the best-kept secrets in Virginia. The visiting public tends to view this site as purely historical, but it's also a wonderful place to enjoy nature."

Part of the reason the birthplace remains off the radar for many is that Washington lived here only the first three-and-a-half years of his life, the park is 45 minutes from the nearest interstate highway, and, frankly, there is little here that physically ties him to it. However, simply walking the grounds, reading the historical notes, and hearing the stories of how generations of Washingtons settled this place lends reality to the early years of Washington.

At the visitor center, we browse through the exhibits and come upon something I did not know: Washington was born not on February 22, but on February 11—according to the Julian calendar that was followed in the British colonies in the early 1700s. When Great Britain switched to the Gregorian calendar in 1752, an adjustment in the number of days meant Washington's birthday would now be celebrated on February 22.

Down a path through a grove of towering junipers, we come to the site of a building foundation, discovered decades ago by archaeologists, that might have been the house where Washington was born, though uncertainty remains. Perhaps 100 feet away, we see the Memorial House Museum, a fine brick home constructed in the 1930s as part of the commemoration of the 200th anniversary of Washington's birth. The house is larger and grander than the house in which the Washingtons lived, but a guided tour of the house does a nice job of connecting the Washingtons to the land and the period, putting into context the era into which George Washington was born.

We eat the lunch we brought at the park's picnic area and then walk it off on the mile-long nature trail that loops around by Popes Creek. Keep your eyes peeled for eagles and ospreys.

As long as you're here, you might not want to miss Stratford Hall, home of the Lee family, which is no more than a 10-minute drive east on VA 3 to VA 214. Make a left on VA 214 and then travel 2 miles to the Stratford Hall entrance. Richard Henry Lee and Francis Lightfoot Lee, the only brothers to sign the Declaration of Independence, grew up here, as did Robert E. Lee, who led Confederate forces in the Civil War. It was Henry "Lighthorse Harry" Lee, Robert's father, who famously eulogized George Washington with, "First in war, first in peace, and first in the hearts of his countrymen."

Stratford Hall was built in the 1730s, a magnificent brick home, particularly considering the limited tools and materials available at the time. The home is open daily for tours, as is the 1,900-acre plantation, which features an exquisite garden, walking trails, and a splendid view of the river from the property's high bluffs. You can even make arrangements to stay at Stratford Hall in a guest house or cabin.

Next door to Stratford Hall, less than a mile down VA 3, is Westmoreland State Park, on a picturesque stretch of the Potomac that is perfect for boating, hiking, and picnicking. For overnight stays, the park offers cabins, lodges, and a campground.

On to Fredericksburg, where we visit Ferry Farm, Washington's boyhood home, on the banks of the Rappahannock. Ferry Farm is on VA 3, about a 45-minute drive from his birthplace. If Washington chopped any cherry trees, this is where he would have done it. Same with that story about him tossing something across a river. The legend is, he threw a silver dollar across the Potomac, which is not true for a couple of reasons: 1) the Potomac is more than a mile wide at Mount Vernon, and 2) there were no silver dollars back then. A step-grandson has said it was a piece of slate Washington flung across the Rappahannock at Ferry Farm, where the river is a more manageable (but still daunting) 250 feet or so these days.

At Ferry Farm, you can tour a replica of the house where Washington grew up and walk its grounds. Young George swam in the river and rode the ferry, which stopped just below the farm, to Fredericksburg. He learned to grow tobacco, wheat, and corn here, and took up surveying. After his father's death in 1743, George spent less and less time at the farm, often visiting his half-brother, Lawrence, at his place at Little Hunting Creek, which later became known as Mount Vernon.

Before leaving Fredericksburg, check out Allman's Bar-B-Q, a venerable barbecue joint on US 1. It's nothing fancy—a small brick building with a few tables and a counter—but the barbecue and slaw are quite good. Dessert? Another Fredericksburg institution, Carl's Frozen Custard, has you covered. Lines are often long at the walk-up window on Princess Anne Street because the old-fashioned custard is so good, but don't be dismayed, the lines usually move fast, in part because the choices are limited to vanilla, chocolate,

WESTMORELAND STATE PARK, JUST EAST OF MOUNT VERNON, OFFERS A VARIETY OF RECREATIONAL ACTIVITIES

or strawberry. Just be ready to order when it's your turn. (Carl's is closed between Thanksgiving and President's Day.)

From Ferry Farm, it's another 45 minutes to Mount Vernon, though there's no real "back road" option because Interstate 95 or US 1 are pretty much the only ways to go. At Mount Vernon, you could stop by, walk through the house, and be on your way, but if you really want to see the place and learn about Washington, you should plan to spend most of the day. Whatever you do, leave time for the Ford Orientation Center, where you should begin your journey, as well as the Donald W. Reynolds Museum and Education Center, featuring twenty-three galleries and theaters and built largely underground so sheep can still graze on a pasture above it. To tell Washington's story, the education center draws on high-tech interactive exhibits such as the 4D theater, where "snow" falls while the general crosses the icy Delaware River on the screen. The museum relies on family artifacts to provide a sense of what life was like for the Washingtons. You can even visit Washington's distillery, which has been reconstructed and is in operation and open for tours (and, occasionally, whisky tastings).

A shrewd businessman and capable farmer, Washington built Mount Vernon into an 8,000-acre estate—but he couldn't have done it without the work of hundreds of enslaved men, women, and children. At the time of his death, the estate's enslaved population was 317. In his will, Washington ordered that enslaved workers be freed at his wife's death, but this turned out to include only a fraction of those who were enslaved. Mount Vernon offers a guided walking tour to highlight the stories of the enslaved people who built and operated Mount Vernon.

When you tour the house itself, you can see the study where he pondered and the bedroom where he died and uttered his last words, "'Tis well." Sit on George and Martha's back porch (or maybe it's the front porch) and admire the unmatched view of the Potomac. Over time, the place has come to look more and more like the home he and Martha made. Recently discovered documentation, coupled with advances in scientific research, has enabled the foundation to update the rooms with authentic wallpaper and other decorative touches and furnishings that allow guests "to see more of the grandeur the Washingtons really wanted you to see," Briney says.

JAMES MADISON

Madison's Montpelier, just outside the town of Orange, is about a two-hour drive southwest of Mount Vernon. While Mount Vernon opened to the public in 1860 and Monticello celebrated its 100th anniversary of being open to the public in 2023, Madison's Montpelier is relatively new to outside visitors.

For more than 100 years, the 2,650-acre estate was in private hands and closed to the public. During that period, the home also had been transformed into something quite different from what it was when James and Dolley Madison lived there: a fifty-five-room mansion covered in pink stucco. Following James Madison's death in 1836, his widow sold the estate, which went through a succession of owners until the DuPont family acquired it in 1900. The last DuPont to own the estate died in 1983, and Montpelier was acquired by the National Trust for Historic Preservation and finally opened to the public. The Robert H. Smith Center for the Constitution was launched in 2003. The completion of an $8.8 million visitor center in 2007, along with the $24 million restoration of the mansion—which included returning the house to its configuration during Madison's time by razing wings that had been added by later owners, reducing the number of rooms from fifty-five to twenty-six and stripping the stucco to reveal the original bare brick—helped transform Montpelier into a full-fledged public attraction. One thing has remained constant through the years: the exquisite view of the Blue Ridge Mountains from the front porch.

Visitors can now tour the house, including the second-floor library where the shy, modest Madison—who drafted the Bill of Rights, authored *The Federalist Papers*, and is called the "the Father of the Constitution"—did his writing. When you go, you also must visit the modern David M. Rubenstein Visitor Center, featuring a theater, gallery, and shop. Tour the formal garden and stroll the walking trails that will take you through horse pastures and wildflower meadows and the old-growth Landmark Forest.

Then there is "Mere Distinction of Colour," a groundbreaking exhibition that opened in 2017 that borrows the phrase Madison himself used, acknowledging the evils of slavery, in his speech at the Constitutional Convention in 1787: "We have seen the mere distinction of colour made in the most enlightened period of time, a ground of the most oppressive dominion ever exercised by man over man."

"Mere Distinction of Colour" includes the reconstructed buildings of Montpelier's enslaved community, just outside the mansion, as well as a moving exhibition on slavery in the cellar. Making it all the more real, visitors can hear the voices of descendants speaking about their enslaved ancestors. The exhibit is the result of decades of archaeological work and other research, as well as long-term engagement with descendants of the enslaved. Other projects over the years have included the restoration of the nearby Gilmore Cabin, which George Gilmore, born into slavery at Montpelier, built for his family following his emancipation following the Civil War. There also is Montpelier Station, the century-old railroad depot and post office at the entrance to Montpelier that the Montpelier Foundation restored in order to document the period of legalized segregation in the first half of the twentieth century. The bathrooms at the depot are labeled "Whites" and "Colored."

Things are very different at Montpelier nowadays. Kyle Stetz, director of education and visitor engagement, says, "We integrate the story of everything and everyone at Montpelier into a single story."

THOMAS JEFFERSON

Thirty miles away, just outside Charlottesville, there's no better place to play the License Plate Game than the parking lot at Monticello on a summer morning. We count no fewer than twenty-five different states represented in the lot, and that's just what we happened to see on our way to the visitor center. Thomas Jefferson's still got it. Two centuries after his death, the third US president remains the big attraction in Charlottesville—his home, his university, his name on roads, churches, and vineyards.

Monticello is an architectural marvel, a place into which Jefferson poured his heart, soul, and much of his money for almost sixty years to make it just right. Of course, Monticello's enslaved population did the heavy lifting. A trip to Monticello begins at the Thomas Jefferson Visitor Center and Smith Education Center, offering learning and shopping before you even get to the house itself. You acquire your tour tickets here (or online). The visitor center is expected to undergo an expansion in advance of the 250th anniversary of the Declaration of Independence in 2026.

It's not a terribly long walk up the hill to the house, but it is uphill, and on a warm day you can become drenched in a hurry. So, we elect to take the shuttle bus to the mansion and walk back—downhill—after our tour. Once at the top of the mountain, we stroll along the garden plateau where more than 300 varieties of vegetables and more than 170 varieties of fruit were cultivated in Jefferson's day. Jefferson dabbled in gardening, weather, design, just about everything. He was a most interesting and interested man. We walk around the small fishpond where Jefferson kept fish for eating and into which a classmate of mine tumbled during a school field trip many years ago. Funny, that's the one thing I remember from that visit. This time, no one in my party gets wet.

When the time arrives for our tour, we enter the house and hear how there was a time, after Jefferson's death, when hay was stored in this jewel of a home and the Levy family saved it from ruin. We marvel at Jefferson's little touches: the great clock in the entry hall, the dumbwaiter, his writing desk. The place is magnificent. It's also constantly changing, with the addition of discovered artifacts from Jefferson's world as well as the restoration and rebuilding of the historic site. A mountaintop restoration project resulted in rebuilt quarters along Mulberry Row, the tree-lined road running alongside the main house, which served as the industrial hub of the plantation: from carriage bays and horse stables to quarters for enslaved people. That project included the restoration of thirty historic spaces, such as the upper floors

JAMES MONROE'S HIGHLAND, MODEST COMPARED TO HIS NEIGHBOR, THOMAS JEFFERSON, IS JUST OUTSIDE CHARLOTTESVILLE

SIDE TRACKS

Colonial Beach

The one-time "playground of the Potomac" is enjoying a revival. Colonial Beach, 15 minutes from the George Washington Birthplace National Monument, is undergoing development as it tries to appeal to vacationers and weekenders seeking a small-town getaway. It checks a lot of boxes: it is on the water, not-far-but-far-enough from Washington and Richmond (about 90 minutes in each case), and living in the Northern Neck community of 4,000 full-time residents is most definitely laid-back. Many people drive golf carts to get around.

Making a comeback is the town's boardwalk, which was one of the attractions in the late 1800s, when Colonial Beach was incorporated as a summer resort for those who lived in Washington, a 40-mile boat ride away, launching the first era of "glory days" as steamboats deposited thousands of DC residents in Colonial Beach. Gambling remains one of the draws, as Maryland, which owns most of the river, operates Riverboat on the Potomac, just off the town's beach. Colonial Beach features the longest public beach in the state, behind Virginia Beach, and new retailers, such as Circa 1892, a wine, cheese, and gourmet food shop, are breathing new life into the place.

"A well-kept secret," says Duke Dodson, the developer behind $25 million in projects around the town.

ONCE KNOWN AS "THE PLAYGROUND OF THE POTOMAC," COLONIAL BEACH IS MAKING A COMEBACK

THE REFURBISHED RIVERVIEW INN, A FEW BLOCKS FROM THE BEACH, HAS A CHARMING RETRO FEEL

of the main house. More recent work includes the restoration of a burial ground for enslaved people and a contemplative site listing the names of those enslaved by Jefferson. The "Getting Word" African American Oral History Project, underway since the early 1990s, preserves the histories of Monticello's enslaved families and their descendants.

We walk down the hill, past Jefferson's grave, and back to the visitor center to watch a movie that brings Jefferson's life into focus. After lunch, we head 2 miles east on VA 53 to Jefferson's neighbor's house: President James Monroe's Ash Lawn-Highland, a modest home that stands in stark contrast to Monticello's splendor. Monroe's original house was so small, our tour guide tells us, that overnight guests might have been offered a blanket to sleep on the floor next to Monroe's canopy bed. In all, Monticello covers 5,000 acres; Ash Lawn-Highland 535. Their homes are reflections of the men: Jefferson was bold, intellectual, and famous; Monroe, the fifth US president, unassuming, deliberative, and, compared with some presidents, relatively unfamiliar to many Americans. But Monroe led a distinguished life of public service, crossing the frigid Delaware River as an 18-year-old soldier with George Washington and later negotiating the Louisiana Purchase on behalf of Jefferson's administration. Said Jefferson, "Monroe was so honest that if you turned his soul inside out there would not be a spot on it."

As long as you're this close, drive into Charlottesville, where you can visit what has been called Jefferson's "masterpiece"—the University of Virginia, which he founded in 1819. Stroll the original "Grounds" (it's never called "campus") that includes the Rotunda and Lawn, designed by Jefferson to be the heart of what he called an "academical village." Tours are available. Adjacent to the grounds, take a walk along the Corner, a stretch of restaurants and shops, central to the lives of UVA students, faculty, and staff. A visit to Charlottesville wouldn't be complete without a stop at the Downtown Mall, about 2 miles east of the Rotunda, where you will find a pleasant mix of more than 150 shops, restaurants, and entertainment venues along a brick-paved pedestrian mall.

IN THE AREA

Accommodations

BOARS HEAD RESORT, 200 Ednam Drive, Charlottesville. Call 434-296-2181. Website: www.boarsheadresort.com. Upscale resort just west of the University of Virginia.

INNS AT MONTPELIER, Orange. Call 540-672-6840. Website: www.innsatmontpelier.org. Collection of bed-and-breakfasts within proximity of James Madison's Montpelier.

RIVERVIEW INN, 24 Hawthorne Street, Colonial Beach. Call 804-224-4200. Website: www.colonialbeachriverview.com. Retro 1950s-style motel.

Attractions and Recreation

CARTER MOUNTAIN ORCHARD, 1435 Carters Mountain Trail, Charlottesville. Call 434-977-1833. Website: www.chilesfamilyorchards.com/carter-mountain-orchard. Pick-your-own orchard with spectacular views near Monticello.

GEORGE WASHINGTON'S MOUNT VERNON, 3200 Mount Vernon Memorial Highway, Mount Vernon. Call 703-780-2000. Website: www.mountvernon.org.

JAMES MADISON'S MONTPELIER, 11350 Constitution Highway, Montpelier Station. Call 540-672-2728. Website: www.montpelier.org.

JAMES MONROE'S HIGHLAND, 2050 James Monroe Parkway, Charlottesville. Call 434-293-8000. Website: www.highland.org.

MOUNT VERNON TRAIL, Mount Vernon. Call 703-289-2500. Website: www.nps.gov/gwmp/planyourvisit/mtvernontrail.htm. An 18-mile-long, paved, multiuse trail that winds along the Potomac River, stretching from George Washington's Mount Vernon to Theodore Roosevelt Island.

THOMAS JEFFERSON'S MONTICELLO, 1050 Monticello Loop, Charlottesville. Call 434-984-9800. Website: www.monticello.org.

THOMAS JEFFERSON'S POPLAR FOREST, 1776 Poplar Forest Parkway, Lynchburg. Call 434-525-1806. Website: www.poplarforest.org.

Dining

BODO'S BAGELS, Charlottesville. Website: www.bodosbagels.com. Popular bagel and sandwich shop at several locations.

CROZET PIZZA, 5794 Three Notched Road, Crozet. Call 434-823-2132. Website: www.crozetpizza.com. Landmark restaurant and bar west of Charlottesville.

MICHIE TAVERN, 683 Thomas Jefferson Parkway, Charlottesville. Call: 434-977-1234. Website: www.michietavern.com. Historic restaurant dating to the 1700s a half-mile below Monticello.

MOUNT VERNON INN RESTAURANT, 3200 Mount Vernon Memorial Highway, Mount Vernon. Call 703-799-5296. Website: www.mountvernon restaurant.com. On George Washington's estate.

Other Contacts

COLONIAL BEACH, Colonial Beach. Call 804-224-7181. Website: www.visit cbva.com. Resort town on the Potomac.

MONTICELLO WINE TRAIL, Charlottesville. Website: www.monticellowine trail.com. More than three dozen wineries within 25 miles of Charlottesville.

OUR LADY OF THE ANGELS MONASTERY, 3365 Monastery Drive, Crozet. Call 434-823-1452. Website: www.olamonastery.org. Monastery where nuns make and sell Dutch-style Gouda cheese to support their mission. Limited hours. Cash or check. No online sales.

9

FROM PIE TO BBQ

A Drive along US 15

ESTIMATED LENGTH: 90 miles

ESTIMATED TIME: Day or two (or more . . .)

HIGHLIGHTS: A little bit of everything representative of Virginia. Considerable history is on this route, primarily traveling US 15, between **Leesburg** and **Gordonsville**: lovely scenery in the foothills, small towns, horse country, **Manassas National Battlefield Park, James Madison's Montpelier**, bed-and-breakfast inns, and wineries. This section of road is part of the larger **Journey Through Hallowed Ground**, a series of itineraries that stretch between Gettysburg, Pennsylvania, and Charlottesville, Virginia, which aims to raise awareness of American history and heritage in the region, featuring battlefields, charming towns, natural beauty, and the homes and birthplaces of no fewer than nine US presidents.

GETTING THERE: Start at either **Leesburg** or **Gordonsville**, depending on whether you want your pie (Leesburg) or your barbecue (Gordonsville) for dessert.

US 15 is a highway that connects the dots of much of Virginia's history. But don't think "highway" means "ugly." US 15 unspools through some of the prettiest countryside in the state. "Gorgeous" is how a friend describes stretches of the road. I decide to include Leesburg as the northern terminus here, even though it is nearly the tip-top of Virginia, deep in Northern Virginia, a region where you wouldn't necessarily go seeking "backroads and byways." And yet . . .

Leesburg is the seat of Loudoun County, one of the fastest-growing counties in Virginia: home to Dulles International Airport and sprawling suburbia. But the rural western part of the county is a step back in time. So much

LEFT: WHEN TRAVELING THROUGH GORDONSVILLE, BBQ EXCHANGE IS A MUST-STOP

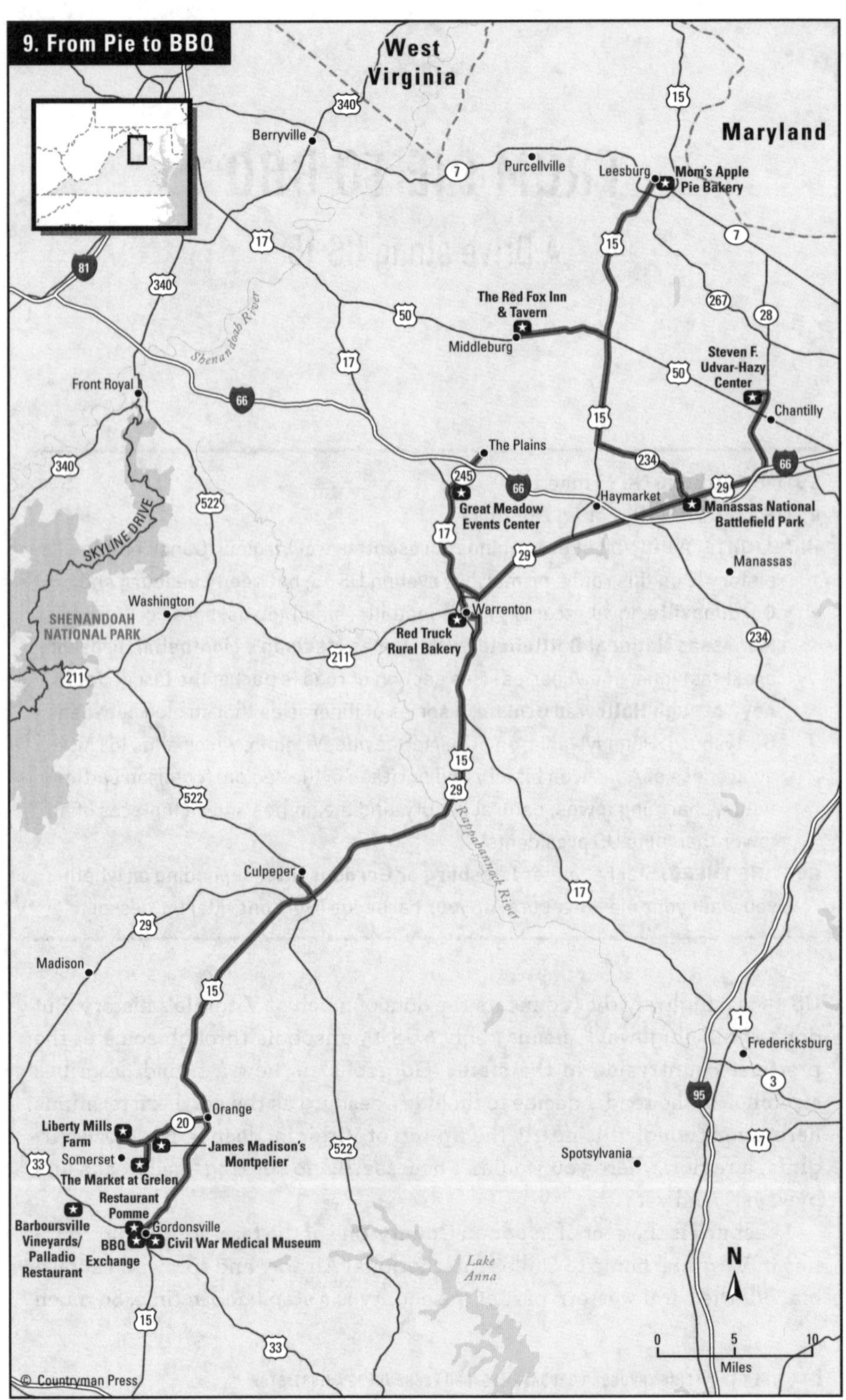
9. From Pie to BBQ
West Virginia
Maryland
Berryville
Purcellville
Leesburg
Mom's Apple Pie Bakery
The Red Fox Inn & Tavern
Middleburg
Steven F. Udvar-Hazy Center
Chantilly
Front Royal
The Plains
Great Meadow Events Center
Haymarket
Manassas National Battlefield Park
Manassas
SKYLINE DRIVE
Shenandoah River
Washington
SHENANDOAH NATIONAL PARK
Warrenton
Red Truck Rural Bakery
Rappahannock River
Culpeper
Madison
Fredericksburg
Orange
Liberty Mills Farm
James Madison's Montpelier
Somerset
The Market at Grelen
Restaurant Pomme
Barboursville Vineyards/ Palladio Restaurant
Gordonsville
BBQ Exchange
Civil War Medical Museum
Spotsylvania
Lake Anna
N
Miles
© Countryman Press

RED TRUCK RURAL BAKERY IN WARRENTON IS A LOCAL FAVORITE, WITH A SISTER SHOP IN NEARBY MARSHALL

so, that Loudoun has about 250 miles of unpaved roads, the most of any county in Virginia. Leesburg also has Mom's Apple Pie, a family-run bakery in a cute little stone building that decades ago was a gas station. It's a fine place to start—or end—this particular journey.

Heading south from Leesburg on US 15, you can hop off on US 50 west, which will take you to Middleburg, a town dating to the 1700s in the heart of Virginia horse-and-hunt country with art galleries, fine dining, and boutique shops. The oldest building in town is the Red Fox Inn & Tavern, which was established in 1728 as Chinn's Ordinary, a midway point between Alexandria and Winchester. A more recent attraction is the National Sporting Library and Museum, dedicated to preserving, promoting, and sharing the literature, art, and culture of equestrian, angling, and field sports.

Onward to Manassas National Battlefield Park, which is about a half-hour southeast of Middleburg. You can show up at the battlefield any time you'd like, but get there, as I did, at dawn and stand in the glorious solitude: in the day's first light, crickets chirp and birds sing as dew drips from the still cannons and deer scamper across the deserted grounds. You don't have to be a Civil War buff to fast develop an appreciation for this place. The visitor center, of course, is not open at dawn, but the property is ripe for strolling or jogging, which a lot of local residents seem to do. You can wait to follow a ranger around, or you can take a self-guided tour of this hallowed ground where thousands were killed and the stage was set for a brutal war of neighbor against neighbor.

The battlefield, site of the first major land battle of the war, and then a

A FIELD OF SUNFLOWERS ON THE SIDE OF US 15 NEAR CULPEPER

second one thirteen months later, used to be on the back roads of the state. Now, it is a rare green space in the suburban sprawl of Northern Virginia. Preservationists and the National Park Service have fought to keep it so, fending off an interstate highway, a shopping mall, a housing development, and even a theme park. Still, the roads that crisscross the park are laden with traffic, particularly at rush hours when commuters are going to work or heading home. The occasional jet from nearby Dulles roars overhead.

Even so, this is a place of great significance and meaning, as your mind drifts back to what transpired here. You can almost hear the cannon fire and the blood-curdling Rebel yell. The first battle, also known as Bull Run for the stream that runs through the park, was fought on a hot Sunday in July 1861, attracting the curious from Washington to bring their picnic baskets and parasols and watch from nearby hillsides. This was supposed to be a skirmish at which Union troops would squelch the Southern uprising. Instead, it ignited the larger conflagration. The Confederates won this battle and the second, but at a steep price for the nation: nearly 4,000 troops were killed and more than 17,000 wounded at both. Scores went missing.

The park features an extensive system of trails, or you can drive to some of the far-flung sites of the 5,000-acre park. Walk the 1-mile Henry Hill Loop Trail, visit the rebuilt Henry House, and pause for a moment at the grave of Judith Carter Henry, the only civilian killed at First Manassas when artillery fire hit her house. Across US 29, visit the Stone House, which served as a field hospital in both battles. Less than a mile north on US 29, you'll find the famed Stone Bridge, with Bull Run trickling beneath it.

You won't want to miss Chinn Ridge, where both battles ended. Of course, at some point you should go by the visitor center, take a look at the artifacts and exhibits, and watch the fine orientation movie that captures the history of the place. There's an extensive bookstore, too.

If you're feeling like a side trip, run up to Chantilly—about a 15-minute drive from the battlefield—to the Smithsonian National and Air Space Museum's Steven F. Udvar-Hazy Center, at the south end of Dulles International Airport. The center has a wonderful display of thousands of aviation and space artifacts, including the Space Shuttle Discovery, a Blackbird SR-71, and a Concorde, in two large hangars. It's open every day except Christmas.

From the battlefield, head south on US 29, joined a few miles later by US 15, toward Warrenton, the seat of lovely Fauquier County and the county's shopping and business hub. You might consider venturing off the road toward the Plains, a dozen miles north on US 17 and VA 245, which goes even deeper into the land of horse farms, and makes for a most pleasant expedition, motoring along tree-lined lanes, rolling green pastures, and long stretches of rail fences. If you get as far as the Plains, you might check out the Great Meadow Field Events Center, where you can catch an occasional steeplechase or regular polo match.

If you didn't satisfy your pie craving in Leesburg, here's another chance: Red Truck Rural Bakery, set in a former gas station in Warrenton's Old Town, serving pastries, sandwiches, coffee, cakes, and, of course, pies.

As you head south on US 15/29, Culpeper comes up in 25 miles. Another historic small town, Culpeper is a nice place for a stop, with museums, antique shops, and a variety of restaurants. Another 20 miles south on US 15 (by this time, US 29 has veered off), as we go by bucolic scenes of pastureland and grazing cattle, brings us to the town of Orange. The town's visitor center is in the old rail station, a good place to stop for brochures and answers to travel questions

THE OLD EXCHANGE HOTEL IN GORDONSVILLE SERVED AS A HOSPITAL DURING THE CIVIL WAR AND NOW HOUSES A CIVIL WAR MUSEUM

Liberty Mills Farm in Somerset has a huge corn maze each fall. Each year it has a different theme, and you can pick your own produce, strawberries, pumpkins, and flowers. Visit their farm store and check out the collection of John Deere vintage tractors, and don't miss the terrific natural views. And if you thought nurseries were just for buying plants, travel a short distance to **The Market at Grelen**, where you can also pick your own fruit, plus it has a great nursery and also a café where you can sit and enjoy lunch and homemade ice cream.

about Central Virginia. Walk along Main Street and check out antique shops and art galleries. James Madison's Montpelier is a 10-minute drive outside town (you can read more about Montpelier in the chapter, Hail to the Chiefs).

Dining options are not a problem here, either, from the upscale Vintage Restaurant on the garden level of the historic Manor House at the Inn at Willow Grove to Forked on Main, in the historic Sparks Building, as well as Silk Mill Grille and My Avocado Mexican Grill. Arranging a stay in this area is made easier by a partnership of area bed-and-breakfast inns—the Inns of Montpelier—that banded together after Montpelier, the home of President James Madison, underwent a major restoration some years ago, and in the process became a major tourist attraction for the first time.

No more than 15 minutes farther south and we find ourselves in Gordonsville, where you can browse a variety of shops along Main Street (US 15). At

GREAT PIES CAN BE FOUND IN AN UNLIKELY LOOKING LITTLE BUILDING IN LEESBURG: MOM'S APPLE PIE, A FAMILY-RUN BAKERY

THE OLD TRAIN STATION IN ORANGE NOW SERVES AS THE TOWN'S VISITOR CENTER

Back in the days when I was traveling around Virginia for the *Richmond Times-Dispatch* with photographer Bob Brown, we were constantly searching out more than good stories. We were also on the lookout for good pie. (Fact is, though, there aren't too many bad pies.) One such place we found was **Red Truck Rural Bakery** in Warrenton, a sweet little shop in a long-ago Esso service station. We stopped there one morning on our way to interview the actor Robert Duvall, who lived nearby, and whom, we had learned, was a fan of the bakery. After ordering our breakfast, we asked the folks running the bakery if Duvall had a favorite pie. Apple, we were told. So, we ordered an apple pie to deliver to Duvall. The interview went great. Duvall later cut the ribbon when Red Truck owner Brian Noyes opened a second, larger location in nearby Marshall. Noyes announced in 2023 he was selling the bakeries to the owners of a local restaurant but said nothing would change—down to the vintage red pickup truck parked outside the Warrenton shop.

Sometime later I came to learn about **Mom's Apple Pie Company** in Leesburg. It, too, is housed in a former gas station, on a triangle-shaped plot of land wedged between two of Leesburg's main roads. Mom's is a tiny store that has room for only a few customers at a time amid display cases stocked with pies, cookies, and breads. On a day I visited, I talked to Tyson Cox, whose mother Avis Renshaw is "Mom" of the bakery's name. But the truth of the matter, Tyson told me, is that most of the pie recipes originated with his dad, Steven Cox.

"But 'Dad's Apple Pie' doesn't have the same ring," Tyson said with a laugh.

The family started out in farming—and still grows many of the fruit and vegetables they use in their pies and quiches—and has been in the pie business since the 1980s. In 2010, *Southern Living* magazine included Mom's blackberry pie in a featured headlined, "The South's Best Pies."

one time, Gordonsville was billed as the "fried chicken capital of the world" because of the townspeople who would greet train passengers with trays of chicken and other fare. Adjacent to the train tracks, you will find the old Exchange Hotel, which was a popular stop for rail travelers before and after the Civil War. During the war, however, it became a hospital where 70,000 troops—Confederate and Union—were treated. Now, it's the Exchange Hotel Civil War Medical Museum, and is said to be haunted.

Across from the hotel is the BBQ Exchange with excellent barbecue (also tofu "barbecue" for vegetarians) and a nice selection of sides and desserts. It's a counter-style place with indoor seating as well as picnic tables outdoors under cover.

IN THE AREA

Accommodations

INNS AT MONTPELIER. Call 540-672-6840. Website: www.innsatmontpelier.org. A partnership of bed-and-breakfast inns within 15 miles of Montpelier, James Madison's home, at Montpelier Station.

THE RED FOX INN & TAVERN, 2 E. Washington Street, Middleburg. Call 540-687-6301. Website: www.redfox.com. Historic inn and restaurant.

Attractions and Recreation

BARBOURSVILLE VINEYARDS, 17655 Winery Road, Barboursville. Call 540-832-3824. Website: www.bbvwine.com. Winery at eighteenth-century estate, with Palladio Restaurant, featuring a northern Italian-inspired menu.

CIVIL WAR MEDICAL MUSEUM AT THE EXCHANGE HOTEL, 400 S. Main Street, Gordonsville. Call 540-832-2944. Website: www.facebook.com/hgiexchange. Former hotel and Civil War hospital.

COX FARMS, 15621 Braddock Road, Centreville. Call 703-830-4121. Website: www.coxfarms.com. Family-run farm market, seasonal festivals, and home of Foamhenge, a styrofoam replica of Stonehenge.

JAMES MADISON'S MONTPELIER, 11407 Constitution Highway, Montpelier Station. Call 540-672-2728. Website: www.montpelier.org. Estate of fourth president of the United States.

MANASSAS NATIONAL BATTLEFIELD PARK, 6511 Sudley Road, Manassas. Call 703-361-1339. Website: www.nps.gov/mana. Site of two major Civil War battles.

STEVEN F. UDVAR-HAZY CENTER OF THE SMITHSONIAN NATIONAL AIR AND SPACE MUSEUM, 14390 Air and Space Museum Parkway, Chantilly. Call 703-572-4118. Website: www.airandspace.si.edu.

Dining

BBQ EXCHANGE, 102 Martinsburg Avenue, Gordonsville. Call 540-832-0227. Website: www.bbqex.com.

FORKED ON MAIN, 124 W. Main Street, Orange. Call 540-308-7660. Website: www.forkedonmain.com. "Modern American eatery with a laid-back vibe."

IT'S ABOUT THYME, 128 East Davis Street, Culpeper. Call 540-825-4264. Website: www.thymeinfo.com. European country cuisine, adjacent to Thyme Market, an upscale deli, in Culpeper's historic district.

MOM'S APPLE PIE COMPANY, 220 Loudoun Street; other location in Round Hill, 35246 Harry Byrd Highway. Call: 703-771-8590. Website: www.momsapplepieco.com.

RED TRUCK RURAL BAKERY, 22 Waterloo Street, Warrenton. A second location in Marshall, 8368 W. Main Street. Call 540-347-2224. Website: www.redtruckbakery.com.

Other Contacts

THE JOURNEY THROUGH HALLOWED GROUND. Website: www.hallowedground.org.

LIBERTY MILLS FARM, 9166 Liberty Mills Road, Somerset. Call 434-882-6293. Website: www.libertymillsfarm.com. Farm market, corn maze, festivals.

THE MARKET AT GRELEN, 15091 Yager Road, Somerset. Call 540-672-7268. Website: www.themarketatgrelen.com. European-style garden shop and cafe.

10

INTO THE HIGHLANDS

"No More Beautiful Place in Virginia"

ESTIMATED LENGTH: 300 miles (from Richmond)

ESTIMATE TIME: At least a few days

HIGHLIGHTS: The beauty of **Grayson Highlands State Park**, one of the premier—and more unusual—places in Virginia. Hiking, camping, or just sight-seeking make it worth the drive to the southwest corner of the state. The park's wild ponies are another draw, and the highest mountain in the state, **Mount Rogers**, is next door. Just down the road is the **Virginia Creeper Trail**, a former rail line and now a 34-mile-long recreational trail, which is a popular destination. The midpoint of the trail is in **Damascus**, which dubs itself "Trail Town USA," given that a number of trails, including the Appalachian Trail, that come through the town.

GETTING THERE: From Richmond, I-64 west to I-81 south to VA 16 to US 58 at Volney, then 10 curvy miles to the park entrance.

I had never heard of Grayson Highlands State Park until I was introduced by the late, great outdoors writer Garvey Winegar. A friend and colleague for many years, Winegar wrote lovingly about Virginia's far southwest, in general, and the park, in particular, many times.

"If I weren't where I am right now, I know where I'd like to be," he started off one column, and then went on to list a half-dozen places around Virginia, Grayson Highlands among them. He once noted how the park's alpine meadows, rocky outcrops, and fir-spruce forests are more reminiscent of "the high country of Montana or Wyoming than Virginia." Another time, he wrote in the *Richmond Times-Dispatch*, my old paper, "This is about as high as it gets in Virginia. On a mountain called Big Pinnacle, you're close to a mile above sea level and can see 360 degrees. In the background, but not loud enough

LEFT: THE GRAZING WILD PONIES OF GRAYSON HIGHLANDS

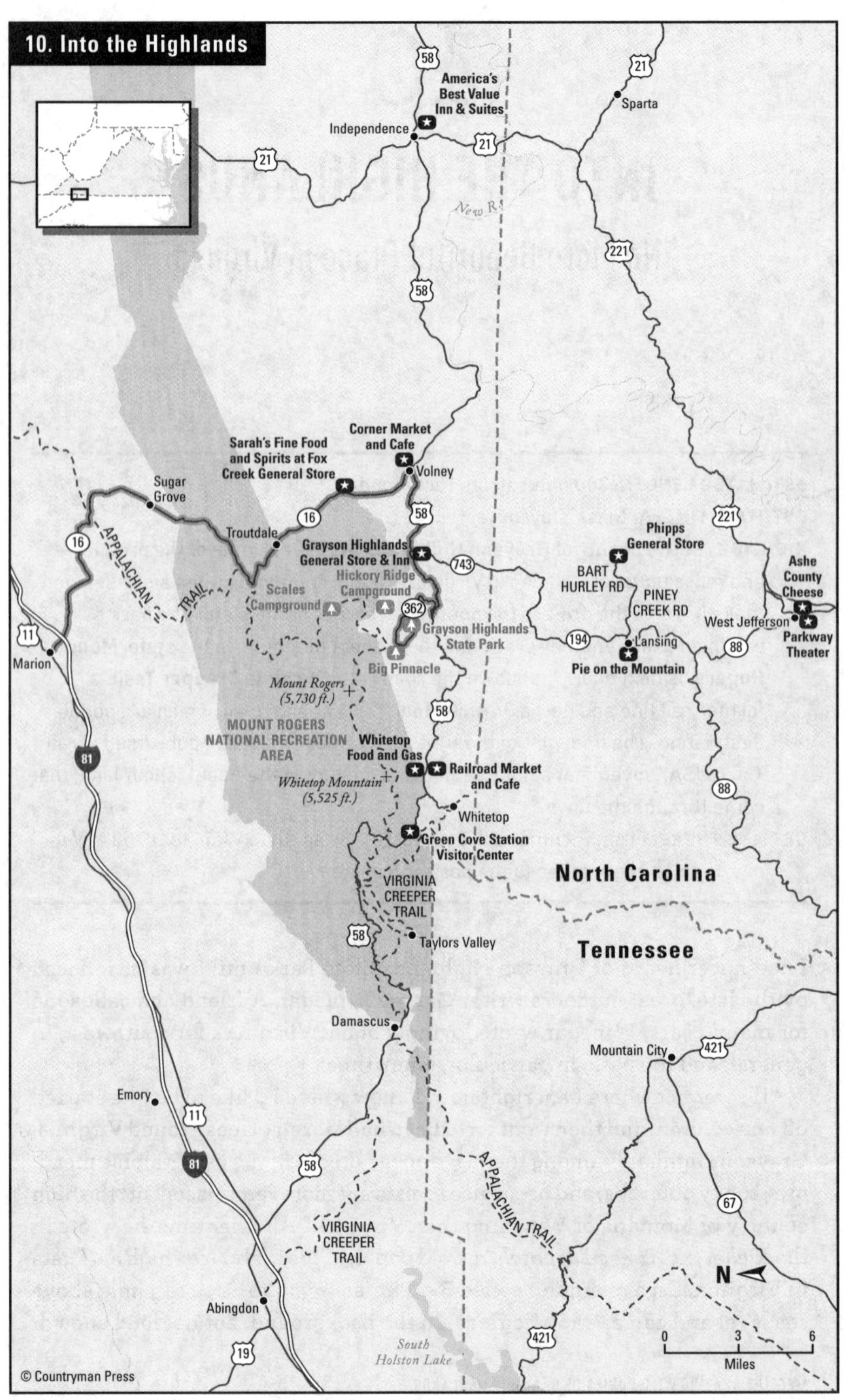

10. Into the Highlands
America's Best Value Inn & Suites
Independence
Sparta
New R.
Corner Market and Cafe
Sarah's Fine Food and Spirits at Fox Creek General Store
Volney
Sugar Grove
Troutdale
APPALACHIAN TRAIL
Grayson Highlands General Store & Inn
Hickory Ridge Campground
Scales Campground
Grayson Highlands State Park
Big Pinnacle
Mount Rogers (5,730 ft.)
MOUNT ROGERS NATIONAL RECREATION AREA
Whitetop Food and Gas
Railroad Market and Cafe
Whitetop Mountain (5,525 ft.)
Whitetop
Green Cove Station Visitor Center
VIRGINIA CREEPER TRAIL
Taylors Valley
Marion
Phipps General Store
BART HURLEY RD
PINEY CREEK RD
Ashe County Cheese
West Jefferson
Parkway Theater
Lansing
Pie on the Mountain
North Carolina
Tennessee
Damascus
Mountain City
Emory
APPALACHIAN TRAIL
VIRGINIA CREEPER TRAIL
Abingdon
South Holston Lake
N
0 3 6
Miles
© Countryman Press

BEAUTIFUL SCENERY IS A HALLMARK OF GRAYSON HIGHLANDS STATE PARK

to drown out birdsong or hawk cry, Cabin Creek rushes off the mountain. We once watched a snowstorm come sweeping up from Tennessee. Awesome."

"In my opinion," he told readers, "There is no more beautiful place in Virginia than Grayson County."

When Garvey Winegar wrote something like that, you could take it to the bank. Sold as I was, it still took me a while to get there. Having spent most of my years in the relative flatlands of Richmond, Southwest Virginia was always largely a rumor to me, mostly because it's a long way out there. The park is only a handful of miles from North Carolina and Tennessee, but, from Richmond, it's a drive of 300 miles, the last few quite challenging. When I finally laid eyes on the place, though, I discovered Garvey was right. It was worth the drive.

THE SUMMIT OF MOUNT ROGERS, THE HIGHEST PEAK IN VIRGINIA AT MORE THAN 5,700 FEET, IS MARKED BY A MEDALLION (ACTUALLY TWO) PLACED BY THE US GEOLOGICAL SURVEY

My family has made the trek almost every year for the last two decades to camp at Grayson Highlands, to wonder at the splendor of the place, and to relish the usually cool summertime temperatures at the highest elevations in Virginia. We hike stretches of the Appalachian Trail, which passes through the park, and often climb the highest mountain in the state, Mount Rogers, located nearby, to its tree-covered summit (i.e., no view). The second-highest, Whitetop Mountain, is only a few miles away.

Before I leave Garvey, I will share one of my favorite lines from the many he wrote. In a column about how, based on his experience, the black bears of Virginia are generally "shy, elusive, timid, even cowardly when it comes to confronting people," he continued, "One should add *none* of the above applies to grizzlies. They wake up dyspeptic and get meaner as the day unfolds." Good thing the nearest grizzly is about 2,000 miles from Virginia. There are black bears in the area around Grayson Highlands, as you would expect in a rural, mountainous region, though encounters with humans are happily rare.

The first time I saw Grayson Highlands, it was an overcast, late-spring afternoon. Daylight was fading, and rain was falling. I was on a newspaper assignment with my colleague, photographer Bob Brown, driving the length of US 58—the longest road in Virginia—and the two-lane road goes past the park's entrance. (US 58 would be another fine travel adventure if you've got a week or two to properly explore it.) US 58 runs westward from the oceanfront at Virginia Beach for more than 500 miles along the southern tier of the commonwealth to Cumberland Gap, in the westernmost corner of the state. A point so far west, in fact, that at Cumberland Gap you are west of Detroit.

In Grayson County, US 58 is mostly a two-lane road, and as you approach the park, it twists and bends, hairpin-like in some places. Large trucks are advised to find another route around the park. I dubbed it "full-bodied driving," as Bob and I made our way toward the park in the rainy twilight. We had to be in Abingdon that evening, so we had time only for a quick spin around the park, but I saw enough to know I wanted to return with my family, which we did later that summer. Now, we rarely miss a year visiting the place, and we are not alone. I've noticed a good many others have made the same discovery. On weekends, in particular, the park can become crowded when visitors flock from not only Virginia but neighboring North Carolina and Tennessee and even farther afield.

The 4,800-acre park was established in 1965 and was originally named Mount Rogers State Park. Besides its beauty, the park has become as well known for its wild ponies, introduced to the park decades ago to graze and maintain the grassy balds on mountaintops. The free-roaming and popular herd is managed by the Wilburn Ridge Pony Association and rounded up every fall for a health-check. A few are auctioned every year.

Though the relatively cold climate at the higher elevations plays a role in the treeless nature of some areas, the rugged beauty of the park was also forged through adversity over time: logging, fire, and the devastating chestnut blight that wiped out billions of American chestnut trees throughout Appalachia in the early 1900s.

The park offers two campgrounds, one of which is dedicated to those who bring horses to enjoy the riding trails in or near the park, including the nearby Virginia Highlands Horse Trail, a 68-mile-long trail in the Mount Rogers National Recreation Area. We don't have horses, but we do have a tent, so we always camp at the Hickory Ridge Campground. The campground also offers yurts, if you prefer walls between you and the great outdoors when you sleep, but for more conventional lodging, you'll have to leave the park. Cabins and other short-term rentals are available within a few miles of the park. For a motel, you'll have to drive 45 minutes to an hour: east to Independence and Galax or west to Abingdon.

HIKING TO ONE OF THE OVERLOOKS AT GRAYSON HIGHLANDS, SUCH AS LITTLE PINNACLE, THE HIGHEST POINT IN THE PARK, ALWAYS AFFORDS A MARVELOUS VIEW AND OFTEN A BIT OF SOLITUDE

Grayson Highlands is very much off to itself, nearly an hour from the closest interstate highway, and that is part of the charm. We usually go for a week, hiking by day and settling in at our campsite at night, preparing dinner on our propane camp stove, and sitting at a cozy fire. On a clear night, walk to one of the open areas and look up: the stars practically leap off the black canvas of the sky. In fact, stargazing is good in a lot of places in the mountains of Southwest Virginia, far from the glow of city lights.

The park offers a number of quite-doable hikes, from those that take you up to soaring views to a trail that takes you down through the coolness of the woods to the aforementioned Cabin Creek, where you can sit on rocks and be mesmerized by roaring waterfalls and enjoy a picnic lunch.

A good first hike, to get the lay of the land, is the Twin Pinnacles Trail, which we start behind the visitor center (you can also start at a trailhead from the Massie Gap parking lot, but it's a pretty steep uphill, so we always start behind the visitor center). The gentle, 1.3-mile loop takes you to the two highest overlooks in the park: Little Pinnacle and Big Pinnacle. Little Pinnacle is the highest at 5,089 feet, compared to Big Pinnacle's 5,068. Little Pinnacle is the smaller overlook of the two (hence the name), but you can enjoy fine views from either, though Big Pinnacle offers more of a 360-degree spectacle. From either, you get a good look at Mount Rogers and Whitetop Mountain.

Massie Gap is the place to start many of the park's hikes, including our annual trek to Mount Rogers via the Appalachian Trail, which is about a 10-mile round-trip that could, depending on how many times you pause to rest, snack, and enjoy the scenery, take you anywhere from about five hours to most of the day. We tend to land in the latter category. How challenging a hike is it? It's not scaling Everest, but the terrain is fairly rocky and there are some definite uphill sections—there is more than 1,000 feet in elevation change from the Massie Gap parking area to the Mount Rogers summit of more than 5,700 feet—so plan accordingly. I wouldn't wear flip-flops, as I've seen some people wearing on the trail. Also be prepared for sudden weather changes. We've experienced a few unexpected thunderstorms over the years, as well as some abrupt changes in temperature.

Almost any time we hike Massie Gap, we encounter wild ponies somewhere along the trail. They're cute and accustomed to people, so they're seemingly quite friendly. The natural inclination is to want to pet them, hug them for a photo, or give them a snack. Don't do any of those things. They're wild, and they could bite and kick. Plus, they fend for themselves in the park and in the adjacent Mount Rogers National Recreation Area, so they shouldn't become dependent on humans for their food. Speaking of food, in late July and early August, your hike might be slowed—a lot—to stop and pick wild blueberries along the trail. Many a summer we've gotten our fill.

As you hike up the fairly steep incline from the Massie Gap parking lot, you meet the Appalachian Trail. Almost a quarter of the AT's 2,200 miles goes through the mountains of western Virginia, and this portion of it comes right through Massie Gap. At the trail intersection, north goes to the right, a direction we hike sometimes to reach the Scales, a grassy corral area where ranchers used to take the cattle to be weighed before taking them down the mountain. It's now a major trailhead and camping spot where several trails, including the AT, converge. It's an 8- to 10-mile loop, depending on which trails you choose. Following the AT is longer but more scenic, as well as more challenging and more pleasant, if that's a possible combination. It's also almost always a less-crowded hike than going to Mount Rogers, which requires a turn to the left at the Massie Gap trail intersection.

You'll almost always find a few people, and on weekends many more, heading to Mount Rogers: thru-hikers on the AT, those on multi-overnight hikes along the trail, or people who simply are taking a day hike to Virginia's highest point. You exit Grayson Highlands and enter the sprawling Mount Rogers National Recreation Area—about 200,000 acres—through a gate just beyond what we jokingly refer to as the "cell phone bench," a nice place to sit, rest, and enjoy the view before continuing on your hike, and also a place to catch up on text messages, emails, and the weather forecast. The cell signal is reliably strong at the bench, a rare occurrence in the park.

After passing through the gate, going up and over Wilburn Ridge is the most challenging part of the hike, a lot of rocky footing, mostly out in the open, but no hanging off the side of a cliff or anything. Lots of places to stop for a drink and admire the view or check out the ponies or herds of their roaming buddies, Watusi cattle, that also graze across the grassy balds. (Tip: After hiking to Mount Rogers for two decades, we suddenly discovered that if you veer off the AT onto the Rhododendron Gap Trail at Wilburn Ridge and then rejoin the AT at Rhododendron Gap, you can make better time and avoid a lot of the rocks. Nice, different views, too.) Less than a mile from the top of Mount Rogers, you come to Thomas Knob Shelter, one of the open-sided shelters for AT hikers. A picnic table and an outhouse off in the woods make this a good place to pause, even for day-hikers.

A half-mile-long spur trail off the AT will take you to the summit, which, as mentioned before, offers no view. As you get close to the top, you enter another world: a deep, dark forest of Fraser firs and red spruce that smells like Christmas. The air turns cool and damp, the ground soggy. Ferns thrive, and moss blankets fallen trees. The scene has been described as more like something you would find in Canada or the Pacific Northwest.

The only way to know you've reached the top is a US Geological Survey medallion affixed to a boulder—and then a second one, maybe 50 feet away, on another boulder at the same elevation. The selfies are somewhat understated, compared to pictures from the tops of other states' highest peaks, but satisfying nonetheless.

Because of the park's location, it's a bit of a drive to anything and anywhere else, but we often take a day and drive the hour to Damascus to ride the Virginia Creeper Trail. I asked friends in the area for other recommendations.

There are various annual festivals in the area, including those at the park: the Albert Hash Memorial Festival (honoring a locally famous instrument-maker) and the Grayson Highlands Fall Festival (including an auction of

PEDALING THE VIRGINIA CREEPER TRAIL, FOLLOWING THE PATH OF AN OLD RAILWAY LINE, IS FUN, SCENIC, AND, ON THE DOWNHILL RUN FROM WHITETOP STATION TO DAMASCUS, IS NOT PARTICULARLY STRENUOUS

SIDE TRACKS

Once a rail line for trains hauling lumber, iron ore, and passengers, the 34-mile-long, multiuse **Virginia Creeper Trail** follows the path of the abandoned rail bed and attracts bikers, hikers, and joggers. The rail line was technically the Abingdon Branch of the Norfolk & Western Railroad, but locally it was known as the Virginia Creeper, whose name came either from the woody vine that grows in this part of the world or, possibly, the sluggishness of the early steam locomotives chugging through the mountains. The trail runs from the Virginia-North Carolina line, just east of Whitetop Station, to Abingdon. Damascus is the midway point.

The 17-mile, mostly downhill stretch from Whitetop Station to Damascus draws the most crowds, particularly on weekends when the trail becomes quite crowded. You can drive to Whitetop Station, but many people prefer to park in Damascus and rely on one of the town's bike shops for shuttle service to the top. The ride itself is fairly easy, but you must be careful because you're going down a gravel path on a wooded, mountain trail. The trestles, particularly the 563-foot-long crossing at Creek Junction, add a little excitement.

You easily can ride the downhill stretch to Damascus straight through in less than a couple of hours, but we like to stop along the way at the visitor center at Green Cove, one of the original depots, as well as at the fast-flowing creeks along the way that beckon kids to skip stones or go wading. We've also made a tradition of stopping for lunch at the cafe in Taylors Valley, a small community about 10 miles from the top. No guarantees the place is open, though, given that it changes hands from time to time, but, if it's open, it's a welcome stop.

The trail flattens for the last few miles into Damascus, which is the end of the line for a lot of cyclists. Of course, you're welcome to continue to Abingdon, which we've done on occasion. That stretch of the trail is slightly uphill, though not exceedingly so, and goes through more farmland. We enjoy stopping at Alvarado Station, another of the restored depots, for a bathroom break. Bonus: The wonderful, riverside park across the street with benches and a shelter. Abingdon is a worthy destination. Just make sure you have a ride waiting for you—or call ahead for a shuttle.

wild ponies); both are held in September. Among festivals outside the park, but close by, are the Whitetop Mountain Maple Festival in March, the Whitetop Mountain Ramp Festival in May (yes, a celebration of wild leeks), and the Whitetop Mountain Molasses Festival in October. You can expect music, food, and fun at all.

There are trout streams to fish and sunsets to savor. Drive up the unpaved, winding road to the summit of Whitetop Mountain, the state's second-highest peak, "and see the sunset below you," says Sharon Compton, a retired school-

YOU GET AN EYEFUL OF SCENERY AT GRAYSON HIGHLANDS, EVEN IF YOU NEVER LEAVE YOUR CAR

teacher who lives outside the park, "Breathtaking." She and her husband Don both have roots in the area and moved from Northern Virginia after retirement. They love the place.

You need to venture a bit to find places to eat, but there are some good ones: Railroad Market and Café in Whitetop, Corner Market and Café in Volney, and Sarah's Fine Food & Spirits at Fox Creek General Store in Troutdale. There's also Whitetop Food and Gas, an old-style country grocery, and Grayson Highlands General Store and Inn, which offers provisions and lodging upstairs.

You can even motor the few miles to North Carolina, which offers more options in a couple of towns—Lansing and West Jefferson—about a half-hour's drive or so from the park. Red Dog Bar & Bistro, Pie on the Mountain, and Black Jack's Pub & Grill are among the promising choices. Phipps General Store in Lansing offers Friday night music jams. You can watch cheese being made at Ashe County Cheese, North Carolina's oldest cheese factory, in West Jefferson. Parkway Theater in West Jefferson shows movies nightly. In fact, the whole town of West Jefferson is a walkable shopping experience.

IN THE AREA

Accommodations

AMERICA'S BEST VALUE INN & SUITES, 155 Rainbow Circle, Independence. Call 276-221-0216. Website: www.redlion.com.

GRAYSON HIGHLANDS GENERAL STORE & INN, 4249 Highlands Parkway, Mouth of Wilson. Website: www.graysongeneralstore.com.

Attractions and Recreation

GRAYSON HIGHLANDS STATE PARK, 829 Grayson Highlands Lane, Mouth of Wilson. Website: www.dcr.virginia.gov/state-parks/grayson-highlands.

MOUNT ROGERS NATIONAL RECREATION AREA, 3714 Highway 16, Marion. Call 276-783-5196. Website: www.fs.usda.gov.

VIRGINIA CREEPER TRAIL CONSERVANCY, 132 W. Laurel Avenue, Damascus. Website: www.vacreepertrail.org. A 34-mile-long recreation trail between Abingdon and Whitetop Station.

Dining

CORNER MARKET & CAFÉ, 4013 Troutdale Highway, Mouth of Wilson. Call 276-579-4440. Website: www.facebook.com/cornermarketcafe.

RAILROAD MARKET & CAFÉ, 16103 Highlands Parkway, Whitetop. Call 276-388-3337. Website: www.facebook.com/profile.php?id=100070920962127.

SARAH'S FINE FOOD & SPIRITS AT FOX CREEK GENERAL STORE, 7116 Troutdale Highway, Troutdale. Call 276-579-6033. Website: www.facebook.com/people/Fox-Creek-General-Store/100060362176167.

Other Contacts

WILBURN RIDGE PONY ASSOCIATION, Rural Retreat. Call 276-266-5952. Website: www.facebook.com/p/Wilburn-Ridge-Pony-Association-100085251856866. Nonprofit organization that cares for the wild ponies at Grayson Highlands State Park and Mount Rogers National Recreation Area.

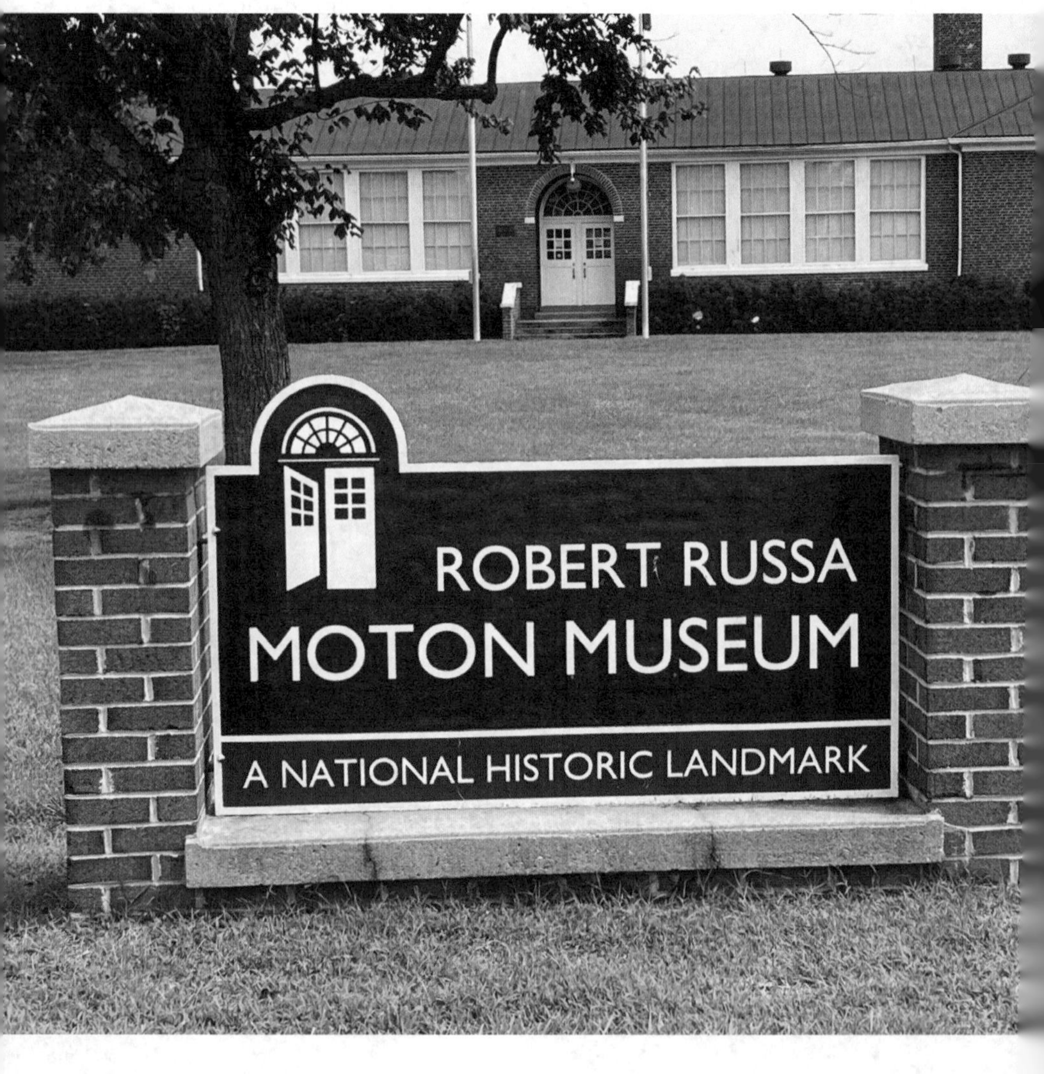
ROBERT RUSSA
MOTON MUSEUM
A NATIONAL HISTORIC LANDMARK

11

ROAD TO WAR, FREEDOM

History Beckons Along US 460

ESTIMATED LENGTH: 100 miles

ESTIMATED TIME: A day-trip or two

HIGHLIGHTS: Civil War-related sites including **General Ulysses S. Grant's headquarters** at **City Point** in **Hopewell**, **Petersburg National Battlefield**, **Pamplin Historical Park & The National Museum of the Civil War Soldier**, and, of course, **Appomattox Court House National Historical Park**, where you can stand in the parlor of the reconstructed home where General Robert E. Lee surrendered to Grant. Be sure to stop in Farmville to visit the **Robert Russa Moton Museum**, the old schoolhouse where Black students stood up for their rights and helped launch the Civil Rights Movement. If you bring your bicycle, you can pedal **High Bridge Trail**.

GETTING THERE: Take I-95 south of **Richmond** to Exit 61A, go east on VA 10, then 8 miles to **Hopewell**. Or south on I-295 from Richmond to Exit 15A, then east on VA 10 for 4 miles to Hopewell. Or north on I-295 to Exit 9A, then east on VA 36 for 2 miles to Hopewell.

Virginia is rich in Civil War history with battlefields—from Manassas, site of the first major battle of the war, to Appomattox, where the conflict came to a merciful conclusion—scattered all over the state. In addition, you will find Civil War–related sites almost everywhere you turn—famous homes, museums, driving tours that connect the dots.

Yet, from a similar time period, there is other history that often has been overlooked. In recent years, a project called Road to Freedom brought attention to people and events prior to the beginning of the war that illustrate "the tenacity and determination of African Americans to self-emancipate," says

LEFT: FARMVILLE'S MOTON HIGH SCHOOL WAS THE SITE OF A 1951 STUDENT PROTEST THAT HELPED LAUNCH THE CIVIL RIGHTS MOVEMENT IN VIRGINIA

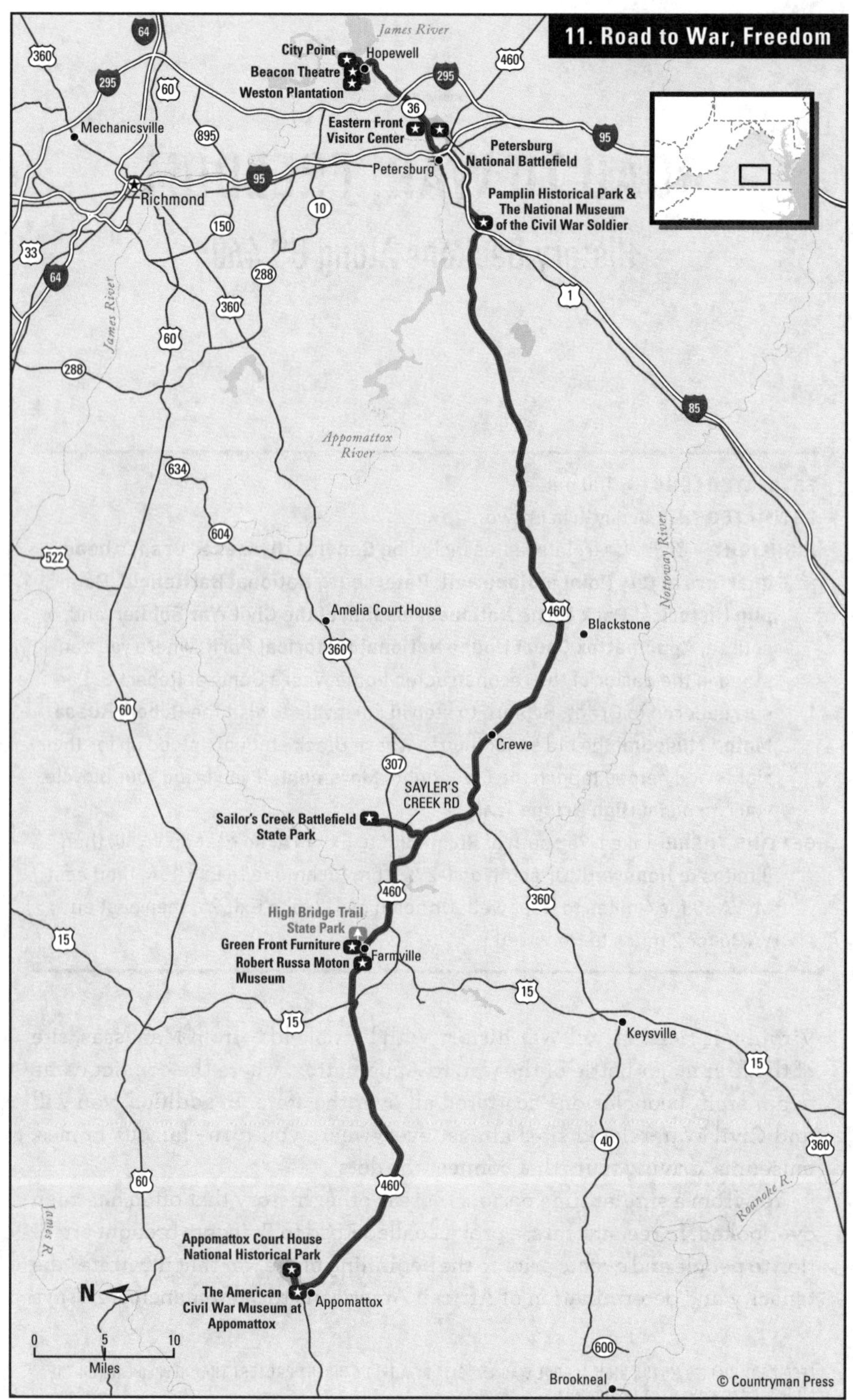

11. Road to War, Freedom
James River
City Point
Hopewell
Beacon Theatre
Weston Plantation
Eastern Front
Visitor Center
Petersburg
National Battlefield
Petersburg
Mechanicsville
Richmond
Pamplin Historical Park &
The National Museum
of the Civil War Soldier
James River
Appomattox
River
Nottoway River
Amelia Court House
Blackstone
Crewe
SAYLER'S
CREEK RD
Sailor's Creek Battlefield
State Park
High Bridge Trail
State Park
Green Front Furniture
Farmville
Robert Russa Moton
Museum
Keysville
Roanoke R.
James R.
Appomattox Court House
National Historical Park
The American
Civil War Museum at
Appomattox
Appomattox
N
0 5 10
Miles
Brookneal
© Countryman Press

GRANT'S HEADQUARTERS AT CITY POINT, NOW A PART OF HOPEWELL, SITS ON A BLUFF ABOVE WHERE THE APPOMATTOX AND JAMES RIVERS CONVERGE

Drew Gruber, executive director Civil War Trails, which developed Road to Freedom in partnership with American Battlefield Trust. The driving tour, aided by a website and a narrative-filled online app, literally gives travelers a road map to visit more than eighty sites where significant events took place. In many cases, there may be little more than a historical marker to indicate the spot, but you are there.

"We believe in the power of place," says Mary Koik, director of communications for American Battlefield Trust, which works to preserve the nation's battlefields and to educate the public about what happened in those places. "It's at the heart of everything we do. It really connects you to the people who were there in a different way. . . . Not to slight any wonderful books or documentaries or museums, but there is something profound about knowing you're standing where these people were and these things happened."

The idea behind Road to Freedom, she says, is "to tell under-represented stories."

Stories like the one about New Market Heights Battlefield, just east of Richmond off I-295, which is the site of a significant though lesser-known Civil War battle in September 1864, in which US Colored Troops (USCTs) were sent to divert Confederate attention from Union movement around Petersburg. The USCT troops performed effectively and bravely while suf-

HIGH BRIDGE, 2,400 FEET LONG AND 125 FEET ABOVE THE APPOMATTOX RIVER, IS THE CENTERPIECE OF HIGH BRIDGE TRAIL STATE PARK, A 31-MILE-LONG RECREATIONAL TRAIL

fering 800 casualties that day. For their particular valor, fourteen Black soldiers were awarded the Medal of Honor, the nation's highest military decoration, a remarkable number considering only twenty-five Medals of Honor were awarded to Black soldiers during the entire Civil War. The site is marked with a historical marker on the north side of Kingsland Road, just east of I-295. Though much of the battlefield has been lost to development, some land has been acquired in recent years for preservation. The National Park Service ultimately would like to include New Market Heights in Richmond National Battlefield Park once it can provide public access. Meantime, through the Road to Freedom app, travelers can take a video tour of the battlefield led by a retired Marine general.

Among the people brought to light by the Road to Freedom tour is Mary Peake, who, in defiance of Virginia law in the years before the Civil War, taught enslaved people and free Blacks to read in Hampton. At one point, she held classes under what became known as Emancipation Oak, a sprawling live oak that still stands near the entrance of Hampton University (on Emancipation Drive). In 1863, the year after she died at age thirty-nine, the tree was the site of a public reading of the Emancipation Proclamation.

Road to Freedom is a good reminder that there are good stories—and meaningful places to visit—all over. Pieces of history from different eras and different perspectives exist side-by-side, or at the next stop along the road, all part of our larger history. This chapter is an example, starting in Hopewell and ending in Appomattox, two significant venues in the Civil War, but also stopping in up-and-coming Farmville, where you will find an inspiring story of youthful (and righteous) courage in the ugly face of segregation, told by an old schoolhouse. Also in Farmville, on a much less serious note, there is furniture shopping, as well as a bike and pedestrian trail on a former rail bed that will carry you over the aptly named High Bridge. It's kind of a thrill.

Hopewell is a sometimes-overlooked city rich in history and friendly people. Hopewell sits at the point where the Appomattox River flows into the James River, a logistically favorable location that, during the siege of nearby Petersburg, inspired General Ulysses S. Grant to set up his headquarters at Appomattox Plantation, on a high bluff overlooking the spot where the two rivers come together. City Point, as this area is known, was one of the busiest seaports in the world during that period, serving as the supply center for 100,000 Union soldiers. President Lincoln sailed here in March 1865 aboard a steamboat, *River Queen,* to meet with Grant and plot the end of the war.

Come to City Point and feel the breeze blowing off the rivers. Visit the plantation, now called Appomattox Manor and a part of the Petersburg

A LIVING HISTORY INTERPRETER DESCRIBES NINETEENTH-CENTURY LIFE AT CLOVER HILL TAVERN FOR VISITORS AT APPOMATTOX COURT HOUSE NATIONAL HISTORICAL PARK

On April 23, 1951, sixteen-year-old Barbara Johns led her fellow students in a walk-out to protest substandard conditions at their school, R. R. Moton High, which served Black students in Prince Edward County. Their two-week strike and lawsuit, in some ways, launched the civil rights movement in Virginia as it became one of the five cases that resulted in the landmark US Supreme Court's *Brown v. Board of Education* decision that struck down legalized racial segregation in schools. Following the ruling, Prince Edward County shut down its schools for five years to avoid integration before the Supreme Court ordered the county to reopen its schools in 1964.

The old schoolhouse in Farmville is now a National Historic Landmark, the **Robert Russa Moton Museum**. It is well worth a visit to browse the permanent exhibition that brings to life that period when students stood up for themselves, and, as it turned out, so many others. Plan to spend a couple of hours, says executive director Cainan Townsend. Admission is free at the museum which is operated in partnership with nearby Longwood University.

Townsend has a personal connection to the Moton story: two great-aunts were among the students who walked out with Barbara Johns, and his father was among many family members who were subsequently locked out of school when the county shut down public education. Moton is a story, he says, of "ordinary people who were able to make extraordinary change." And these ordinary people were young people, who came together in collective action to push for that change and showed resilience and courage in the process.

One other important point: "This is not exclusively Black history," Townsend says, "This is American history."

National Battlefield, and tour the mansion that was in near ruins after the war but has since been restored. Walk the grounds and peek inside the modest log cabin Grant used as his headquarters. It hasn't been here all along. After the war, the cabin was presented as a gift to Philadelphia, where it was a tourist attraction but eventually suffered from neglect and vandalism. After the National Park Service purchased Appomattox Manor in 1979, it returned Grant's cabin to City Point and restored it. While in Hopewell, you might check and see if there's a show at the Beacon Theatre, the old movie house that underwent a multimillion-dollar restoration, reopened in 2014, and is once again a gem in the city's once-moribund downtown.

The Eastern Front of Petersburg National Battlefield is less than 15 miles west of Hopewell. Take VA 36 west from Hopewell to I-295 and head south to Exit 3B and then west on US 460 to the entrance. The park actually includes thirteen separate sites with three visitor centers along a 33-mile route. The Eastern Front visitor center tells the story of the siege of Petersburg and is the best place to go if you have time for only one stop. But if you have a full day to drive the entire route, which includes the Western Front at Five Forks, where a dramatic Union victory ensured the collapse of Petersburg and Richmond, you'll be glad you did.

We like to take our bikes to the main site and ride along the paved tour road and, on occasion, the off-road trails that twist and turn through the woods. The pedaling is easy and makes for a great way to see the park. Don't miss the site of the Battle of the Crater, a July 1864 clash that began with Union soldiers' construction of a 500-foot-long tunnel under the Confederate line. Union troops set off an explosion beneath the Confederates, instantly killing scores of Southern troops and creating a ghastly crater 30 feet deep. However, the battle proved to be a disaster for Union troops, many of whom advanced into the crater and to their deaths as the Confederates recovered and counterattacked.

Aside from the national park sites, you really should save some time for the stunningly good Pamplin Historical Park & The National Museum of the Civil War Soldier, a private and innovative park located 9 miles west of the Eastern Front site on US 460. Dr. Robert B. Pamplin Jr., a businessman and philanthropist in Portland, Oregon, whose family owned land in this area in the 1800s, purchased the property in the early 1990s to preserve a line of well-maintained earthworks constructed by Confederate troops, and the land-preservation effort turned into something much more when Pamplin set up an interpretative center and made plans to construct a more elaborate attraction, now a 424-acre park.

VISITORS CAN PEER INTO THE ENTRANCE OF A RE-CREATION OF THE UNION TUNNEL AT PETERSBURG NATIONAL BATTLEFIELD

A note about Civil War tourism: check out Civil War Trails. Gruber, its executive director, describes his organization as "an open-air museum." It works with communities to share their stories and connect visitors with historic sites spanning six states, including Virginia. As of 2024, its suggested driving tours (printable brochures are available at www.civilwartrails.org) include interpretative signage at more than 1,500 sites. The program aims to put travelers in the footsteps of those who

THE RESTORED BEACON THEATRE IN HOPEWELL HOSTS CONCERTS AND OTHER EVENTS

lived through the Civil War—generals, soldiers, citizens, and the enslaved—and in so doing dispel the notion that the war was "just a white, male, military story," Gruber says.

One of the Civil War Trails's suggested drives is "Lee's Retreat," which is somewhat the route we're taking.

Back on US 460, we continue west and make a slight detour a few miles before Farmville to Sailor's Creek Battlefield State Park, site of the April 6,

1865, battle that crippled General Robert E. Lee's army and led to the Confederate surrender 72 hours—and less than 50 miles—later at Appomattox Court House. At the time of our visit, the park superintendent was Chris Calkins, a historian and author of note, who took us through the Hillsman House, which was converted into a field hospital during the battle. He pointed out bloodstains still visible on the wood floor. He told us about the battle, which really consisted of separate engagements, during which the Confederate army suffered 7,700 casualties, after which Lee is reported to have said, "A few more Sailor's Creeks and it will be all over—ended—just as I have expected it would end from the first."

Calkins says there is reason to believe there is a mass Confederate grave within the park. "This is sacred soil," he says.

In Farmville, we jump ahead a century and then some with the Robert Russa Moton Museum, a former segregated high school and now a National Historic Landmark that is the birthplace of a student-led Civil Rights Revolution. We have shopped a number of times at Green Front Furniture, with almost a million-square-feet of showroom space in renovated tobacco warehouses, and ridden our bikes at High Bridge Trail State Park. Farmville also has good restaurants and a trendy new hotel that isn't really new at all.

We head to Appomattox Court House. You can retrace Lee's steps by

APPOMATTOX MANOR IS A FORMER PLANTATION HOME IN HOPEWELL THAT WAS USED AS UNION HEADQUARTERS DURING THE SIEGE OF PETERSBURG NEAR THE END OF THE CIVIL WAR

SIDE TRACKS

Farmville is an old tobacco market town on US 460, about 70 miles west of Petersburg. It's the home of **Longwood College**, and **Hampden-Sydney College** is just outside town. Farmville, a town of 7,000, also attracts lots of visitors shopping for furniture. **Green Front Furniture** fills thirteen renovated tobacco warehouses, wall to wall and floor to ceiling, with furniture, rugs, and all sorts of furnishings—including statues and other decorative garden art—at discount prices.

We stop for dinner at **Charley's Waterfront Café**, housed in a historic tobacco warehouse, overlooking the Appomattox River. One of the Green Front warehouses is next door. Family-friendly, Charley's offers seafood, steaks, and pasta, as well as soups and sandwiches. My Cajun chicken alfredo was quite good.

High Bridge Trail State Park, a 31-mile-long, rails-to-trails, multiuse path for hiking, biking, and horseback riding, comes through downtown Farmville, which is about the midway point. The trail's signature piece is High Bridge, which is nearly a half-mile long and soars 160 feet above the Appomattox River. It's a wonderful, well-used cinder path with several parking lots and access points along the way.

Lodging options in Farmville include the renovated **Hotel Weyanoke**, which originally opened in 1925 and immediately became a gathering place for movers and shakers. After undergoing a major renovation, it reopened as a boutique hotel in 2018, with restaurants on site including Taproot Tavern and Catbird, on the rooftop terrace.

following Virginia's Retreat, an official tourism trail of twenty-five stops with audio and visual interpretation at each site. The suggested time to devote to that trail alone is two days. Having the interest but not the time on this jaunt, we opt to drive US 460—the most direct route to Appomattox Court House, roughly 90 miles from Petersburg. US 460 becomes the backroads equivalent of an interstate highway—four lanes with a grassy median in between—particularly west of Farmville. You get the feeling, though, that much of the area along the route hasn't changed significantly in the days since Lee headed west from Petersburg with Grant in pursuit. Except for occasional small towns, farmland and thick woods dominate the landscape.

Before you get to Appomattox Court House, you might consider a stop at a fairly new addition to the area: the American Civil War Museum at Appomattox, the western satellite location of the Richmond-based museum, located at the intersection of US 460 and VA 24, just down the road from the Appomattox Court House National Historical Park. The American Civil War Museum at Appomattox, tells the story of the closing days of the Civil War and the beginning of what came next.

Appomattox Court House National Historical Park probably has never received the widespread attention or appreciation it deserves. Tucked in the countryside of south-central Virginia, the understated park gives the appearance of a bucolic little village, which it was, but little hint of the momentous event that occurred here when Lee ended his desperate dash for supplies and reinforcements and decided discretion was indeed the better part of valor. The restored village, 2 miles northeast of the town of Appomattox on VA 24, looks very much as it did in 1865, when Lee and Grant met here.

We arrive in early afternoon and begin our look around at the visitor center, which is the reconstructed courthouse. The original burned to the ground in 1892. The visitor center provides context and perspective through artwork and artifacts, including the tabletop on which the terms of surrender were signed and the white towel that was the Confederates' first flag of truce.

We stand on the porch of the original Clover Hill Tavern, a popular spot in those days because of its location on the Richmond-to-Lynchburg stagecoach road. In an extensive and detailed monologue, a costumed interpreter tells us about life in the village in the 1860s.

We walk over to the McLean House, the reconstructed home where the surrender took place on April 9, 1865. The original house was dismantled in 1893, with plans to rebuild it elsewhere as a tourist attraction. The idea never came to fruition, and many of the original building materials were lost to damage and decay. Using detailed specifications and archaeological evidence, the National Park Service reconstructed the house on the original foundation. We stand in the parlor where Lee and Grant quite possibly saved a nation: adversaries who ended a most uncivil war in a most civil manner. Grant offered generous terms of surrender, Lee accepted, and the nation moved on. The house, by the way, was owned by Wilmer McLean, a businessman who earlier owned a home at Manassas, the site of the first major land battle of the war, four years earlier.

My favorite story from our tour was this: On the stage road, three days after the surrender, Grant assigned General Joshua Chamberlain to accept the formal surrender of arms from Lee's soldiers. As the ragged Confederate troops trudged into the village to lay down their weapons, Chamberlain called his men to attention and had them salute the Confederates as they approached. No cheers or taunts, just simple honor, respect, and dignity.

IN THE AREA

Accommodations

BABCOCK HOUSE BED AND BREAKFAST INN, 250 Oakleigh Avenue, Appomattox. Call 434-352-7532. Website: www.babcockhouse.com. Set in an 1800s Victorian house, serving farm-to-table meals.

HOTEL WEYANOKE, 202 High Street, Farmville. Call 434-658-7500. Website: www.hotelweyanoke.com. Boutique hotel.

Attractions and Recreation

THE AMERICAN CIVIL WAR MUSEUM AT APPOMATTOX, 159 Horseshoe Road, Appomattox. Call 434-352-5791. Website: www.acwm.org.

APPOMATTOX COURT HOUSE NATIONAL HISTORICAL PARK, 111 National Park Drive, Appomattox. Call 434-352-8987. Website: www.nps.gov/apco.

GREEN FRONT FURNITURE, 316 N. Main Street, Farmville. Call 434-392-5943. Website: www.greenfront.com. More than a dozen warehouses of furniture and furnishings.

HIGH BRIDGE TRAIL STATE PARK, 6888 Green Bay Road, Green Bay. (Park office.) Call 434-315-0457. Website: www.dcr.virginia.gov/state-parks/high-bridge-trail. Biking and hiking trail that runs through Farmville.

PAMPLIN HISTORICAL PARK AND THE NATIONAL MUSEUM OF THE CIVIL WAR SOLDIER, 6125 Boydton Plank Road, Petersburg. Call 804-861-2408. Website: www.pamplinpark.org.

PETERSBURG NATIONAL BATTLEFIELD, 5001 Siege Road, Petersburg. Call 804-732-3531. Website: www.nps.gov/pete.

ROBERT RUSSA MOTON MUSEUM, 900 Griffin Boulevard. Call 434-315-8775. Website: www.motonmuseum.org. National Historic Landmark and museum.

SAILOR'S CREEK BATTLEFIELD STATE PARK, 6541 Saylers Creek Road, Rice. Call 804-561-7510. Website: www.dcr.virginia.gov/state-parks/sailors-creek.

Dining

ANDRADE'S INTERNATIONAL RESTAURANT, 7 Bollingbrook Street, Petersburg. Call 804-722-0344. Website: www.facebook.com/andradesinternational.

BAINE'S BOOKS AND COFFEE, 205 Main Street, Appomattox. Call 434-229-8157. Website: www.bainesbooks.com.

CHARLEY'S WATERFRONT CAFÉ, 201 Mill Street, Farmville. Call 434-392-1566. Website: www.charleyswaterfront.com. Lunch and dinner overlooking the Appomattox River.

K&L BARBECUE, 5 Cavalier Square, Hopewell. Call 804-458-4241. Website: www.kandlbbq.com. Low-key, local favorite.

LONGSTREET'S DELI, 302 N Sycamore Street, Petersburg. Call 804 722-4372. Website: www.longstreetsdeli.com. Sandwiches, specialty wines, and beers.

TAPROOT TAVERN, 202 High Street, Farmville. Call 434-658-1200. Website: www.taprootfarmville.com. Located in Hotel Weyanoke, along with Catbird, a rooftop terrace restaurant.

WALKER'S DINER, 307 N. Main Street, Farmville. Call 434-392-4230. Website: www.facebook.com/walkersdeliciousdiner. Classic (and tiny) small-town diner, serving breakfast and lunch.

Other Contacts

CIVIL WAR TRAILS. Website: www.civilwartrails.org.

ROAD TO FREEDOM. Website: www.battlefields.org/learn/civil-war/road-freedom.

12

THE VALLEY PIKE

A Journey on US 11

ESTIMATED LENGTH: 300 miles

ESTIMATED TIME: 3 days

HIGHLIGHTS: Uncoiling through fertile farmland, US 11 stitches together a series of splendid towns and cities such as **Lexington**, **Staunton**, **Harrisonburg**, **New Market**, **Woodstock**, and **Strasburg**. Lovely scenery dominates the drive. You will find Civil War history along the way and a number of venerable colleges and universities worth visiting even if they're not your alma mater, such as Lexington neighbors **Virginia Military Institute** and **Washington and Lee University**. You can drive over a natural wonder like **Natural Bridge** and walk through one of the numerous caverns—Endless, Luray, or Shenandoah, among others. Surprises include the **American Shakespeare Center** in Staunton, the **Route 11 Potato Chips** factory near Mount Jackson, and the **Green Valley Book Fair**, where you can browse among the stacks of a half-million discount-priced new books. The southernmost stretch includes **Roanoke**, with its museums and restaurants, as well as other worthy stops, including artsy **Abingdon**, **Draper Mercantile** (along **New River Trail State Park**) and **Big Walker Lookout and Country Store**.

GETTING THERE: This drive along US 11 stretches between **Winchester** (near the West Virginia line) to the north and **Bristol** (on the Virginia-Tennessee line) to the south. Winchester is just off I-81, about 15 miles south of the West Virginia line. US 11 parallels I-81 the entire distance and, in some stretches, is I-81.

LEFT: THE ONE-LANE MEEMS BOTTOM BRIDGE NEAR MOUNT JACKSON IS A STEP BACK IN TIME

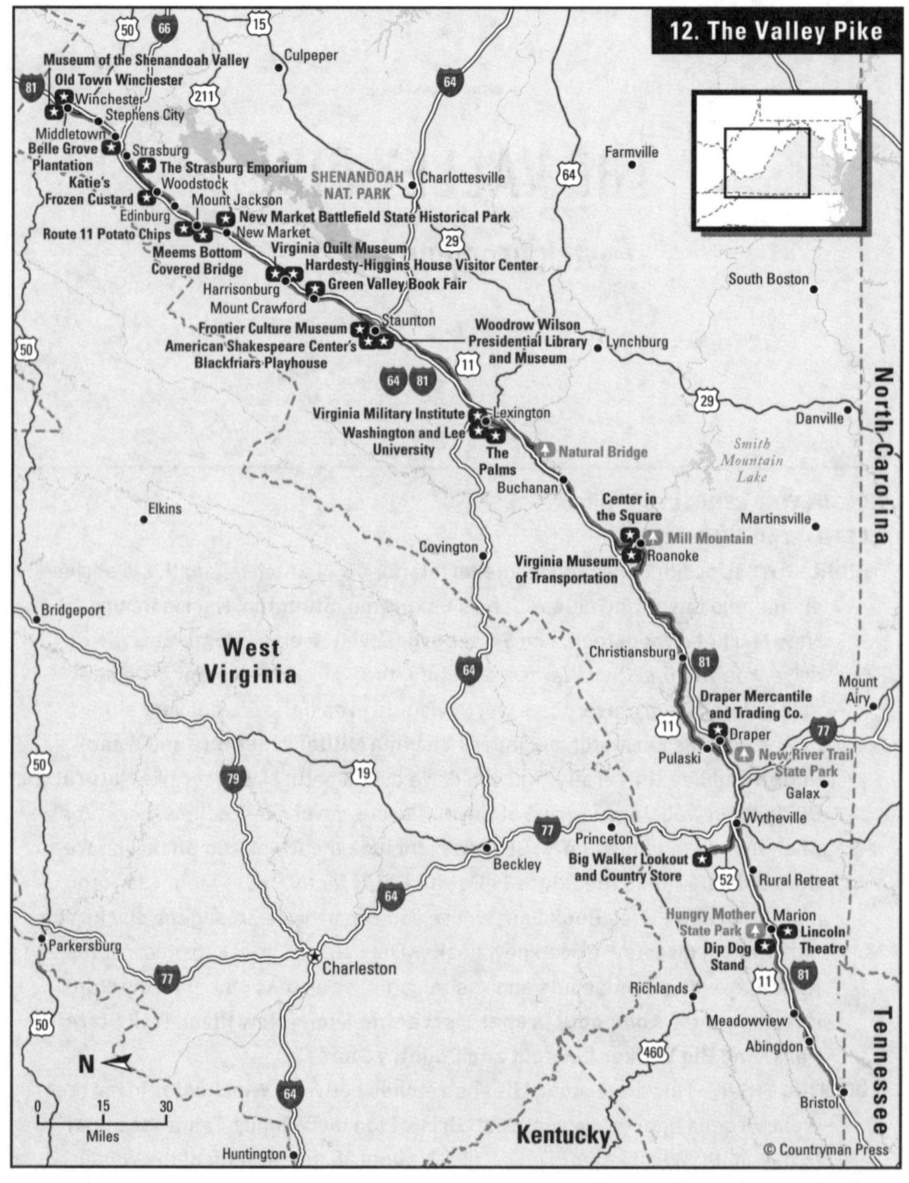

Following the path of an old trail favored by Native Americans long before the English and other immigrants arrived, US 11 runs down the mountainous spine of Virginia for more than 300 miles, from Winchester in the north to Bristol in the south. (In all, US 11 extends from upper New York to Louisiana, one of the nation's old, great roadways.) In Virginia, it offers the fetching scenery of valley farmland and small-town America, a world away from interstate highway travel—but in reality usually only a mile or less from I-81, which replaced it beginning in the 1960s as the primary artery through the western valley of Virginia. In fact, the interstate is sometimes visible from US 11, and on several occasions the old road crisscrosses the newer highway.

In the 1700s, pioneers and traders poured into the valley, using this route as a thoroughfare to a new life or to the next state. It became known as The Great Wagon Road. In the early 1800s, the commonwealth of Virginia partnered with a private firm to develop a large section of the trail into an actual road with tolls. In effect, the Valley Turnpike was one of the nation's first highways. During the Civil War, it served as an avenue for troop and artillery movement. The history runs deep.

The tolls are gone, and most of the traffic today is local. Those merely passing through speed past on I-81, not knowing what they're missing. You can certainly drive US 11 from border to border, Winchester to Bristol, but be aware that US 11 and I-81 merge as one at times, and have a good map handy if you try to follow the road through Roanoke.

Let's start at Winchester, a city of about 25,000, site of the Shenandoah

YOU WILL FIND WIDE OPEN SPACES OF FARMLAND, AS WELL AS ATTENTIVE COWS, ALONG US 11

Apple Blossom Festival every spring and the home of the late singer Patsy Cline, which is open to the public as a museum. There's also the Museum of the Shenandoah Valley, which interprets the art, history, and culture of the valley, and the Old Town pedestrian mall, which historically was part of Route 11 and is now home to outdoor cafés and shops and is perfect for an enjoyable stroll. With sufficient time, you might consider a walking tour of the city's historic district to admire the architecture and to drop by one of the numerous museums, such as Stonewall Jackson's Headquarters Museum or George Washington's Office Museum.

Head south on US 11 and within 10 miles you'll come to Stephens City, which has, among its attributes, an honest-to-goodness drive-in movie theater. The Family Drive-In, just south of Stephens City, has two screens, a playground, and, of course, a concession stand. Family pets are even allowed. The theater operates, naturally, during warm-weather months.

Midway between Middletown and Strasburg, about 15 miles south of Winchester, you'll find Cedar Creek and Belle Grove National Historical Park. Belle Grove Plantation was the magnificent eighteenth-century home of future-president James Madison's sister Nelly. On Belle Grove Road, just west of US 11, the mansion is open for tours. Nearby is Cedar Creek Battlefield, site of a critical Union victory in 1864 that, coupled with other events, helped secure Lincoln's reelection, which had been far from a certainty.

Another 5 miles south on US 11 brings you to Strasburg, one of the great little towns along the valley road. Strasburg has numerous antique shops in its historic downtown, none more impressive than The Great Strasburg Emporium Antiques, which houses more than sixty antiques and art dealers, at 160 N. Massanutten Street, at the intersection of US 11 and VA 55.

By the time we get to Woodstock, another dozen miles down the road, we are ready for ice cream, so we pull into Katie's Frozen Custard, a little stand in front of a motel at US 11's intersection with Fairground Road. The medium cups of chocolate-and-vanilla swirl come piled high with frozen goodness and hit the spot. We sit at a patio table and enjoy the treat as we watch the traffic pass.

US 11 slices through the middle of these towns, the roadway passing a few feet from handsome old homes with rocking chair porches and residents quite happy to offer a smile and a wave. Drive through on a weekend and you might happen upon a street festival or a series of yard sales that beckon you to stop.

Fresh, warm potato chips might just do the same. We continue south on US 11, through Edinburg and then Mount Jackson. Just south of Mount Jackson, we turn right on Caverns Road and then make another right on, yes, Caverns Road, before making yet another right on Industrial Park Road, which brings us into a nondescript industrial park, as you might have guessed, and then a sign for Route 11 Potato Chips. If you like potato chips, this stop is a must. Consider it educational, if you must.

Not far from the Route 11 chips factory, you can take a drive through time—and a covered bridge. You find Meems Bottom Bridge, spanning the north fork of the Shenandoah River, on Wissler Road, just west of US 11. At

I've long been a fan of **Route 11 Chips**, but I'd never had the opportunity to visit the nerve center of the operation until now. As factories go, this one is not exactly mammoth, but it's nice and relatively new and a far cry from where the company began in the 1990s, in an old feed store up the road in Middletown. The popularity of the hand-cooked chips necessitated the move to bigger quarters.

We arrive when they're actually cooking and bagging the chips, so we wander from window to window watching the process (you can't actually go in the kitchen or shoot photos, and there's not all that much to see anyway). Watching chips being made is all well and good, but the big attraction to being here is sampling them. Employees generously put out baskets of the various flavors of Route 11 chips, some of them still warm: barbecue, dill pickle, sweet potato, Chesapeake crab. You get the idea. A hand-lettered sign above a basket containing Mama Zuma's Revenge habanero-flavored chips carries a warning: VERY HOT! Always up for a dare, I try a few. The sign was right. This is where I should point out it's always a good idea to keep a cold bottle of water in your vehicle.

The samples are in the same room with the counter where you can purchase chips, and the marketing ploy seems to work famously. Customers are leaving carrying many bags of chips. We are no different, but choosing among the dozen or so flavors takes a few minutes. I'd be happy to buy one of each, but I'm trying to maintain a shred of dignity and be a model of moderation for the daughter who's with me. We settle on four flavors, buy several big bags, and go on our way. At least two of the bags are open by the time we reach the car. Moderation today; self-restraint tomorrow.

IF YOU'RE A FAN OF POTATO CHIPS, THE ROUTE 11 CHIPS FACTORY NEAR MOUNT JACKSON IS A REQUIRED STOP

A CHARMING CITY, STAUNTON OFFERS SURPRISES FOR THE UNSUSPECTING, LIKE THIS GIANT WATERING CAN AT A BUSY INTERSECTION

slightly over 200 feet, it's the longest covered bridge still remaining in Virginia. We drive across the one-lane bridge, make a U-turn, and do it again. Built in the 1890s, the bridge was burned by vandals in 1976, and then rebuilt with some of the salvaged original timbers, undergirded with steel beams and concrete piers. So as old bridges go, this one's pretty sturdy.

A 20-minute jaunt to the west on VA 263 will bring you to lovely Orkney Springs and Shrine Mont, a conference and retreat center operated by the Episcopal Diocese of Virginia. Groups and individuals are welcome. The Cathedral Shrine of the Transfiguration is an open-air cathedral where public services are held Sundays, early April through mid-November. The four-story Virginia House, built in 1875 and formerly the Orkney Springs Hotel, is on the National Register of Historic Places. Homestyle Southern meals are a hallmark of Shrine Mont. The fried chicken alone is worth the drive.

New Market is next up, a charming little town that, like others along the way, was built right on the valley road. You could easily spend a week or more traveling US 11, stopping at each town, poking around the shops and museums, spending the night, and moving on to the next one in the morning. Civil War battlefields can be found up and down the valley, but the battlefield at New Market is particularly noteworthy because cadets from Virginia Military Institute, some as young as 15 years of age, fought alongside the Confederate army and helped defeat the Union army. In the 1864 battle, 57 cadets were wounded and 10 were killed; the battle remains a proud milestone in the history of the school we will visit in Lexington. You can walk in the cadets' footsteps at the 300-acre New Market Battlefield State Historical Park.

Go 20 miles south of New Market and find Harrisonburg, a thriving college town of more than 50,000. Home of James Madison University, Harrisonburg offers much in the way of shopping, touring, and walking, if you're of a mind to stop and look around. A good place to get your bearings is the Hardesty-Higgins House Visitor Center on Main Street (US 11), which is also home to the Valley Turnpike Museum, which offers great history on how this road came to be. Just down the street is the Virginia Quilt Museum, which is the official quilt museum of the commonwealth of Virginia, celebrating the state's quilting heritage and displaying numerous quilts that are both lovely and rich in history. For a quick bite to eat, we pull over at Bar-B-Q Ranch, an

PORTIONS OF THE STONE PIERS OF THE BUCHANAN SWINGING BRIDGE WERE CONSTRUCTED IN 1851; THE 366-FOOT-LONG BRIDGE SPANS THE JAMES RIVER, ADJACENT TO US 11

ARTIST AND ENTERTAINER MARK CLINE, BEING PHOTOGRAPHED AT HIS ENCHANTED CASTLE STUDIOS BY NOW-RETIRED *RICHMOND TIMES-DISPATCH* PHOTOGRAPHER BOB BROWN, IS THE CREATOR OF DINOSAUR KINGDOM II

old-style drive-in with curb service and a dining room, a couple miles north of downtown. A barbecue sandwich with slaw, fries, and hush puppies is just what I need, but the place also offers more extensive meals, such as country-fried chicken and rib-eye steak. There are also a number of more upscale restaurants around town, as well as a venerable custard-style ice cream place: Kline's Dairy Bar, which was established in 1943 on the ground floor of the Kline's family home in Harrisonburg. Now there are several locations around Virginia, including two in Harrisonburg. We stopped at the one on US 11 as you head south through town.

Less than 10 miles south of Harrisonburg, you come to Mount Crawford. Cross over the I-81 interchange, go a little over a mile, and turn left on VA 681 at the sign that reads Green Valley Book Fair. If you like books, you're in for a treat. The family-run operation typically has a half-million books for sale at discount prices.

Staunton, at the crossroads of I-81 and I-64, is a handsome, historic town with much to do and see. (Before we go any farther, you should know it's pronounced *STAN-ton*, not *STAWN-ton*. Now, on with the trip.) Visit the Frontier Culture Museum, a living history museum featuring reconstructed working farms from the seventeenth, eighteenth, and nineteenth centuries, representing the immigrants who settled the valley and worked the land, and take in a production at the American Shakespeare Center's Blackfriars Playhouse, described as the world's only re-creation of Shakespeare's indoor theater. It truly captures the magic of a Shakespearian production. Check out Gypsy Hill Park, a sprawling 214-acre municipal park that's a haven for walking, biking, and rollerblading, offering playing fields, a swimming pool, and even a miniature railroad.

Walk down Beverley Street, in the heart of the historic district, and drop in at Camera & Palette, a camera shop and museum with hundreds of old cameras and local historical photographs, or grab a bite at one of the restaurants along the way. In fact, Staunton has become known for its restaurants, places like Mill Street Grill (located in an old flour mill), Zynodoa, and The Shack, which indeed looks something like a shack, but has gained a national reputation for its remarkable food. Or just stroll or drive around town and admire the Victorian architecture, look around an art gallery, and take note of the eye-catching landmark sculptures created by the late local artist Willy Ferguson: a giant watering can and flower pots at Greenville Avenue and Coalter Street, an oversized open book at the Staunton Public Library, a huge plow at the intersection of Statler Boulevard and New Hope Road, and the mammoth goose-quill pens and scrolls at Beverley and New Streets at the Pen & Paper Shop. To learn more about one of Staunton's most famous residents, visit the President Woodrow Wilson Library and Museum (and birthplace) on Coalter Street. If you're looking for a place to stay, the Hotel 24 South, a 1924 palace renovated in 2005 and next door to the Blackfriars Playhouse, might fit your needs. It was formerly known as the Stonewall Jackson Hotel.

As you head south of town, there are a couple of other popular, but very different, dining experiences waiting: Wright's Dairy-Rite, an old drive-in with curb service, or the Edelweiss German Restaurant, a good choice for German food in a rustic setting. There's also Kathy's Restaurant, where the pancakes are famous and breakfast is served all day. My first time there, I not only met owner Kathy Lacey, who opened the place in 1986, but also her 88-year-old mom, Ellen Anderson, who had stopped by to drop off a few apple pies she'd baked that morning. That's known as good timing. My piece of pie came topped with vanilla ice cream and whipped cream.

Lexington, a city of about 7,000 almost 40 miles south of Staunton on US 11, largely revolves around two of Virginia's most venerable institutions of higher learning: Virginia Military Institute and Washington and Lee University, two schools that in some ways couldn't be more different—VMI is a state school in a military environment, W&L a private university where uniforms are something the football team wears—but they have been next-door neighbors since the 1800s.

The **Green Valley Book Fair** started as an offshoot of the Evans' family auction business. The first one took place in 1971 in the family's barn, although it didn't take long for the occasional fair to outgrow that space. The fair is still held on the old family farm, but the books have been moved to warehouse-type buildings totaling 25,000 square feet. The book fair, open Tuesday through Saturday, features 20,000 to 30,000 titles and a total of roughly 500,000 volumes: novels, history, science, religion, art, cooking, gardening, and shelves and shelves of children's books. Pretty much everything. Even better than the variety? The prices are 60 to 90 percent below retail.

The books are primarily "returns" from publishers, meaning they're new and in good shape, but simply didn't sell. You're not likely to see many current bestsellers, but you might see them in a year or two.

"I think right away we knew we were on to something," says Michael Evans, of those early days with the weekend sales of used books that his father had acquired. "The first one was successful enough that we did it again. It was one of those things that just grew organically. It really propelled itself. We were selling them, so we had to find more books, and in finding more books we needed more room, and every time we found a new source for books we found out we could sell those."

The fair draws people from all over Virginia and the mid-Atlantic, and from around the country and world.

"We know that folks come in a lot from out of state," Evans tells me. "We're not sure if it's planning to come to the book fair and do other things, or if it's planning to do other things and just making sure it's when the book fair is open."

WITH A HALF-MILLION BOOKS AT DISCOUNT PRICES, THE GREEN VALLEY BOOK FAIR IN MOUNT CRAWFORD IS A READER'S PARADISE

My fifteen-year-old daughter and I browse the three levels of bookshelves and stacks for a couple hours. Adults sit on benches, reading their newfound prizes; small children crawl under the tables with a volume of *Curious George* or some other favorite and turn the pages contentedly. The place is like a library on steroids. My daughter, an avid reader, picks out an armful of books to buy. As we settle into the car, she beams and describes the experience.

"That," she says without hesitation, "was awesome."

We park our car at VMI and begin our tour of both schools, both of which are happy for visitors to come by. At first blush, VMI is a bleak-looking place with its dull-colored buildings and spartan barracks, but in my years of traveling to schools around Virginia, I've never found people warmer and more hospitable than those who study, work, and teach at VMI. This is a place of great camaraderie and fierce loyalty, which shines through in any conversation with anyone associated with VMI.

Other than simply walking around the post—that's the preferred description, instead of campus—and soaking in the history of the place, the best places for visitors to go include the George C. Marshall Museum, which honors Marshall, a VMI graduate, Army chief of staff, and architect of the Marshall Plan to rebuild western Europe after World War II, and the VMI Museum in Jackson Memorial Hall. There is also the VMI Museum, which is open seven days a week, where among the noteworthy items on display is the mounted hide of Little Sorrel, the warhorse of General Thomas "Stonewall" Jackson, a professor of natural philosophy at VMI. In the same display case, we see Jackson's desk and the raincoat he wore when he was mortally wounded by shots fired by his own men. In the world of odd little facts, Jackson is buried in Lexington, but his left arm, amputated after being shattered by gunfire, is buried in a cemetery near the Chancellorsville battlefield.

We walk over to the leafy W&L campus, marked by stately buildings with large columns. Something else you'll see at both VMI and W&L that you wouldn't have seen in early years are women: once male-only, both schools now enroll women.

A walking tour is a fine way to see Lexington. We wander through a weekly farmers' market and a bookstore, and finally over to The Palms, a popular restaurant on West Nelson Street in a building that has previously housed a grain and feed store and an ice cream parlor. A debating club held its weekly debates on this site in the 1800s, and also developed a public library here for the city. The Palms has a historic yet funky feel with its stamped-tin ceiling and brightly painted booths. Ceiling fans turn slowly overhead. The Hot Brown—a sandwich of shaved roast beef, caramelized onions, smoked bacon, jalapeños, and mozzarella on a roll—tops the lunch menu. If you want something more or something different, there are lots of other restaurants within walking distance to choose from. And on the way into town, on a hilltop, is Devils Backbone craft brewery. Bring a growler.

Natural Bridge is 15 miles to the south of Lexington on US 11. Privately owned for many years—for a time, even by Thomas Jefferson—Natural Bridge is now a state park. At the heart of the park is a 200-foot-tall natural arch carved out of limestone by Cedar Creek over the last, say, few hundred thousand years. You can walk down to the foot of Natural Bridge—and it actually is a bridge, as US 11 runs across the top of it—by navigating a stairway of 137 steps and then following the paved walkway along the creek.

NATURAL BRIDGE IS A NATURAL WONDER THAT ACTUALLY IS A BRIDGE FOR US 11 TRAFFIC

We stroll beneath the bridge and spot, more than 20 feet above the creek, the initials "G W," which some believe George Washington carved when he came to survey the bridge in 1750. The park also includes forests, meadows, and 10 miles of hiking trails.

A convenient place to stay is across the street from the park at Natural Bridge Historic Hotel and Conference Center, which is not affiliated with the state park. Since US 11 parallels I-81 closely, there is never a shortage of chain hotels along the way, but you will also find numerous bed-and-breakfast inns and one-of-a-kind lodging possibilities like Natural Bridge Historic Hotel. When we stayed there, our spacious room had a private porch with a screen door to invite in cool mountain breezes.

As long as you're in the area, you ought to consider stopping by Dinosaur Kingdom II, the brainchild of Mark Cline, a local entertainer and artist who's been dubbed the "P. T. Barnum of the Blue Ridge" for the public art he produces out of his Enchanted Castle Studios. Perhaps his most renowned creation was Foamhenge, a full-scale reproduction of Stonehenge made of beaded foam blocks that he erected on a hilltop in Natural Bridge as an April Fool's stunt. It drew visitors from around the world, but after more than a decade, he had to vacate the property, so he sold Foamhenge to Cox Farms in Fairfax County, where Foamhenge still resides today.

Dinosaur Kingdom II, tucked in the woods just north of the state park on US 11, is a roadside attraction in the fullest sense. It is a 16-acre stroll through Cline's rollicking imagination, revealing, as he says, the "untold story"—untold for a good reason—of how dinosaurs changed the course of the Civil War. It's as silly as it sounds, though presented with such flair and humor that you can't help but laugh out loud, or at least shake your head in amazement (and admiration).

THE OBSERVATION TOWER AT BIG WALKER LOOKOUT OFFERS A MAGNIFICENT VIEW OF THE COUNTRYSIDE

Onward we go. A dozen miles south of Natural Bridge is Buchanan, a small town on a horseshoe bend in the James River, which was devastated by a November 1985 flood caused by the remnants of Hurricane Juan.

"It really just destroyed the people's spirit," says Harry Gleason, who was Buchanan's Downtown Revitalization Program manager, hired to oversee the town's rebirth.

In the four decades since the flood, buildings have been renovated, and people and businesses have moved back into the historic downtown. An old movie house has been revitalized, and you can get a sandwich at the soda fountain at Ransone's Drug Store. When I visited, then-Mayor Larry Hall's cellphone ringtone chimed the theme from "The Andy Griffith Show."

Buchanan gained prominence in the late 1800s as the western terminus of the James River and Kanawha Canal. The river still plays an important role in the life of the town, now as a place for kayaking and canoeing. Buchanan's signature attraction is the 366-foot swinging bridge that spans the James.

And just so you know, the town's name is pronounced *BUCK-cannon.*

Once you get to Roanoke, you ought to drive to the top of Mill Mountain, where you will find the famous 100-foot-tall illuminated star and a matchless view of the city. The Virginia Museum of Transportation is an excellent and appropriate stop since Roanoke grew up around the railroad. The steam locomotives are something to see. Walk through the downtown farmers' market and find your way to Center in the Square, which is a home for cultural organizations. After a $30 million renovation, Center in the Square is home to several museums—a children's museum, a science museum, a history museum of African American culture, a museum of Western Virginia—as well as an aquarium, a theater, and one of the best views of downtown and the Blue Ridge beyond from its "green" rooftop.

An hour south of Roanoke is tiny Draper. The reason for our stop is Thee Draper Village, which formerly was Draper Mercantile, a landmark of a general store that, in recent years, has been rescued and revitalized and is once again a thriving part of the community. Debbie Gardner and her family purchased the vacant building and breathed new life in it and the surrounding area. The Village now houses a coffee shop, a restaurant, a small market, and has become a community gathering space. You can also rent bicycles, which is perfect considering the Village is on the New River Trail State Park, a 57-mile recreational path that follows an abandoned railroad right-of-way. Thee Draper Village also includes short-term housing rentals along the trail under the banner of New River Retreat.

"They've brought it back from the dead is what they've done," Bill White told me on my first visit a few years ago. White grew up in Draper—he used to play upstairs at The Merc when his grandfather managed the place years ago—and returned frequently. This was a Sunday afternoon, and White was enjoying live music provided by local musicians.

Once you get to Wytheville, you might consider a slight break in the US 11 action and take US 52 for a dozen miles or so to Big Walker Lookout and Country Store, a longtime attraction where you can stretch your legs, buy an ice-cream cone, listen to a little picking on the front porch, and, if you're game, climb to the top of a 100-foot-tall tower for a spectacular view of the countryside.

Ron Kime grew up on Big Walker Mountain, where his parents built a

THE REVIVED DRAPER MERCANTILE HAS BECOME A GATHERING PLACE FOR LOCALS AND A CONVENIENT STOP FOR CYCLISTS RIDING NEW RIVER TRAIL STATE PARK

business and a life. His family has welcomed tourists for about 70 years. The coming of I-77 in the early 1970s diverted traffic and business away from the store and observation tower his family operated, but he's survived. A fire that destroyed the original store didn't stop him either.

"My father said he knew somewhere there was a place that was meant for him," Kime tells me, "and he found this mountain here."

The steel tower remains the centerpiece of the place. Kime says years ago, from the top, you could see five states—Kentucky, North Carolina, Tennessee, West Virginia and, of course, Virginia. Kentucky and Tennessee have faded from view on all but the clearest days because of increasing haze. Rather than promise a view of a certain number of states, his pitch now is, "Only the birds see more."

Farther down US 11, we take a slight side trip into Rural Retreat, where we find an old train depot—made famous in a 1957 O. Winston Link nighttime photo that showed a station agent giving a lighted signal to a steam locomotive—that was about 20 minutes from being torn down or moved a few years ago and now is in the process of being restored.

Twenty minutes farther down the road is Marion, a town rebounding from tough times because of the loss of manufacturing jobs.

"It's an overnight success that's taken 20 years to happen," says Ken Heath, executive director of community and economic development for the town where he was born and raised.

Marion is the gateway to the popular Hungry Mother State Park. The town features the General Francis Marion Hotel, a fine old hotel that's been renovated to its former splendor. Just down the block, the Lincoln Theatre, a glorious old movie house—named for a local family, not the former president—has been restored and now hosts the nationally syndicated "Song of the Mountains" public television program. The town's old schoolhouse was revived as a school of music, and even the old post office on Main Street has a new function, selling sandwiches instead of stamps as Macado's, a regional restaurant chain.

A short distance south of Marion is the famous Dip Dog Stand, an institution along US 11 known for its battered red weenie, a hot dog that is deep-fried and then slathered in mustard. The menu is long and varied, but the Dip Dog is the true attraction here. When I visited, a regular customer advised me to order two. Tacked on the wall are photos of fans from around the world holding red bumper stickers that read, "Got Dip Dogs?"

Before we reach Tennessee, we drive through Abingdon and Bristol, which are covered in the chapter on the Crooked Road.

IN THE AREA

Accommodations

THE GEORGES, 11 N. Main Street, Lexington. Call 540-463-2500. Website: www.thegeorges.com. Boutique hotel occupying five historic structures in the heart of downtown.

HOTEL 24 SOUTH, 24 S. Market Street, Staunton. Call 540-885-4848. Website: www.hotel24south.com. An iconic Southern hotel in the historic downtown district, built in 1924 and renovated in 2005.

NATURAL BRIDGE HISTORIC HOTEL AND CONFERENCE CENTER, 15 Appledore Lane, Natural Bridge. Call 540-291-2121. Website: www.naturalbridgeva.com. More than 150 guest rooms, fine dining, and cocktail lounge. Within walking distance of Natural Bridge.

SHADOW MOUNTAIN ESCAPE, 1132 Jewell Hollow Road, Luray. Call 540-843-0584. Website: www.shadowmountainescape.com. Elegant cabins with a "touch of traditional Europe."

Attractions and Recreation

AMERICAN SHAKESPEARE CENTER BLACKFRIARS PLAYHOUSE, 10 S. Market Street, Staunton. Call 540-885-5588. Website: www.americanshakespearecenter.com. Shakespeare's works performed in a re-creation of the first indoor theater in the English-speaking world.

BIG WALKER LOOKOUT AND COUNTRY STORE, 8711 Stoney Fork Road, Wytheville. Call 276-663-4016. Website: www.virginia.org/listing/bw-country-store/13186/.

DINOSAUR KINGDOM II, 5781 S. Lee Highway, Natural Bridge. Call 540-464-2253. Website: www.dinosaurkingdomii.com. Fun roadside attraction.

FRONTIER CULTURE MUSEUM, 1290 Richmond Road, Staunton. Call 540-434-0309. Website: www.frontiermuseum.org. Tells the story of the pioneers and immigrants who settled the valley through living history demonstrations and re-created farmsteads.

GREEN VALLEY BOOK FAIR, 2192 Green Valley Lane, Mount Crawford. Call 1-800-385-0099. Website: www.gobookfair.com. A book-lover's paradise, with an estimated 500,000 discount-priced books for sale at the fair, which is open for six sessions each year.

MUSEUM OF THE SHENANDOAH VALLEY, 901 Amherst Street, Winchester. Call 888-556-5799. Website: themsv.org. Chronicles the valley's art, history, and culture through a historic house, formal gardens, and museum galleries.

NATURAL BRIDGE STATE PARK, 6477 S. Lee Highway, Natural Bridge. Call 540-291-1326. Website: www.dcr.virginia.gov/state-parks/natural-bridge.

THE PATSY CLINE HISTORIC HOUSE, 608 S. Kent Street, Winchester. Call 540-662-5555. Website: www.facebook.com/PatsyClineHistoricHouse.

ROUTE 11 POTATO CHIPS FACTORY, 11 Edwards Way, Mount Jackson. Call 540-477-9664. Website: www.rt11.com. Watch chips being made, then help yourself to samples. Also a retail outlet.

SHRINE MONT, 217 Shrine Mont Circle, Orkney Springs. Call 540-856-2141. Website: www.shrinemont.com. Conference and retreat center for groups and individuals. Early spring to mid-November. Operated by the Episcopal Diocese of Virginia.

THEE DRAPER VILLAGE, 3054 Greenbriar Road, Draper. Call 540-994-5659. Website: www.draperisfordreamers.com.

VIRGINIA QUILT MUSEUM, 301 S Main St, Harrisonburg. Call 540-433-3818. Website: www.vaquiltmuseum.org.

Dining

BAR-B-Q RANCH, 3311 N. Valley Pike, Harrisonburg. Call 540-434-3296. Website: www.bar-b-qranch.com. Old-style drive-in with a dining room. Barbecue, fried chicken, hush puppies.

DIP DOG STAND, 2035 Lee Highway, Marion. Call (276) 783-2698. Website: www.dipdogs.net.

PINK CADILLAC DINER, 4347 S. Lee Highway, Natural Bridge. Call 540-291-2378. Website: www.facebook.com/ThePinkCadillacDiner.

THE PALMS, 101 W. Nelson Street, Lexington. Call 540-463-7911. Website: www.thepalmslexington.com.

THE SHACK, 105 S. Coalter Street, Staunton. Call 540-490-1961. Website: www.theshackva.com.

Other Contacts

ROANOKE TOURISM. Website: www.visitroanokeva.com.

SHENANDOAH VALLEY TRAVEL ASSOCIATION. Call 800-847-4878. Website: www.visitshenandoah.org.

CENTER IN THE SQUARE, 1 Market Square, Roanoke. Call 540-342-5700. Website: www.centerinthesquare.org.

VIRGINIA SCENIC RAILWAY, Staunton. Call 434-391-9772. Website: www.virginiascenicrailway.com. Tourism train excursions through the Shenandoah Valley, departing from the Amtrak station in Staunton.

13

MOUNTAIN HIDEAWAYS

Highland, Bath, and Alleghany Counties

ESTIMATED LENGTH: 175 miles

ESTIMATED TIME: Weekend

HIGHLIGHTS: The spectacular beauty of the forested mountains and lush valleys of Virginia's two least-populated counties: **Highland County**, home of maple sugar camps and the annual **Maple Festival** each March, and **Bath County**, home of healing waters and **The Homestead**. Enjoy superb classical music in an exquisite barn-turned-concert hall at **Garth Newel Music Center**, stroll across **Humpback Bridge** in Covington, take a hike at **Douthat State Park**, be awed by the scenic drive through **Goshen Pass** by taking Route 39 along the Maury River, and then be amazed by the breathtaking view of the spectacular **Falling Springs Falls**—all punctuated with a down-home meal and a slice of pie at **Mrs. Rowe's Restaurant** in Staunton.

GETTING THERE: From Staunton, at junction of I-81 and I-64, go west on US 250 to Monterey, south on US 220 to Warm Springs, east on VA 39 through Goshen Pass, and north on VA 42, which will bring you back to US 250 and Staunton. Alternatively, you can stay on VA 39 all the way to Lexington. Or stay on US 220 all the way to I-64 and Covington and just loop back to Staunton by way of I-81.

The countryside quickly unfolds before you as you leave behind the interstate highways and Staunton and head west into the highlands. US 250 follows the historic route of the Staunton-to-Parkersburg Turnpike, an old toll road built in the 1800s to help open the western frontier by connecting the Shenandoah Valley with the Ohio River. We're not going as far west as the Ohio on this trip, just Monterey, a very small but attractive town and the county seat of Highland County—sometimes referred to as Virginia's

LEFT: THE MOUNTAINS RIPPLE TO THE HORIZON ACROSS HIGHLAND COUNTY

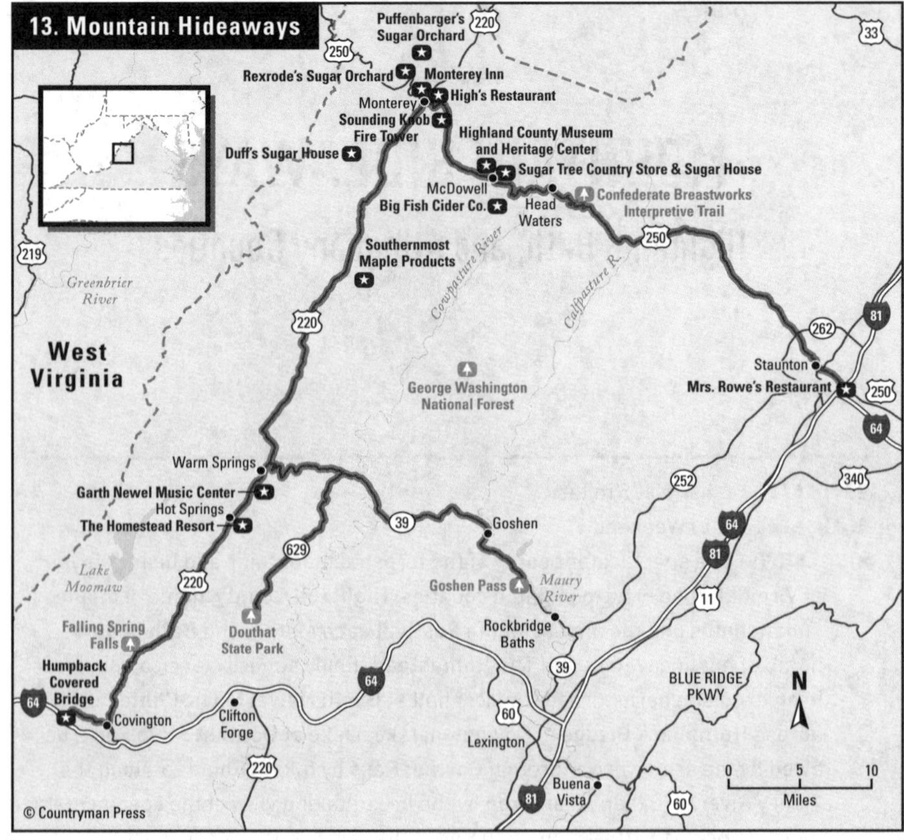

"Little Switzerland." It also has a lot of sugar maple trees, but that's getting a little ahead of the story.

The drive between Staunton and Monterey covers less than 45 miles, but the going is slow in stretches when you're climbing or descending mountain switchbacks. You'll appreciate the simplicity of the first part of the route, scenic, two-lane driving through valley farmland; it gets a little more demanding once you leave Augusta County and enter Highland, which has a population of only 2,300, the smallest among Virginia counties. Or as Chris Swecker, executive director of Highland County Chamber of Commerce, says, "We don't look at that as a negative." What Highland lacks in people, it makes up for in beauty.

The road carries you into the George Washington National Forest. A stretch-your-legs-time arrives with a turnoff for the Confederate Breastworks Interpretative Trail, atop Shenandoah Mountain, where Confederate soldiers constructed a trench-like fortification during the early part of the Civil War. Walk a short loop trail that follows the remnants of the trench.

CLIMBING THE RESURRECTED, 80-FOOT-TALL SOUNDING KNOB LOOKOUT FIRE TOWER AFFORDS A SPECTACULAR VIEW OF MONTEREY HAMILL D. "SKIP" JONES JR.

From here, you get a striking view of the valley where we're headed. Drive through the community of Head Waters, which is Headwaters Presbyterian Chapel, a few houses, and little more. Cross the Cowpasture and Bullpasture Rivers, near *their* headwaters; a couple of counties downstream, the rivers flow together and help form the James River.

Here's McDowell, a town that was the site of a bloody Civil War battle

A good place to start—or end—this drive is at **Mrs. Rowe's Restaurant**, a landmark on US 250, just east of Staunton. Mrs. Rowe's is one of my go-to places. I like to stop and pick up a pie or cookies to take home, or, if I have time, sit and enjoy a meal. Mrs. Rowe's served comfort food before it was known as comfort food. Yet, Mrs. Rowe's nearly never happened.

Mildred DiGrassie was a divorced mother of three running a restaurant in the small town of Goshen in the late 1940s when Willard Rowe met her. Rowe (rhymes with "wow") had a barbecue place 30 miles away in the not-as-small town of Staunton. But his restaurant wasn't doing as well as hers, so when they decided to marry, he figured he'd sell his and move to Goshen. He found no buyers, however, so Mildred sold her restaurant and they moved to Staunton.

Good thing. Otherwise, many of us would never have gotten to know the woman who became known as "the Pie Lady." In Staunton, she introduced some of her customers' favorites—such as fried chicken, meatloaf, and pies—to his restaurant, which they renamed Rowe's Seafood and Steakhouse. The restaurant expanded and really soared when I-81 was built, just a few hundred yards to the west.

Willard Rowe died in 1972, and Mildred carried on, eventually with a new name because customers began calling it "Mrs. Rowe's," which had a nice ring to it. Mildred loved her customers and never really retired, says her son Mike DiGrassie, who ran the restaurant for many years. She died in 2003 at age 89, still coming into the restaurant near the end.

"There used to be a chair at the counter . . . and she would sit there all day long and talk to the customers and tell everybody what they were doing wrong," says her grandson, Aaron DiGrassie, with a laugh.

Aaron, who now runs the place, came to love cooking while working at the restaurant as a teen when his dad put him on the 5:30-a.m. shift on weekends to keep him out of trouble. He attended culinary school and enjoys putting his modern touches on his grandmother's recipes, tweaking the menu and taking pride in making food from scratch.

Any pressure running a restaurant that bears his grandmother's name?

"Absolutely," he says, taking a break from the kitchen where he had been making cobbler for 250 people for an event the next day for the restaurant's flourishing catering business. On the other hand, working at a place where staff and customers are like family is "a lot of fun."

AARON DIGRASSIE IS FOLLOWING IN THE FOOTSTEPS OF HIS GRANDMOTHER, MILDRED ROWE, FOR WHOM THE RESTAURANT IS NAMED BOB BROWN

in 1862. Union troops were moving toward Staunton, attempting to occupy the South's breadbasket, the fertile Shenandoah Valley. Confederate troops successfully repelled them, the victory marking the beginning of General Thomas "Stonewall" Jackson's Valley Campaign. You can walk or drive to different sites where the battle was fought. A good place to start is the Highland County Museum and Heritage Center, located in an 1851 house that served as a hospital during the battle. It has also been a stagecoach stop and hotel.

Near the center of town, you'll find Sugar Tree Country Store & Sugar House, where you can buy apple butter, pottery, and handcrafted toys, but the signature products are, as you might expect, maple-related. This is one of the local operations that makes and sells pure maple syrup, made from the cold, clear sap of sugar maples growing nearby. The annual Maple Festival, held the second and third weekends of March, is the county's biggest happening celebrating the late-winter rising and running of the sap. If you like pancakes—and even if you don't—you'll love this event.

For an uncommon opportunity (and a great view), turn onto Sounding Knob Tower Road a couple of miles before you reach Monterey and drive 1.3 miles on the dirt road to the old, rebuilt fire lookout tower that sits atop Jack Mountain. You're welcome to climb the 80-foot tower during daylight hours at no charge. Just be careful.

Sounding Knob Tower was built in 1935 for the Virginia Department of Forestry by Civilian Conservation Corps workers. The tower was staffed until the 1960s and then sat abandoned for decades before being dismantled in 2002 and acquired by Steve Good of Highland Welding and Fabrication, who salvaged and stored the aging components. In 2016, Hamill D. "Skip" Jones, Jr., purchased the pieces and paid Good to repair and reassemble the fire tower. No public funds were involved.

"I always loved coming here as a boy," Jones told me in a phone interview from Highland in 2023. "I remember, as a kid, climbing the fire tower. It was such an attraction back then."

All the steel, as well as the nuts and bolts, had to be cleaned and regalvanized before it was put up again in 2017 on land Jones inherited from his father that overlooks Monterey. The present location is a few miles from the top of Sounding Knob, where the tower was originally situated, but it's on the same mountain ridge, Jones said, just closer to Monterey.

We drive the final few miles into Monterey on US 250, which becomes Monterey's Main Street, and where it crosses US 220, you will find the county's only traffic signal. Just beyond the intersection is the Highland Inn, the town's iconic grand hotel with its magnificent rocking-chair porches that dates to 1904, when it was known as the "pride of the mountains." I stayed there on a visit years ago, but the inn was closed temporarily in 2024 as it underwent a major restoration (and fundraising campaign to pay for it). Its

SHALLOW RIVERS RUNNING THROUGH LUSH VALLEYS LEND BEAUTY TO HIGHLAND AND BATH COUNTIES

owner, the nonprofit Blue Grass Resource Center, plans to reopen the inn for lodging and dining once the work is complete.

The Highland Inn was Monterey's only hotel, but the area has a number of short-term rentals available, as well as bed-and-breakfasts, including Arbogast Inn, a restored Victorian bed-and-breakfast on Main Street, and Monterey Inn, which opened in 2023 just two doors from the Highland Inn. Another lodging option is the Curly Maple, which offers suites with kitchens—Suite Spots—above a former general store that has grocery items and prepared food.

Down the street, still on Main, is High's Restaurant, housed in one of the county's oldest buildings. There's history here—in its past, the building has been a saloon and a brothel—as well as good, substantial food, served in a friendly atmosphere. A couple of blocks away, over on Spruce Street, is Big

Fish Cider Co., which features award-winning hard ciders made with locally grown apples and traditional techniques.

After eating at High's, as the sun sets behind the nearby mountains, my son and I decide to walk off dinner. Merely a 20-minute drive on a squiggly mountain road from West Virginia, Monterey is so small you can cover a lot of it in just a few minutes. Although it's August, the evening air is cool, a most pleasant departure from the flatlands whence we've come.

From Monterey, head south on US 220, but if you have the time, you ought to visit a local sugar camp or two. In addition to Sugar Tree Country Store & Sugar House in McDowell, others include Puffenbarger's Sugar Orchard in Blue Grass, Rexrode's Sugar Orchard in Hightown, Duff's Sugar House south of Monterey, and Southernmost Maple at Bolar, at the Bath County line. The Virginia Maple Syrup Trail website is a good place to find a list of sugar camps and more information.

Some syrup makers use miles of plastic tubing running through the forest to gather the sap in central collection points; others collect it the old-fashioned way: in buckets. All use one style of evaporator or another to reduce the sugar water to syrup. Regardless of how they produce the syrup, their busy time is in the late winter when the sap, or sugar water, begins to trickle through the trees as the air temperatures creep above freezing. The annual Maple Festival brings thousands of visitors into tiny Highland.

The county also has established a Barn Quilt Trail. Barn quilts are the painted wooden quilt blocks on many barns and houses in Highland, and you're invited to drive around the back roads looking for dozens of them on the official trail. For directions and the stories behind each one, visit the Barn Quilt Trail website.

We have a 30-mile drive south on US 220, along the Jackson River for a ways, to Warm Springs, where you can "take the waters." Bath County, which has the second-lowest population among Virginia counties with about 4,000 residents, developed around the warm, mineral spring waters that bubble to the surface in natural pools and are viewed by some as having healing powers. The Omni Homestead Resort, a legendary mountain oasis that has attracted the rich and famous from around the world, was established before the American Revolution, just down the road in Hot Springs. Thomas Jefferson, as an old man suffering from what he described as rheumatism, soaked in one of these pools, protected then by a wooden, octagonal-shaped building. You can still soak in the 98-degree waters in the recently restored eighteenth- and nineteenth-century bathhouses—a woman's bathhouse was constructed in the 1800s—at the rate of $30 for a 50-minute soak.

The Homestead is the signature destination in these mountains, with

Who is Garth Newel? Nobody.

It's a Welsh phrase meaning new hearth or new home, and it was the name given a property in Bath County when Williams Sergeant Kendall, a painter, and his wife, Christine Herter Kendall, moved here in the 1920s to raise Arabian horses.

That farm is now the **Garth Newel Music Center**, a haven for chamber music set on a serene mountainside, in Warm Springs, just off US 220.

"It's a real heaven on earth for me," says Evelyn Grau, who was the center's artistic director when I first visited years ago. Grau, who plays viola, came here in the early 1980s as a guest artist. After several years, she just decided this is "where I wanted to be."

MUSICIANS AT GARTH NEWEL MUSIC CENTER IN WARM SPRINGS REHEARSE IN A CONCERT HALL THAT WAS ONCE A RIDING RING FOR ARABIAN HORSES

We sit in the concert hall—the old riding ring—with its wood walls and floors, soaring ceiling, and stone fireplace, sunlight streaming in the large windows that look out onto the countryside.

"It's a very warm sound," Grau says of the acoustics in the hall. Intimate, too. White plastic patio chairs are arranged in rows for the next concert. Everyone has a good seat. Audience members are only feet away from the musicians, who perform on a slightly raised wooden stage. A violinist, cellist, and pianist are rehearsing, talking about crescendos, and playing Haydn. It is a rare treat.

skiing, golf, and horseback riding, among other activities, but the hills are full of fine bed-and-breakfast inns and rustic cabins for the renting. Nearby Douthat State Park, 25 miles to the southeast on VA 629, is another option for cabins and camping, plus it has more than 40 miles of hiking trails and a 50-acre lake for swimming and trout fishing.

Our destination today is a place you might not necessarily expect to find on a secluded mountainside: Garth Newel Music Center, a one-time farm for Arabian horses that has been transformed into a sanctuary for world-class music and gourmet food. The exquisitely rustic concert hall is a former indoor riding ring. The center fulfills its mission of celebrating chamber music amid great natural beauty, set on 114 acres, through year-round public concerts and education programs. It also offers fine meals served in the concert hall after performances. Lodging is even available.

You can turn back toward Staunton from Warm Springs, heading east on VA 39, which will carry you, just over 20 miles away, to Goshen, a tiny town on the Calfpasture River. Continue following VA 39 east to Goshen Pass, one of the most scenic stretches of road in Virginia, along the Maury River. You might consider swimming, tubing, or canoeing—or if you'd prefer to stay dry, hiking a trail on the north side of the river—while you're here. Pack a picnic and make an afternoon of it. Rockbridge Baths is another 10 miles to the east on VA 39. From there, turn north on VA 252 and head toward

AGAINST A MOUNTAIN BACKDROP, HEADWATERS CHAPEL IS JUST EAST OF MCDOWELL, ON US 250

TOP: SUGAR TREE COUNTRY STORE IS A MCDOWELL OUTPOST FOR MAPLE SYRUP
BOTTOM: HUMPBACK BRIDGE NEAR COVINGTON IS VIRGINIA'S OLDEST COVERED BRIDGE

Staunton, 30 miles away, at which point you might want to start the loop all over again.

Or you can skip VA 39 and head south on US 220 for a lovely ride and a look at Falling Spring Falls, an 80-foot waterfall that will be on your right as you head south, 5 miles north of Covington. It's visible from a pullout on US 220, or you can venture closer and enjoy an overlook and picnic area. Once you reach Covington, you really ought to check out Humpback Bridge, one of the few remaining covered bridges in the United States that was built higher in the middle than on either end, giving it a humpback appearance. The 100-foot-long bridge was built in 1857 and spans Dunlap Creek. It's a nice place for a picnic.

IN THE AREA

Accommodations

HIDDEN VALLEY BED AND BREAKFAST, 2241 Hidden Valley Road, Warm Springs. Call 540-839-3178. Website: www.hiddenvalleybb.com. The nineteenth-century home, Warwickton, is an historic landmark nestled in a valley along the Jackson River.

MONTEREY INN, 32 W. Main Street, Monterey. Call 540-495-0070. Website: www.montereyinnva.com. Bed-and-breakfast in a restored 1905 Victorian home.

OMNI HOMESTEAD RESORT, 7696 Sam Snead Highway, Hot Springs. Call 800-838-1766. Website: www.thehomestead.com. Golf, ski, spa.

Attractions and Recreation

DOUTHAT STATE PARK, 14239 Douthat State Park Road, Millboro. Call 540-862-8100. Website: www.dcr.virginia.gov/state-parks/douthat.

GARTH NEWEL MUSIC CENTER, 403 Garth Newel Lane, Hot Springs. Call 540-839-5018. Website: www.garthnewel.org.

HIGHLAND COUNTY BARN QUILT TRAIL. Website: www.highlandcounty.org/barn-quilt-trail.

HIGHLAND COUNTY MUSEUM AND HERITAGE CENTER, 161 Mansion Road, McDowell. Call 540-396-4478. Website: www.highlandcountyhistory.com.

HIGHLAND MAPLE FESTIVAL, second and third weekends every March. Call 540-468-2550. Website: www.highlandcounty.org. Visit sugar camps to see how maple syrup is made. Eat pancakes. Wear warm clothing and boots.

VIRGINIA MAPLE SYRUP TRAIL. Call 540-468-2550. Website: www.virginiamaplesyrup.com.

Dining

BIG FISH CIDER, 59 Spruce St., Monterey. Call 540-468-2827. Website: www.bigfishcider.com.

COUNTRY CAFÉ, 6156 Sam Snead Highway, Hot Springs. Call 540-839-2111. Website: www.facebook.com/countrycaferestaurant1994. Family-style dining.

THE CURLY MAPLE, 174 W. Main Street, Monterey. Call 540-468-1250. Website: www.facebook.com/thecurlymaple. General store with restaurant on the first floor and lodging—Suite Spots—on the upper levels of a historic building.

FORT LEWIS LODGE, 603 Plantation Way, Millboro. Call 540-925-2314. Website: www.fortlewislodge.com. Historical family-owned inn open April through October.

HIGH'S RESTAURANT, 73 West Main Street, Monterey. Call 540-468-1700. Website: www.highsrestaurant.com. Café with home cooking.

MRS. ROWE'S RESTAURANT, 74 Rowe Road, Staunton. Call 540-886-1833. Website: mrsrowesrestaurantandbakery.com. Southern cooking, including great pies, in a family setting.

WATERWHEEL RESTAURANT, at the Inn at Gristmill Square. Old Mill Road, Warm Springs. Call 540-839-2231. Elegant country setting. Website: www.gristmillsquare.com.

Other Contacts

ALLEGHANY HIGHLANDS OF VIRGINIA. Website: www.visitalleghany highlands.com.

VISIT BATH, 2696 Main Street, Hot Springs. Call 540-490-1111. Website: www.discoverbath.com. Bath County tourism.

14

GARDEN SPOT

Burke's Garden of Tazewell County

ESTIMATED LENGTH: 75 miles

ESTIMATED TIME: 2 days

HIGHLIGHTS: A visit to **Burke's Garden**, Virginia's highest valley. History at the **Historic Crab Orchard Museum** in Tazewell. Incomparable dining in a cheerfully funky atmosphere at **Cuz's Uptown Barbecue**, which provides a fine place to sleep, too. Take a spin on "**Back of the Dragon**," a twisty and scenic section of VA 16 that winds through the mountains between Tazewell and Marion and is Virginia's only designated motorcycle route.

GETTING THERE: From the intersection of I-77 and I-81 near Wytheville, take I-77 north through Big Walker Mountain Tunnel to Exit 64, Rocky Gap, and go south on VA 61 before turning onto VA 623, which is the only paved road into the Garden and will take you up and over the mountain into the valley.

There's nothing particularly backroad-ish about I-77 as it hurtles between mountains through Southwest Virginia. However, what most intrigued my then-twelve-year-old son on his first visit to this part of the world was when the road went *through* a mountain as it does at Big Walker Mountain Tunnel, between the towns of Wytheville and Bland. Now, that's cool. So, that's where our journey begins.

Big Walker Mountain Tunnel was an engineering marvel when it opened in 1972, and it's still pretty remarkable. It's 4,200 feet long and took five years to build at a cost of $50 million, at the time the most expensive single project undertaken on the Virginia interstate system. All that, and you can change lanes inside it, too, which is unusual for a tunnel.

Drive another 20 miles north and you can do it all over again at BWMT's cousin, the 5,400-foot-long East River Mountain Tunnel, near Bluefield at

LEFT: THE SPECTACULAR VIEWS STRETCH FROM MOUNTAIN TO MOUNTAIN IN BURKE'S GARDEN

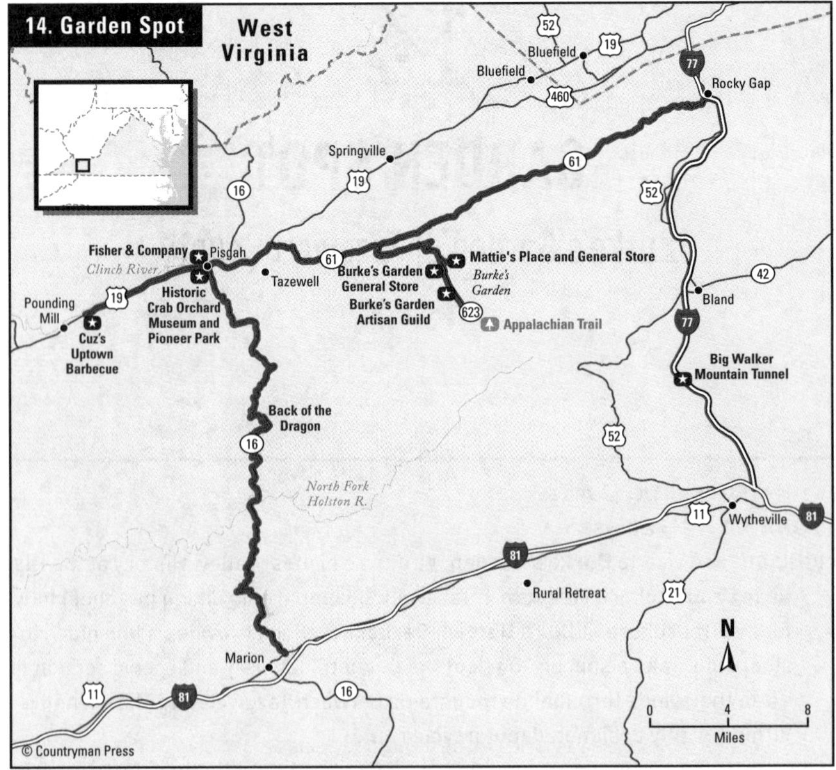

the Virginia-West Virginia line. But that's past our turnoff at Rocky Gap, where we catch VA 61, a pretty 20-mile drive that will carry us to the turnoff at VA 623 for Burke's Garden.

Known as God's Thumbprint because of the way it looks from aerial views, Burke's Garden is a bowl-shaped valley. How it came to be is open to conjecture. The giant crater might have been created when a meteor crashed into it or when a mountaintop collapsed in on itself. However it happened, the place is fertile and green in the summer and makes for a lovely scene.

The Garden, as locals call it, is about 9 miles long, 5 miles wide, more than 3,000 feet above sea level, and accessible by only one paved road: VA 623, steep and twisting as it climbs over the mountain from Tazewell, the nearest town. Lush and fertile, the Garden was for a long time a farming community, though fewer residents farm there now than a generation or two ago; cattle are the primary agricultural commodity. The Garden has maybe 200 year-round residents and perhaps twice that number who live there during the warmer months and head south when winter rolls in. Signposts near the entrance to the valley provide the names of those who live here year-round with distances and directions to their homes. The phone directory is a single sheet of paper, and community potluck suppers are commonplace. The sign over the front door of the old post office says simply, in hand-scrawled cursive, "God's Land."

This also is the kind of place it is: "Yesterday, I walked with the kids to the mill dam, climbing the rocks on the edge of the pond, picking Queen Anne's Lace, and watching the water tumble into a hypnotic swirl beneath the bridge; it was very affordable therapy," Charlotte Whitted told me when I first visited the place years ago. "All my workday stress just washed with the water straight through the gap. After chatting with several neighbors that drove or biked by, we all raced for the front yard hammock."

Back then, Whitted's family ran a 60-acre farm in the Garden, and she also was executive director of the Historic Crab Orchard Museum and Pioneer Park in Tazewell. She's since retired from the museum and moved from the Garden, but she still owns the farm and rents out her former home, Weatherbury Cottage, as an Airbnb. She still loves the Garden.

We stayed at Weatherbury Cottage on our most recent visit, and it was a perfect home base for exploring the Garden or, if you've got the time, just kicking back and taking it easy. It even has an office if you need to get some work done. It has big mountain views and is also a short walk down the road from Mattie's Place, an Amish general store with homemade food,

SIGNPOSTS SERVE AS THE BURKE'S GARDEN DIRECTORY, DIRECTING VISITORS TO RESIDENTS' HOMES THROUGHOUT THE VALLEY

HISTORIC CRAB ORCHARD MUSEUM AND PIONEER PARK NEAR TAZEWELL PRESERVES APPALACHIAN CULTURAL HERITAGE

snacks, souvenirs, and bike rental. Mattie's cinnamon buns are particularly outstanding.

Several roads meander through the Garden. Take any of them, and enjoy the scenery: the long and empty straightaways, the wide-open pastures, and the seamless mountain backdrops. Don't worry. You won't get lost. At some point, all of the roads simply end or come back to the others. Just be careful. You never know when you might encounter a herd of cows crossing the road. They have the right-of-way here. If you're feeling particularly adventurous, you're welcome to take the gravel road at the end of VA 623, on the east side of the Garden, up to a small parking area near its intersection with the Appalachian Trail. We chose not to and, instead, drove to the southeastern end of the valley, parked on the side of the road away from anyone's driveway, and walked up a rutted path to meet the AT, which follows the ridgeline and leads to a series of unmatched views of the Garden.

The valley is named for James Burke, a member of a 1748 survey team that camped in the area and left potato peelings. Burke returned a year later to find a crop of potatoes waiting for him. Native Americans hunted the valley for centuries, but European pioneers didn't settle here until the 1800s. According to local legend, the Vanderbilt family thought the Garden so beautiful they wanted to construct a family castle. But local landowners declined to sell, and the Vanderbilts settled for building Biltmore, America's largest home, in Asheville, North Carolina.

A warning: There's usually not a lot of excitement in the Garden. Stop for a cold drink, a sandwich, and homemade baked goods at Mattie's Place or the Burke's Garden General Store. In the winter, you might find locals gathered around the potbellied stove, sharing the news of the valley. That's about it. The Garden does have a bed-and-breakfast inn—the Parsonage Guest House—and several short-term rentals, such as Weatherbury Cottage. But there are no gas stations, no public schools (the kids attend the public schools in Tazewell, although the old Burkes Garden school building is used by the burgeoning Amish population as a schoolhouse for their children). Burke's Gardeners even lost their post office when the long-time postmaster died. The old building now houses the wares of the Burke's Garden Artisan Guild, and it's open seasonally.

What you get when you come to the Garden is a glimpse of a different sort of life in a different sort of place. It's great for sight-seeing, and because there is usually not a great deal of traffic, it's wonderful for biking, though the terrain is far from perfectly flat. A good time to visit the Garden is its Fall Festival, held the last Saturday of September each year, but anytime over the summer is ideal. David Schlabach, a farmer and member of the Amish community, says even in the hottest part of the summer he's never seen the temperature reach 90 degrees. (It should be noted we visited in mid-October and hiked around the Garden in near-freezing temperatures with snow flurries flying.)

A few words about the Garden's Amish residents. Decades ago, a number of Amish families lived in the Garden but eventually moved on when there wasn't enough land available to establish a sustainable community. Then came Schlabach and his wife, Mattie. David had been looking for a mountain place where he could farm, where the summers would be relatively cool and the winters not terribly long. Many years ago, while lying on his living room floor in Kentucky on a Sunday afternoon, perusing an atlas, he was intrigued by the looks of a place he found on the map: Burke's Garden.

"I saw this little round circle with a crook of a road going into it, and it stopped in the middle," he recalled. "I told Mattie I believe we needed to check that area out." It was another 10 years before they actually laid eyes on Burke's Garden. "Once we did see it," David says, "we knew this was the place."

They moved to Burke's Garden in 2012. David is a partner in a beef-cattle operation; Mattie operates Mattie's Place. Family has followed them, then word-of-mouth brought others. By 2023, eighteen Amish families had settled in Burke's Garden, making for a thriving Amish community, David says.

The Amish, in general, are known for their devotion to plain living and strict adherence to religious beliefs, eschewing much modern technology and maintaining a separation from the wider world. The Amish of Burke's

ROAD SIGNS CAUTION MOTORISTS IN BURKE'S GARDEN TO BE AWARE OF AMISH REISDENTS AND THEIR HORSES AND BUGGIES

Garden use horses and buggies for transportation, so be mindful as you drive the roads. When Amish school lets out, children race home on what, from a distance, appear to be bicycles but are actually foot-powered scooters, seen in some Amish communities as a simpler and more traditional alternative to pedal-powered bikes.

The Amish live off the public power grid, not bringing electricity into their homes—though they use solar panels to generate energy to power lights, refrigerators, and water pumps. Some have landline telephones, but keep them in small structures some distance from their homes, David says, "so that way we won't be interrupted by the phone if we're having family time or devotions."

Though the Amish have a strong foothold in the Garden, David says there is no desire to make Burke's Garden an Amish-only community.

"Definitely not," he says, noting that Amish communities are tight-knit by nature, and when you have too many people in the community, disagreements often arise, and it can become difficult to work things out to everyone's satisfaction. In addition, "We depend a lot on the English people for our transportation and jobs, and so they're a vital part in our community. We really need to keep them here and have them be the biggest population."

Head out of the Garden the way you came in and make your way to the Historic Crab Orchard Museum and Pioneer Park, just west of Tazewell, about 17 miles to the west on US 19/460. The museum preserves and promotes Appalachian cultural heritage, depicting life on the American frontier from the viewpoint of pioneers and Native Americans. The museum is built on the Big Crab Orchard archaeological site where American Indians lived and hunted for thousands of years. The first European settlers arrived in 1770 and named the place because of the abundance of wild crabapple trees.

Cuz's Uptown Barbecue, housed in a former dairy barn, is a quirky combination folk-art museum and restaurant with a down-home feel, though the fare is a lot more elaborate (hand-cut steaks, a variety of seafood, and distinctive touches such as cheesy egg rolls and mac-and-cheese made "skanky" with the addition of blue cheese) than what you would normally find in a restaurant described as "down-home." The food is outstanding, and the people warm and welcoming. It's open only between March and Thanksgiving, four days a week (Wednesday through Saturday), adding to its eccentric feel. Though off the beaten path, Cuz's is far from a secret. It was selected by Urban Matter as among the "15 Best Remote Restaurants Hidden Around the World."

Mike and Yvonne Thompson started in 1979, encouraged by a family friend, "Cuz," who suggested a restaurant would be a good use for the idle barn on Mike's family's property. Over the years, Cuz's has survived a couple of major fires and then, the biggest blow of all, the death of Mike, the restaurant's irreverent, bigger-than-life personality and a genius in the kitchen, just before he turned 70. But Yvonne has carried on with the love and support of her employees, many of whom have worked there for decades, and loyal customers.

Born in Hong Kong, Yvonne came to the United States as a teen under sponsorship of an uncle who operated a popular Chinese restaurant in St. Louis, where she learned how challenging the restaurant business can be. She went to college, majored in journalism, and had two job offers when she graduated: one was the *Richlands News-Press* in Tazewell County. She took it and arrived in this lovely but remote part of Virginia in 1976 with all of her belongings packed in a Volkswagen. She figured she would stay a couple of years and then move on to a bigger newspaper, but an editor set her up on a blind date with Mike. They married in 1977 and opened the restaurant two years later.

Pounding Mill is a long way from Hong Kong. "I used to think I was just made to go into this business because Mike wanted to cook," Yvonne tells me. "I always said it was a tough business, and it is hard, but I really have learned to fall in love with the job and the place." She calls it "my life's work."

Go to Cuz's. Eat. If you can, stay in one of the two cabins on the top of the hill behind the restaurant. There's such a good vibe here.

"First time you come through the door, you're a stranger," says Mike Oder, the restaurant's long-time head chef. "After that, you're family."

TOP: A PLEASANT MORNING AT ONE OF THE HILLSIDE CABINS ABOVE CUZ'S UPTOWN BARBECUE, AN EXCEPTIONAL RESTAURANT IN POUNDING MILL
BOTTOM: YVONNE THOMPSON AND HER LATE HUSBAND, MIKE THOMPSON, WERE THE CREATIVE AND CULINARY FORCES BEHIND CUZ'S UPTOWN BARBEQUE

The museum features exhibits of unearthed pottery and tools, as well as displays of mining, medicine, and music. We wander over to see what I've heard are the two most popular items in the museum: "The Varmint" and "Old Hitler." Both are stuffed. The Varmint is a notorious coyote that killed scores of sheep in Burke's Garden before being shot in the 1950s. Old Hitler was a black bear that caused the same sort of havoc a few years earlier.

Outside, we find more than a dozen log cabins and stone structures—all original and dating to the early 1800s—which offer an up-close view of life during pioneer days and serve as a perfect stage for the museum's living history programs. We roam around the rest of the park, which includes a smokehouse, a cobbler's shop, a springhouse, an apple house, and a family dwelling. We peek in a large barn and see a Model T Ford, replicas of the McCormick reaper, and a horse-drawn hearse. The museum has a cottage for rent on the property for travelers.

Across US 19/460, we visit the museum's restaurant, Fisher & Company, housed in a 1907 general store and specializing in barbecue, but serving all sorts of other good things.

Back on the highway, we head southwest toward Pounding Mill—Pounding Thrill, as some know it—and one of my favorite places: Cuz's Uptown Barbecue. It's about a 10-mile drive, but you'll know when you arrive: just look for the brick silo, the red barn, and the weather vane on the roof that looks like a pig. It is. The two bigger-than-life cement pigs next to the silo, painted sky blue and fire red, also will also confirm you've arrived.

Walk inside and the place dazzles with quirkiness: wall murals of fish and pigs, superhero figures, a Richard Nixon mask, a bronze hippo, Chinese lanterns, and lots more. It's a feast for the eyes—and the appetite. I sample the deep-fried catfish, barbecued pork ribs, and homemade bread before my dinner arrives: prime rib with burgundy gravy. Even the beer tastes colder here.

We're staying the night at Cuz's, in one of the two cabins on the hilltop behind the restaurant. Our cabin has a loft bedroom, a whirlpool tub, and a stone fireplace. In the morning, I make a pot of coffee and enjoy it on the porch that looks across a hillside covered in wildflowers. The restaurant and the highway are in the distance below us. Cows graze in the next pasture. A creek trickles past the cabin. A low cloud hugs the mountain behind us. I pour a second cup.

If you have the time, you might make a point of driving the "Back of the Dragon," a 32-mile stretch of VA 16 between Tazewell and Marion, featuring more than 400 curves. The mountainous road is popular among motorcyclists, but cars are welcome, too. Just don't expect to travel too quickly. You won't want to miss the delicious scenery—or the next curve.

AS ALMOST EVERYWHERE ELSE IN THE VALLEY, CHARLOTTE WHITTED'S AIRBNB OVERLOOKS A BUCOLIC SCENE

IN THE AREA

Accommodations

THE PARSONAGE GUEST HOUSE, 7322 Burke's Garden Road. Call 276-970-6862. Website: www.vrbo.com/749443.

WEATHERBURY COTTAGE, Burke's Garden. Website: www.airbnb.com/rooms/746347710694416532.

Attractions and Recreation

HISTORIC CRAB ORCHARD MUSEUM AND PIONEER PARK, 3663 Crab Orchard Road, Tazewell. Call 276-988-6755. Website: www.craborchardmuseum.com. Tribute to Appalachian cultural heritage. Also has a cottage for rent.

Dining

BURKE'S GARDEN GENERAL STORE, 6156 Burke's Garden Road, Burke's Garden. Call 276-472-4444. Website: www.virginia.org/listing/burkes-garden-general-store/12576/. Market and prepared foods.

CUZ'S UPTOWN BARBECUE AND CABINS, 15746 Governor George C. Peery Highway, Pounding Mill. Call 276-964-9014. Website: www.cuzs.com. Fun restaurant with innovative menu. Hillside cabins. Restaurant is open March through November.

FISHER & COMPANY, 1735 Pisgah Road, Tazewell. Call 276-385-1150. Website: www.facebook.com/fisher-company-183034755234120.

MATTIE'S PLACE, 920 Gose Mill Road, Burke's Garden. Call 276-647-2222. Website: www.heartofappalachia.com/places/matties-place. Market, baked goods, sandwiches, and other prepared foods. Bicycle rental.

Other Contacts

BACK OF THE DRAGON. Website: www.backofthedragon.com. Virginia's only designated motorcycle route, featuring 32 miles and more than 400 curves.

TAZEWELL COUNTY TOURISM, 163 Walnut Street, Bluefield. Call 800-588-9401. Website: www.facebook/visittazewell.

Doug Rogers

15

END OF THE ROAD

Mathews by the Bay

ESTIMATED LENGTH: 75 miles (from Richmond)

ESTIMATED TIME: Day trip or weekend

HIGHLIGHTS: Walking around the town of **Mathews**, kayaking or canoeing, driving around the county to find the tiny post offices with names such as **Moon** and **Onemo** and getting a look at the historic and restored **New Point Comfort Lighthouse**.

GETTING THERE: To reach Mathews from Richmond, drive east on I-64 to Exit 220 (West Point), VA 33, and follow that to VA 198, which will take you to Mathews.

Mathews is not the sort of place you reach by accident. Getting here requires a 75-minute drive from Richmond and numerous turns on roads that bear little resemblance to major highways. And if you go too far, you run the risk of splashing into the Chesapeake Bay—or at least into one of the numerous creeks and inlets that sketch the jagged outline of this piece of Virginia that is dearly loved by those who know it best. And it's not so much what you see here—though it is surely lovely—but how it *feels* here.

"It's not a place you pass through," says Bette Dillehay, director of the award-winning Mathews Memorial Library, which has attracted national attention, a source of great pride and rightly so in the small community. "If you're here, you *meant* to be here."

Dillehay knows Mathews well. She grew up here—"We have two groups of people," she says, "'come-heres' and 'been-heres,' and I'm a 'been-here'"—and she still lives here part-time, though she also lives in Richmond where she worked in state government. At one point, she was the state's deputy secretary of technology and also oversaw the state's Y2K transition as director of the Century Date Change Initiative.

LEFT: NEW POINT COMFORT LIGHTHOUSE, RECENTLY RESTORED, WAS CONSTRUCTED DURING THOMAS JEFFERSON'S PRESIDENCY DOUG ROGERS PHOTOGRAPHY

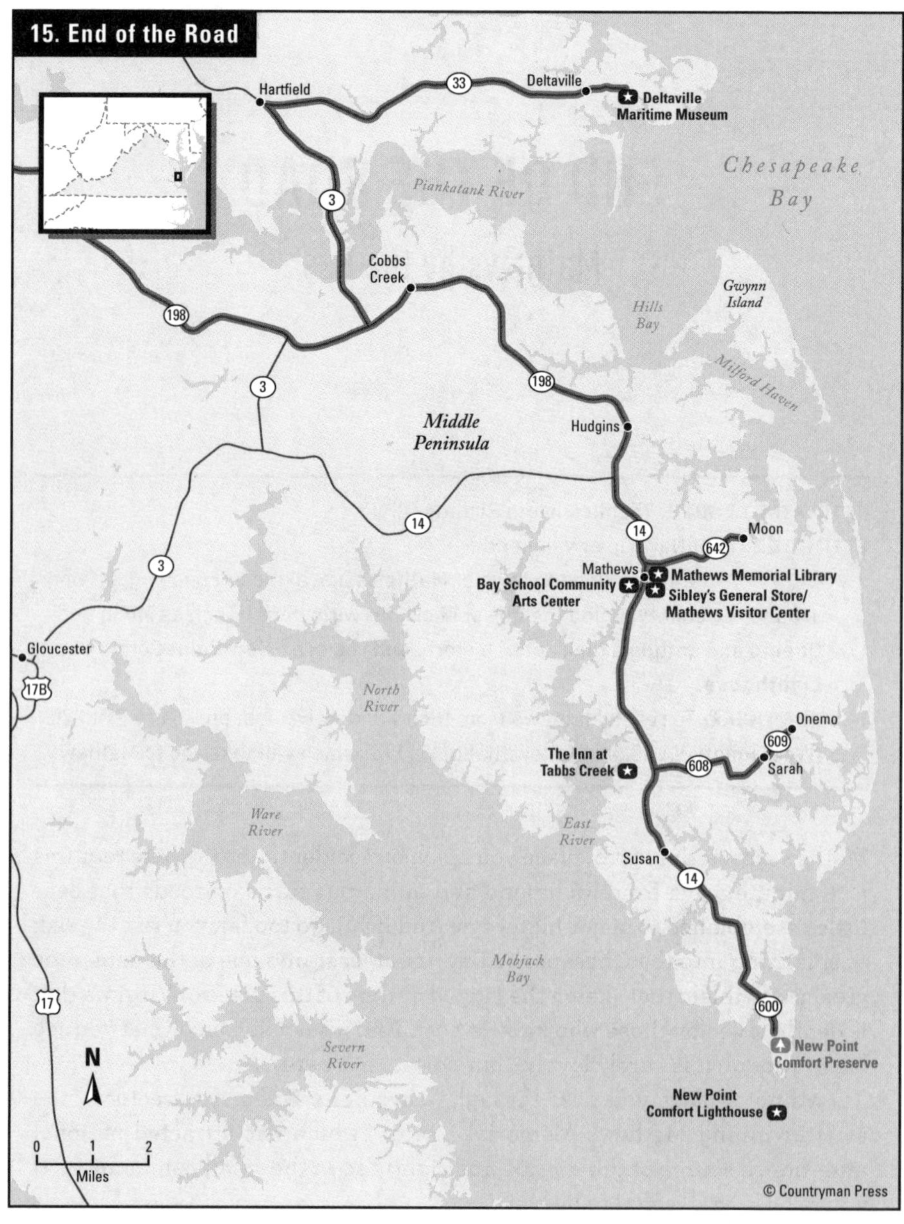

"I think the thing that draws people here is the sense of quietness," she said. "I know people who say, 'I come here to escape.' But it's also a place to connect." And the way to connect in Mathews is through art, or recreation, or just a shared sense of wanting to get away but not be too isolated.

Mathews is a small place—the second-smallest county, land-wise in Virginia, with a population of about 9,000—but it can seem pretty large when

THE RESTORED NEW POINT COMFORT LIGHTHOUSE SHINES AGAIN AFTER A LONG PERIOD OF DARKNESS
DOUG ROGERS PHOTOGRAPHY

you're driving around. The county has more than 200 miles of shoreline, counting rivers and bays and everything else, meaning its country roads meander here and there and everywhere, occasionally coming to abrupt halts when dry land runs out. In Mathews, there are more lighthouses (two) than traffic lights (none), and you can't help but love a place like that.

On to the town of Mathews, where a good first stop would be Sibley's General Store, which is now the Mathews Visitor Center. You can pick up maps and brochures, browse handmade items from local artisans, and acquire a handsome Mathews ball cap. You also can get a heaping helping of history. Sibley's dates back to the late 1800s, but there is evidence of an older general store—perhaps from around 1815—in a building behind Sibley's. Mathews was formed as a county in 1791.

Sibley's is right in the center of Mathews, which, given its size, is very walkable, meaning you can shop, learn, and eat—even put in a kayak for a paddle—all within a few steps of wherever you are in town. Just down the street from Sibley's is the aforementioned library, which is a real gem. Housed in an old bank building, the library was awarded in 2005 the Institute of Museum and Library Service's National Medal for Museum and Library Service, the nation's highest honor given to museums and libraries for service to the community. The Mathews library was one of the first in Virginia, Dillehay tells me; the community began raising money for it in 1922. The library had just opened a brand new expansion for teens when I made my first visit to Mathews in 2014. The library also used to hold tea dances, at which the average age was about 75. As Dillehay told me at the time, "We have live music and they dance like crazy."

Dillehay adds, "What we try to do is have programs that really match the community. It's more than just a library."

The Bay School Community Arts Center, a nonprofit arts organization, is on the same side of the street as the library, and is another good place to stop. It offers studio classes, conducts outreach programs in the community for those who cannot attend a traditional art class, and also holds exhibitions and sells artwork through its Art Speaks Gallery.

Assorted shops around town might get your attention, as well as several places to eat. I'm most familiar with Richardson's Café, in an old corner pharmacy, where you can slide into a booth or sit at the old soda fountain. You can get sandwiches or seafood or just about anything else. The pies and cakes are really something, too. The White Dog Bistro, in the historic courthouse, offers casual and upscale dining. There's a Mexican restaurant, a Chinese restaurant, and a pizza place in close proximity—pretty decent offerings for a small town.

Mathews historically was a boatbuilding center, but now it's a recreational attraction with boating and fishing, kayaking, and canoeing. Right in town, there's the Put In Creek Park, a kayak and canoe launch facility. The waterways around Mathews are popular with canoeists and kayakers, and

THE MATHEWS MEMORIAL LIBRARY HAS WON NATIONAL ACCOLADES MATHEWS COUNTY VISITOR & INFORMATION CENTER

SIBLEY'S GENERAL STORE IS BOTH HISTORIC AND HOME OF THE MATHEWS VISITOR CENTER
MATHEWS COUNTY VISITOR & INFORMATION CENTER

there are multiple launch sites around the county. Check at Sibley's for maps and directions.

You've got to see New Point Comfort Lighthouse, the third-oldest lighthouse on the Chesapeake Bay, which was commissioned in 1804 by Thomas Jefferson, opened in 1805, and survived the War of 1812 and the Civil War. The 55-foot-tall, octagonal sandstone lighthouse went dark for decades until a major restoration was completed in 2021. The lighthouse, shored up by structural repairs, gleams again as years of old paint and biological growth were blasted off, eroded sandstone blocks were repaired, and fresh white paint applied. As the cherry on top, a new solar light flashes at the same frequency—every four seconds—as the light did more than a century ago.

Reed Lawson, president of the Mathews County Historical Society, who has long been involved in restoring the lighthouse, tells me watching it come back to life was "exhilarating, momentous! Mathews County's icon has been rescued, revived, and strengthened." The entire project was long in the making and very complex. My friend Dennis Baker, a former director of Virginia State Parks, who retired to Mathews and became active in community affairs before eventually returning to Richmond in later years, describes the completion of the lighthouse restoration as "quite a miraculous happening for a small community on the Chesapeake Bay like us."

When it was built, the lighthouse stood on an island of about 100 acres at the entrance to Mobjack Bay, just off Mathews' southernmost peninsula, and was reachable by foot at low tide. However, erosion and centuries of storms and shifting sands have reduced the island to a postage stamp-size piece of land, far from shore. You can view the lighthouse from the elevated

SIDE TRACKS

Mathews County's neighbor to the north on the Middle Peninsula is Middlesex County, which is home to **Deltaville**, a town well worth a visit. Deltaville was known as the "Boatbuilding Capital of the Chesapeake Bay," and honoring that heritage is the **Deltaville Maritime Museum**, which has risen from the ashes of a devastating fire in 2012 to become bigger and better than ever.

The museum is up and running again and "a far cry" from the original museum, a modest operation founded in 2002 in a repurposed ranch house to preserve the area's boatbuilding heritage, according to John England, a member of the museum's board and a longtime volunteer.

"What we put back is just night and day difference," said England, who among other things headed the project to restore the F.D. Crockett, a 1920s-era buyboat that now serves as the museum's floating ambassador.

A primary exhibit of the museum is a simulated boatbuilder's shop with everything but the spiderwebs and sawdust. A partially constructed deadrise workboat, the sort of vessel that has long been Deltaville's calling card, is part of the display.

"The museum started because we were the boatbuilding capital of the bay," says Bill Powell, president and events director of the museum and Holly Point Nature Park.

Deltaville lies on the Chesapeake Bay at the eastern end of the Middle Peninsula, an area distinguished by its rivers, creeks, and marshes. It's easy to see why boating, sailing, and fishing are favorite pastimes here, and the museum covers that entire history. A particularly interesting exhibit is its collection of toy pond boats, some more than a century old. The museum also offers summer concerts at its waterfront stage, weekly covered-dish socials at its cozy tea house (all are invited) and a family boatbuilding workshop each summer.

"All of us love the water," Powell says. "We love this area."

A SIMULATED BOAT-BUILDER'S SHOP IS A CORE EXHIBIT OF THE DELTAVILLE MARITIME MUSEUM

observation walkway at New Point Comfort Preserve and from the Bayside Landing, which has sheltered picnic tables and a somewhat distant view of the lighthouse. Better yet, find a friend with a boat for an up-close look at the lighthouse.

If you're going to stay a while in Mathews—and you really should—there are no chain hotels or motels. Your choices are primarily cottages, though there is also The Inn at Tabbs Creek, a farmhouse on the water that Greg and Lori Dusenberry restored and modernized into the county's only bed and breakfast, which aims to appeal to outdoor enthusiasts. Bring your kayaks, or use one of theirs.

"No doilies here," Lori says with a laugh. "Our goal is to be a little less traditional and a little more laid-back."

It's fun just to drive around Mathews, take in the sights, and marvel at the interesting little communities whose names derive from the tiny post offices that serve or served them, such as Moon. Retired longtime postmaster Shirley Snow, whom I meet while gathering material for a piece in the *Richmond Times-Dispatch*, says the story she always heard was that Moon got its name by accident when the store owner's handwriting on the postal application in the early 1900s was misread. He wanted it to be called "Noon"—for when the mail would be delivered—but postal authorities read it as "Moon."

Snow says hers was "the best job in the world."

"People would come pretty much the same time every day," Snow says when I meet her on the porch of the old, shuttered Moon post office that's been replaced by a modern structure down the road. "You knew all about their families. You became part of their families, and they became part of yours."

Susan is the name of another small post office, and there used to be one called Sarah, but it's now defunct. Then there's Onemo. It's pronounced *o-NEE-mo*, but, according to the local story, it originated as "One More" post office, as in *ONE-mo*.

"It's the only story I've ever heard," says Charlotte Crist, postmaster relief, when I stop in at the Onemo post office, a cute little building that looks like a glorified tool shed. She has a plate of homemade oatmeal-chocolate chip cookies for her customers.

Jay Black grew up near Onemo, went away to school, and returned, and now lives with his wife, Lori, in Moon. He now works as an investment advisor across the Rappahannock River on the Northern Neck—not far as the gull flies, but quite a commute on the roads that weave and wind here and there on their way to any destination in these parts. But he loves Mathews—the place, the people, and the stories that come with it—and when he's not working, he serves as a tour guide around the county. He tells the story of how children used to have to take a boat to school because all of the rivers and creeks made it far too long a walk on dry land. If the weather was bad and they couldn't get

THE DELTAVILLE MARITIME MUSEUM HAS RISEN FROM THE ASHES AFTER A DEVASTATING FIRE IN 2012

home by boat after school, they would hunker down with friends or relatives on the school side of the water, go to school the next morning, and finally return home the following evening.

"You didn't think about it at the time," he says. "It's just what you did. Kids complain now if the bus doesn't let them off right in front of their house."

Black has a personal connection to the aforementioned Sarah post office. His great-grandfather operated a store and the post office was part of it.

"The post office was named for my great-grandmother, Sarah," Black says. "It just makes my heart sing when I pull up a Google Map every once in a while and it'll say, 'Sarah.' "

I get the feeling Mathews makes a lot of people's hearts sing, including those who haven't known Mathews all along. More and more retirees are finding Mathews to be a perfect place to unwind. People like Baker, who in his role as director of Virginia State Parks, was familiar with lots of perfect places around the state. Mathews, though, won his heart.

"An absolutely wonderful, wonderful experience," he says.

When she stops to think about it, Shirley Snow, the retired Moon postmaster, marvels there are so many "come-heres" in Mathews.

"Most everybody has come from somewhere else," she says, "and it always amazes me they find us because we are at the end of the road."

IN THE AREA

Accommodations

THE INN AT TABBS CREEK, 384 Turpin Lane, Port Haywood. Call 804-725-5136. Website: www.innattabbscreek.com.

Attractions and Recreation

DELTAVILLE MARITIME MUSEUM AND HOLLY POINT NATURE PARK, 287 Jackson Creek Road, Deltaville. Call 804-776-7200. Website: www.deltavillemuseum.com.

Dining

RICHARDSON'S CAFÉ, 12 Church Street, Mathews. Call 804-725-7772. Website: www.facebook.com/Richardsonscafe.

SOUTHWIND PIZZA, 44 Church Street, Mathews. Call 804-725-2766. Website: www.facebook.com/southwindpizza. Pizza and most everything else.

WHITE DOG BISTRO, 68 Church Street, Mathews. Call 804-725-7680. Website: www.thewhitedogbistro.com.

Other Contacts

MATHEWS COUNTY VISITOR INFORMATION CENTER, 239 Main Street, Mathews. Call 804-725-4229. Website: www.visitmathews.com.

16

SKYLINE DRIVE

Shenandoah National Park's Scenic Road

ESTIMATED LENGTH: 105 miles

ESTIMATED TIME: 4 hours

HIGHLIGHTS: **Skyline Drive**, a pleasant though curvy mountain road, is the only public road in **Shenandoah National Park**, so it's hard to get lost. Go in October, and you can enjoy the turning of the leaves. Plan to make lots of stops at overlooks, visitor centers at Milepost 4.6 (**Dickey Ridge**) and 51 (**Big Meadows**), picnic grounds, and hiking trails, including 101 miles of the Appalachian Trail. Side trips include hiking **Old Rag**, a nearby mountain that is one of the most popular destinations for hikers in the Mid-Atlantic, or **Luray Caverns**.

GETTING THERE: The road has four access points along its 105-mile length: **Front Royal**, near I-66 and US 340, **Thornton Gap**, at US 211, **Swift Run Gap**, at US 33, and **Rockfish Gap**, at I-64 and US 250. Though a haven of wild, natural beauty, **Shenandoah National Park** is a short drive from nearby population centers. **Front Royal**, the northern end of the park, is less than 75 miles from **Washington DC**. **Rockfish Gap**, the southern end of the park, which connects to the **Blue Ridge Parkway** to the south, is about 90 miles from Richmond.

Skyline Drive courses over, around, and occasionally through the Blue Ridge Mountains. The centerpiece of Shenandoah National Park, the scenic drive was designed in the 1930s as a way to provide Americans who were quickly falling in love with their cars a leisurely drive through the mountains. It is still so.

I've been visiting Shenandoah National Park since I was a child, often on autumn trips to view the changing colors of the foliage. While fall is a most popular time to visit, summer is great, too. Even winter is interest-

LEFT: LOW STONE WALLS AND LONG, SCENIC VIEWS MAKE THE SKYLINE DRIVE ONE OF THE PRETTIEST DRIVES ANYWHERE

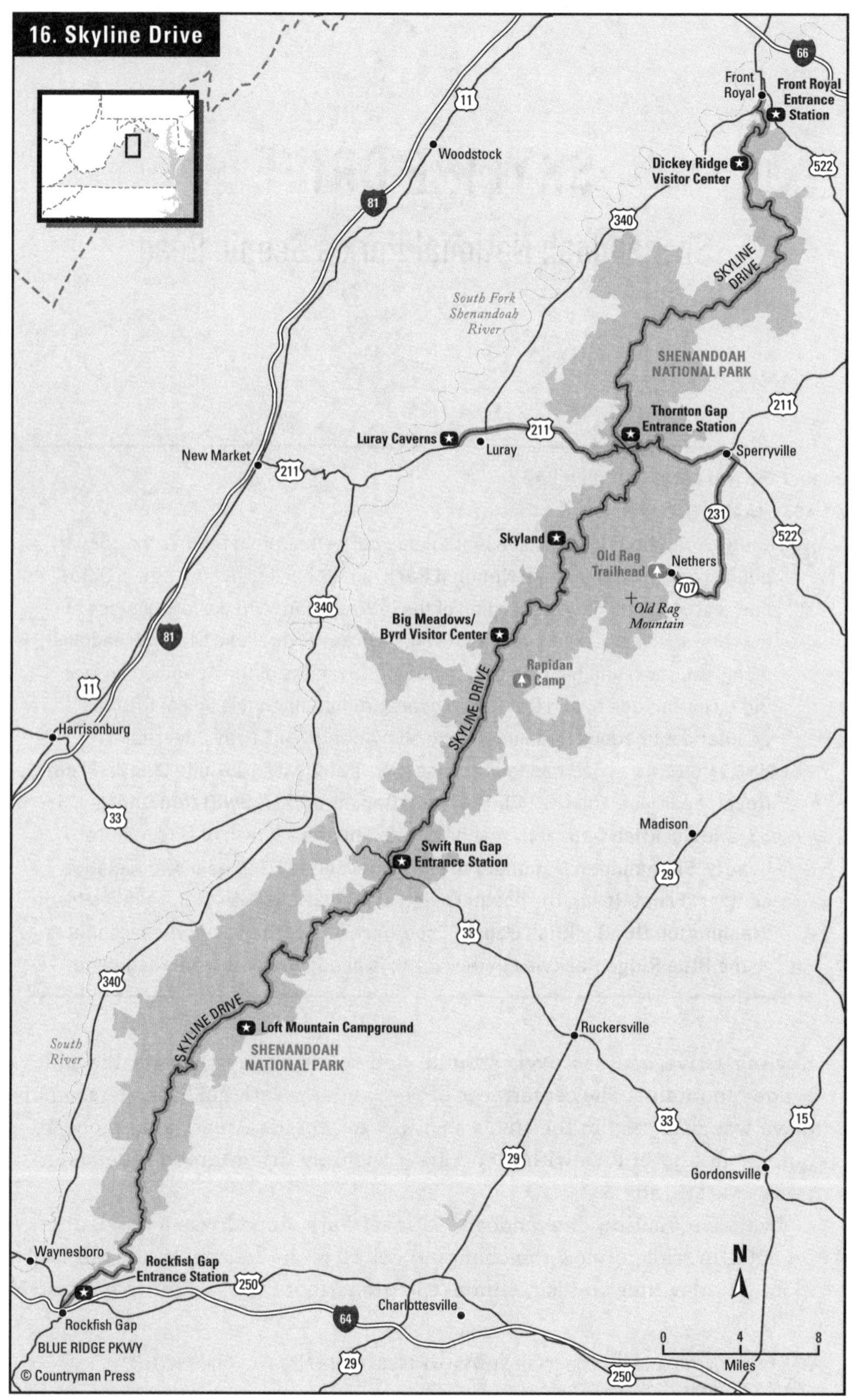
16. Skyline Drive
Front Royal
Front Royal Entrance Station
Woodstock
Dickey Ridge Visitor Center
Skyline Drive
South Fork Shenandoah River
Shenandoah National Park
Thornton Gap Entrance Station
Luray Caverns
Luray
New Market
Sperryville
Skyland
Old Rag Trailhead
Nethers
Old Rag Mountain
Big Meadows/ Byrd Visitor Center
Rapidan Camp
Harrisonburg
Madison
Swift Run Gap Entrance Station
Loft Mountain Campground
Shenandoah National Park
South River
Ruckersville
Gordonsville
Waynesboro
Rockfish Gap Entrance Station
Charlottesville
Rockfish Gap
Blue Ridge Pkwy
© Countryman Press
N
0 4 8
Miles

AT BIG MEADOWS LODGE, A FAVORED PERCH IS A WINDOW SEAT

ing, although make sure Skyline Drive is open. While the park is open, the road is sometimes closed because of inclement weather, and most services are shut down between November and April. A quick note about fees: Since Skyline Drive is in a national park, an entry fee is charged. Skyline Drive is often confused with Blue Ridge Parkway. The roads are similar in that they are scenic, mountain roads administered by the National Park Service, and they meet at Rockfish Gap—the southernmost point of Skyline Drive and the northernmost point of Blue Ridge Parkway. But there is no charge to drive the Blue Ridge Parkway, in many places a narrow right-of-way slicing through private land. One more thing about Skyline Drive: The maximum speed limit is 35 mph, so there's no need to be in a rush.

Now, back to our trip. Skyline Drive was largely a project of the Civilian Conservation Corps, the Great Depression-era jobs program. CCC workers cut roadways, flattened slopes, built overlooks, installed low stone walls and guardrails, and landscaped much of the roadside with trees and shrubs. Besides appealing to Americans and their cars, the construction of Skyline Drive served two other major purposes: to bring a national park to the East and to present a shining example of success amid the nation's economic despair.

Start at Front Royal and come south. Dickey Ridge, a visitor center with exhibits, a film, and picnic grounds, comes up at Milepost 4.6. Overlooks pop up every few miles, if not more often. I stop at several coming from the north, shooting photographs at each, admiring the view of the valley below. I am far from alone, even on a weekday, because it's October, usually the peak leaf season; the parking areas at overlooks are active as people are enjoying the mountains turn autumn red and gold. The northern half of Skyline Drive offers more waysides for food and gas; the southern has more overlooks. There's no shortage of views anywhere.

As a side trip, travel a few miles west on US 211 from Thornton Gap to the town of Luray and visit Luray Caverns, one of the world's most popular natural wonders. A half-million visitors come by every year to tour the massive cave with ceilings 10 stories high. "Hear rocks sing" was the Luray slogan for years, and you really can when they fire up the Great Stalacpipe Organ in the caverns' cathedral room. The walkways are well lit. You won't feel claustrophobic. The temperatures are perpetually cool. Plus, you can see intriguing rock formations, like the famous fried eggs, sunnyside up. Be sure to bring your imagination.

If going underground is not your idea of a good time, Luray Caverns also offers a car museum, a garden maze, and a rope adventure park. Then there's a "singing tower"—a 117-foot-tall carillon of 47 bells, the largest one weighing more than 3 tons. Recitals are held regularly in the warm-weather months.

Back on Skyline Drive, I head for Skyland, at Milepost 42, the highest point on Skyline Drive at about 3,600 feet. It began as a nineteenth-century resort and is now a motel and restaurant, with a spectacular valley view to the west through the huge windows in the dining room. When the sun is setting, everyone in the dining room will stop and look.

I've stayed in the past at Skyland, which has a cabin feel to it with its lodge buildings set in the woods or perched on the edge of a mountain. Deer roam along roadsides and through the resort, and black bears are prevalent throughout the park. As a result, you have to be careful with food. The deer and bears are not alone. One evening on a previous trip, a sleepless toddler and I went for a walk around the property and came within a few feet of another critter: a skunk. We walked very quietly and quickly back to our room, returning unscathed (and smelling no worse than when we left).

East of Skyland and well off the Skyline Drive, but still within the park, is Old Rag, a popular mountain for hikers. Despite the crowds it attracts, Old Rag is no stroll in the park. The approximately 8-mile round-trip hike to the top of the 3,200-foot mountain is strenuous, featuring rock scrambles and steep climbs. The payoff: spectacular panoramic views. You can

FREQUENT OVERLOOKS BECKON MOTORISTS TO STOP, ENJOY THE VIEW, AND SNAP A FEW PHOTOS

access the trailhead at Nethers, off VA 600. Take note: Between March 1 and November 30, hikers need to purchase an Old Rag day-use ticket in advance. The requirement was initiated to alleviate overcrowding on the mountain.

From Skyland I head south for another 9 miles to Big Meadows, just about the midway point on Skyline Drive, and, as the name suggests, a spectacular open, grassy expanse favored by wildflowers and deer. Besides hikes and ranger-led tours, Big Meadows also offers a camp store, restaurant, lodging, and campground. In the visitor center, I walk through a fine little museum that focuses on the not-so-easy development of the park, including unpleasant episodes such as the uprooting of mountain people from their land. I drive to the Big Meadows Lodge, a structure built with stones cut from Massanutten Mountain in the 1930s. It's also a nice place to sit awhile, either inside or on the deck, and take in the valley view.

Just south of Big Meadows, you will come to a parking area for Milan Gap, at Milepost 52.8, a nondescript pull-off except it's the trailhead for the Mill

ON A REASONABLY CLEAR DAY, YOU CAN SEE PRETTY MUCH FOREVER FROM THE DECK AT BIG MEADOWS LODGE

Prong Trail, a 4.1-mile round-trip hike that will lead you to Rapidan Camp, the summer retreat built by President Herbert Hoover so he and his wife, Lou Henry, could escape the heat and humidity of Washington summers. I hiked to the summer White House on an earlier visit to Shenandoah: a winter hike in near-zero temperatures with my son's Boy Scout troop. We stopped to rest and eat our peanut butter sandwiches for lunch on the deck of the Brown House, which has been restored to its 1929 appearance. Of course, you can avoid crossing icy streams and having your drinking water freeze by walking the trail in June instead of January.

Keep going south, stopping at overlooks to peer either west into the valley or east into the foothills rippling toward the coast. Enjoy a picnic or take a short hike. Just watch your time. Stops every few miles will eat up your day. Of course, there are not many better ways to spend a day. Finally, you're at Rockfish Gap, the end of the road. You can go west on I-64 toward Staunton or east on the highway toward Richmond. Or, if you haven't had enough of pretty drives, keep straight and continue on the Blue Ridge Parkway.

IN THE AREA

Accommodations and Dining

BIG MEADOWS LODGE AND SKYLAND RESORT, Shenandoah National Park. Call 877-847-1919. Website: www.goshenandoah.com. Historic motels and cabins, and full-service dining in a mountain setting.

GRAVES MOUNTAIN FARM AND LODGE, 205 Graves Mountain Lane, Syria. Call 540-923-4231. Website: www.gravesmountain.com. Family-owned rustic mountain retreat.

SHADOW MOUNTAIN ESCAPE, 1132 Jewell Hollow Road, Luray. Call 540-843-0584. Website: www.shadowmountainescape.com. Timber-frame cabins exuding European charm.

Attractions and Recreation

SHENANDOAH NATIONAL PARK, 3655 Highway 211 East, Luray. Call 540-999-3500. Website: www.goshenandoah.com. Skyline Drive is the centerpiece of the mountainous park, stretching for 105 miles from Fort Royal to Rockfish Gap. Hiking, camping, and scenic overlooks.

LURAY CAVERNS, 101 Cave Hill Road, Luray. Call 540-743-6551. Website: www.luraycaverns.com. Open every day, tours every 20 minutes.

17

BE PREPARED TO STOP

Blue Ridge Parkway

ESTIMATED LENGTH: 220 miles
ESTIMATED TIME: 2 days
HIGHLIGHTS: Called America's Favorite Drive, the **Blue Ridge Parkway** twists its way through the southern Appalachian range, providing views that deserve to be framed and displayed on gallery walls. The parkway, managed by the National Park Service, is America's longest linear park, stretching for 469 miles through twenty-nine Virginia and North Carolina counties. The road is always open—24 hours a day, seven days a week—although sections are closed at times for maintenance or inclement weather. There is no fee. **Humpback Rocks**, **Peaks of Otter**, and **Meadows of Dan** offer diversions along the way for exploring, dining, and lodging. **Roanoke** is the largest city along the parkway. Stop at **Chateau Morrisette Winery** for a sip of wine or a bite to eat, or settle into your lawn chair or spread your blanket on a hillside at the **Blue Ridge Music Center** amphitheater for an evening of mountain music.
GETTING THERE: Take I-64 to Exit 99, near Waynesboro, then follow the signs to the Blue Ridge Parkway.

When you turn onto the Blue Ridge Parkway, as we did at Rockfish Gap—the northern terminus of the road, Milepost 0—it's important to keep this in mind: Don't be in a hurry. The parkway is the ultimate Sunday Drive: a leisurely, picturesque experience with maximum 45-mph speed limits, no 18-wheelers, and no billboards, but also—and more significantly as far as safety goes—deceptively dangerous curves and steep drop-offs. Take your mind off the road for too long to admire a view or search for a deer, and you might find yourself in a grove of trees, or, worse, lurching down a mountainside.

The National Park Service provides many places along the road for

LEFT: MABRY MILL, NEAR THE SOUTHERN END OF VIRGINIA'S STRETCH OF THE BLUE RIDGE PARKWAY, IS ONE OF THE MOST PHOTOGRAPHED SPOTS IN THE STATE

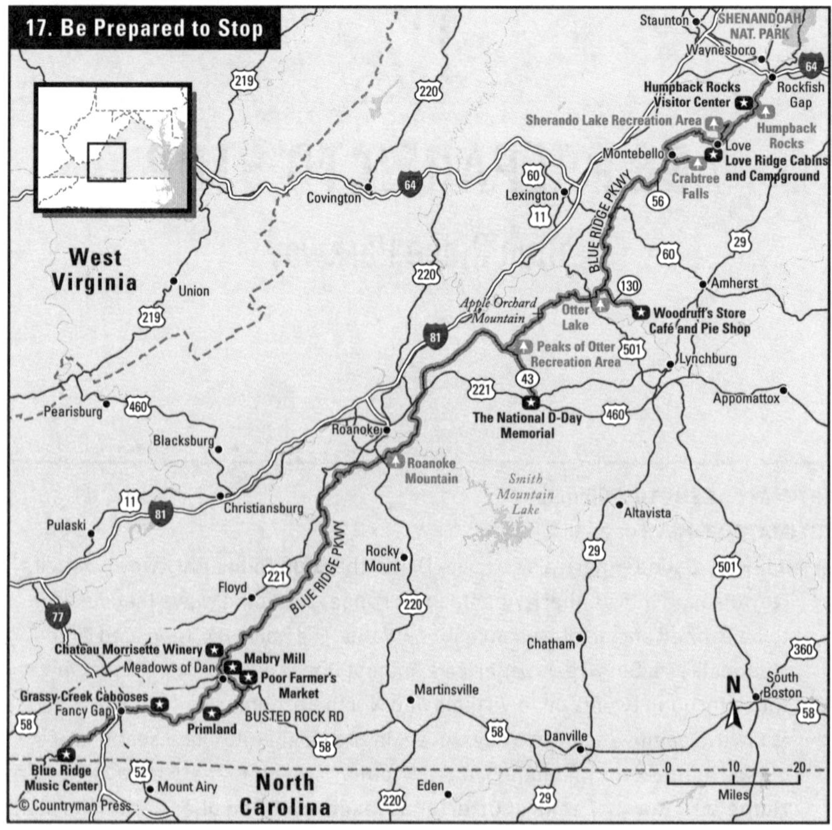

you to pull off and park and marvel at the scenery. (It should be noted that the parkway, as a linear park, is extremely narrow, shrinking to a width of 200 feet at times. Land on the immediate sides of the road is owned by the National Park Service, but beyond that is private property.) We stop at the first major one we come to, Humpback Rocks Visitor Center, just before Milepost 6, which features a mountain farm museum with a log cabin, barn, and other nineteenth-century buildings that have been relocated here from nearby homesteads. A short trail leads through the farm that comes alive in summer, and on spring and fall weekends, with living history demonstrations by park rangers and volunteers in period clothing. On the weekend afternoon when we show up, we encounter a bonus: a local bluegrass band picking on a small stage, as visitors sit beneath a shade tree enjoying the music.

The farm path leads across the parkway to a parking and picnic area for Humpback Gap Overlook and another trail, which accesses the Appalachian Trail. For the price of a moderately strenuous climb of less than a mile to Humpback Rocks, the reward is a spectacular view.

Down the road we come to Love, a tiny community at Milepost 16. If you need a place to stay, turn at VA 814 and travel a few hundred feet to Love Ridge Mountain Lodging, where there are mountain homes, cabins, and campsites available. The parkway doesn't allow commercial businesses or even signs along the road, so it helps to know where to look.

When you think of the parkway you might think of far-off valley vistas, but we also find creeks and lakes to hike along, tucked in the woods alongside the road. Otter Lake, at Milepost 63, is a nice place to stretch your legs and, from the looks of a small crowd with rods and reels on the banks, to fish. The lake is just south of Otter Creek, where there is a campground, and just north of the lowest point on the parkway, just below 650 feet, at the James River. The bridge crossing the river marks the beginning of a big, 13-mile climb to the highest point on the parkway in Virginia: 3,950 feet at Apple Orchard Mountain. The highest elevation on the parkway is at 6,500 feet at Richland Balsam, south of Mount Pisgah, North Carolina.

After Apple Orchard Mountain, we come down to Peaks of Otter, at Milepost 86, one of the more famous stops along the parkway, with a lodge and lake-view restaurant. At the visitor center, we find a museum and nearby a campground and several trails. The Sharp Top Trail is a 1.6-mile strenuous hike that begins near the camp store and leads to a panoramic view. In the

THE MOUNTAIN FARM MUSEUM AT HUMPBACK ROCKS VISITOR CENTER IS A GOOD PLACE TO STRETCH YOUR LEGS AND LEARN ABOUT LIFE IN THE MOUNTAINS IN TIMES PAST

A VISIT TO THE NATIONAL D-DAY MEMORIAL IN BEDFORD IS A MOVING EXPERIENCE

past, we've hiked the 3.3-mile Harkening Hill Loop, which begins behind the visitor center and includes some steep terrain on the way to another superb view. We take a stroll around Abbott Lake, next to the restaurant, which is less than a mile and, just that, a stroll.

The thing about driving the parkway is that your inclination is to stop at every overlook, walk every trail, and shoot pictures at every opportunity. The problem, of course, is if you do that it will take you just shy of forever to reach your destination. Pick your spots. One of the spots we pick is the 4-mile, one-way driving loop on Roanoke Mountain, starting at Mile Post 120. Several overlooks along the way provide views of the city of Roanoke and Roanoke Valley.

Past Roanoke, the parkway opens into farmland with split-rail fences marking pastures dotted with hay bales. At Milepost 171, we reach the turn-off for Chateau Morrisette Winery, going west on Black Ridge Road and then south on Winery Road. Chateau Morrisette is one of two wineries in the neighborhood; Villa Appalaccia, 2 miles north, on VA 720, is the other. I've stopped at Chateau Morrisette in the past to shop for a few bottles of wine in the impressive hospitality center. Tastings and tours are also available. The winery's restaurant is next door. I've never been fortunate enough to arrive when one of the periodic music festivals is held on the lovely grounds. I can imagine enjoying a nice glass of merlot as music drifts across the mountainside. You can also swing over to the fine little town of Floyd, just a few miles away. (I cover Floyd in the chapter on the Crooked Road.)

Now, though, we are heading to Meadows of Dan, but, first, Mabry Mill, perhaps the most-photographed spot on the parkway. The rustic mill, at Milepost 176, couldn't be in a prettier setting, with a pond in the foreground,

The 469-mile-long **Blue Ridge Parkway** is typically the National Park Service's most visited unit. It connects the **Shenandoah** and **Great Smoky Mountains** national parks, stretching from Rockfish Gap in the north to the southernmost point near Cherokee, North Carolina. Almost 220 miles of the parkway is in Virginia.

Construction of the parkway began in 1935, during the Great Depression, as a way to create jobs. Thousands of Civilian Conservation Corps workers built much of the parkway, working with private contractors, state and federal highway departments, and Italian and Spanish stonemasons. The road was completed in sections for the next 52 years, the final portion—around Grandfather Mountain, North Carolina—opening in 1987.

The parkway is a favorite drive for motorcyclists as well as motorists, particularly in autumn when the leaves turn, but besides the beauty, everyone must take note of the descending radius curves that require drivers to tighten their steering as they go through them. Keep an eye out, too, for bicyclists, hikers, deer, and, on occasion, sheep. Keep this in mind, too: During the winter months, parts of the parkway often are closed because of snow or ice.

THE PARKWAY GENTLY BENDS THROUGH THE COUNTRYSIDE SOUTH OF ROANOKE

trees surrounding it, and the parkway running alongside it. As long as you stop—you have to shoot a picture, remember?—you might as well take a walk on the interpretive trail, which provides a glimpse into life in these hills in years past. Across the parking lot from the mill is a gift shop. The adjacent restaurant closed at the end of 2023 with plans to reopen in 2025.

Two miles down the road, we come to Meadows of Dan, a pleasant village where the parkway crosses US 58, with several shops, a few places to eat, and a candy factory. A highway bypass, part of a major expansion of US 58, allows you to skirt the little town entirely. But if you have the time, don't, for reasons beyond the fact that even at the height of the summer the nights are refreshingly cool.

"People are kind here," one resident told me years ago. "They'll call and say, 'I'm going down the mountain to Stuart or Mount Airy or Galax—and it's a long way down the mountain—and they'll say, 'Need anything?'"

SIDE TRACKS

Depending on your available time and your sense of adventure, a number of attractions await just a few miles off the parkway:

Crabtree Falls, the highest vertical-drop, cascading waterfall east of the Mississippi River. A trail leads to a series of overlooks for viewing the falls. Leave the parkway near Milepost 27, and head east for 6 miles through the village of **Montebello**. Website: www.nelsoncounty.com.

Roanoke, the largest urban area along the parkway. Four exits off the parkway—between Mileposts 105 (US 460) and 121 (US 220)—take you to Roanoke, just a few miles to the west. Website: www.visitroanoke.com.

Sherando Lake Recreation Area, part of the George Washington National Forest, two lakes for swimming, boating, and fishing, plus camping and hiking. Milepost 16. Take VA 814 west for 4.5 miles to the park. Website: www.fs.usda.gov.

Another is the **National D-Day Memorial Foundation** in Bedford. Leave the parkway near Milepost 86, at Peaks of Otter, and head southeast on VA 43 for 13 miles to Bedford. The address is 3 Overlord Circle, Bedford. Website: www.dday.org.

No community suffered more than Bedford in the landing operations of the Allied invasion of Normandy that began June 6, 1944. Bedford, a town of just more than 3,000, lost 23 young men in the invasion—19 in the first assault wave on Omaha Beach and four others in follow-up battles or from other circumstances related to D-Day. The Bedford Boys have come to be known far beyond the foothills of Virginia.

The giant arch, the statuary, and the water effects in the pool that simulate gunfire faced by troops tell pieces of D-Day's chilling story. It's a moving memorial, never more so than when you see the names of the 4,413 Allied troops who died etched on tablets encircling the plaza.

In Meadows of Dan, you can buy groceries and gas at Poor Farmer's Market—or hand-spun, hand-dyed yarns and spinning fiber at Greenberry House. A few hundred yards east of the parkway, you'll find Nancy's Candy Co., a candy factory and store. They'll be glad to have you watch while they make fudge, chocolates, and other goodies. Free samples, too. Sammy Shelor, one of America's best banjo pickers, is a resident of Meadows of Dan, which is on the Crooked Road, the state's designated musical heritage trail that winds through Southwest Virginia.

We will spend the night at a nearby cabin, Poor Farmer's Cabin, owned by Felecia Shelor, who also happens to be the proprietor of Poor Farmer's Market, where we pick up a few provisions to make dinner. Private cabins for rent are prevalent around the parkway, particularly this stretch through Southwest Virginia. Shelor rents the cabin on her farm north of town. The cabin, perched on a hill set against a rhododendron backdrop, has a kitchen, a bath, a soft bed, and a sweet view of the surrounding countryside.

For breakfast, we head to town to Shelor's old-style country store, a gathering spot for locals and a destination for visitors, who seek locally grown vegetables, hoop cheese, or fried pies. You can play checkers on the porch and fill the tank at the gas pumps out front. We eat breakfast there: country ham biscuits and hot coffee. We pick up a jar of local honey, too.

FOR GAS AND FOOD IN MEADOWS OF DAN, POOR FARMER'S MARKET IS A POPULAR STOP

ANGELA SCOTT AND HER FAMILY HAVE TURNED WOODRUFF'S CAFE AND PIE SHOP INTO A HAPPY DESTINATION

If you'd like something more than a jar of honey and you have fairly deep pockets, you might want to consider Primland, a 14,000-acre, luxury resort with golf, hunting, a mountaintop lodge, and even an observatory. Primland is southeast of Meadows of Dan.

Just down the parkway from Meadows of Dan at Milepost 180, we find Mayberry Presbyterian Church, one of the half-dozen rock churches once ministered by the Rev. Bob Childress, the mountain preacher who brought spirituality and education into the hills and hollows of the region. His life is chronicled in the book *The Man Who Moved a Mountain* by Richard C. Davids. His grandson, Stewart Childress, left a business career to continue his grandfather's legacy and attend seminary. For many years he served as the pastor at two of the churches, including Mayberry.

"It's a calling," Childress has told me. "I feel like it's something where I can actually make a difference. I never really felt like I made that much of a difference in corporate America."

Just south of the church is Mayberry Trading Post, a general store constructed in the 1890s as the Mayberry post office. We hop back on the

If you like pie (and nice people), visit **Woodruff's Store Café and Pie Shop**. Says proprietor Angela Scott, with a smile, "We just have sandwiches so people can have lunch before they have pie."

Woodruff's is 10 minutes east of the Blue Ridge Parkway, on VA 130, in Amherst County, in a little community called Agricola (though the official address is in Monroe, at 3297 Elon Road). It's a small, family-run place that's open only a few days each week, and you need to call ahead to make sure they have fresh pies available. Even if they don't have pies, it's worth the trip.

For years, the two-story cinderblock building was a general store operated by Angela Scott's parents; it was also the family's home. The store closed in 1983 and mostly sat vacant for the next 15 years until Scott decided to reopen it, though she wasn't quite sure what she wanted to sell. She started a deli and made a few pies, which the customers seemed to like. A few years later, when it came time to get a new sign after a motorist plowed through the old one, Scott told a sign-maker friend to add "pie shop" to the name of the place. Good thing. Customers travel there from all over the state and beyond. Woodruff's has been featured in national publications, and Al Roker even came to see them to do a piece for NBC's *Today Show*.

As a small operation, Woodruff's has a limited menu: a few kinds of sandwiches and, when the weather turns cool, pinto beans and cornbread. The pie selection is widely varied, including seasonal fruit pies.

Scott and her sisters run the shop, and for many years their charming mother, Mary Fannie Woodruff, held court at a back table as a sort of official greeter. Their mom died in 2021 at the age of 104. Her spirit lives on.

Scott tells me that business was slow after she first opened, and some days they didn't have a single customer. Scott was tired, as she was waiting tables at night at another restaurant to keep money coming in, and she was discouraged and about ready to give up. She recalls her mom telling her to keep the faith. "It's going to be all right," her mom told her. "I just believe it's going to work out." Her mom was right.

IF YOU LIKE PIE—AND NICE PEOPLE—THE WOODRUFF CAFÉ AND PIE SHOP IS A MUST STOP

CHATEAU MORRISETTE WINERY IN FLOYD COUNTY HAS WINE TASTINGS, A RESTAURANT, AND OCCASIONAL MUSIC FESTIVALS

parkway and head toward the North Carolina border. Before we get there, though, we pass Orchard Gap, at Milepost 193, where an unusual sort of lodging exists: Grassy Creek Cabooses, featuring three train cabooses converted into cabins and another cabin constructed to look like an old depot. All have whirlpool tubs and unmatched views of the surrounding mountains.

Now, here's a dining tip: If you're close to Fancy Gap, near Milepost 200, stop at the Lake View Restaurant, just off the parkway on US 52. There's not much of a lake to view, but the food is great. A family diner, the Lake View is unpretentious and always busy when I show up. I can't ever get past the fried chicken, which is outstanding. Another tip: order the outstanding coconut crème pie *before* dinner just so they don't run out by dessert time. That happened to a friend once. But it won't happen again.

The hills come alive with country, bluegrass, and old-time mountain music at the Blue Ridge Music Center, an outdoor amphitheater and indoor interpretive center at Milepost 213, just before the North Carolina state line. The music center is operated by the National Park Service and the National Council for the Traditional Arts. If you're lucky enough to see an outdoor show, pack a picnic dinner, bring a lawn chair, and find a spot on the tiered hillside. Like the parkway itself, the music center is a no-hurry zone. Sit back, relax, and tap your toes to the music.

IN THE AREA

Accommodations

GRASSY CREEK CABOOSES, 278 Caboose Lane, Fancy Gap. Call 276-398-1100. Website: www.grassycreekcabooses.com.

LOVE RIDGE MOUNTAIN LODGING, 45 Royal Oaks Lane, Love. Call 1-540-943-7625. Website: www.loveridgeva.com. Cabins and camping.

PEAKS OF OTTER LODGE, 85554 Blue Ridge Parkway, Bedford. Call 866-387-9905. Website: www.peaksofotter.com. Lodging and dining.

Attractions and Recreation

BLUE RIDGE MUSIC CENTER, Music Center Road, Galax. Call 276-236-5309. Website: www.blueridgemusiccenter.org.

MAYBERRY PRESBYTERIAN CHURCH, 1127 Mayberry Church Road, Meadows of Dan.

PRIMLAND, 2000 Busted Rock Road, Meadows of Dan. Call 855-876-6593. Website: www.primland.com. Resort featuring golf, hunting, lodging, horse-back riding.

Dining

LAKE VIEW RESTAURANT, Fancy Gap Highway, Fancy Gap. Call 276-728-7841. Family dining.

WOODRUFF'S STORE CAFE AND PIE SHOP, at 3297 Elon Road. Call 434-384-1650. Website: www.woodruffspieshop.com.

Other Contacts

BLUE RIDGE PARKWAY, National Park Service. Website: www.nps.gov/blri.

MEADOWS OF DAN, off the Parkway at Milepost 178. Website: www.visitmeadowsofdan.com.

THE
CROOKED
ROAD
VIRGINIA'S HERITAGE
MUSIC•TRAIL

18

THE CROOKED ROAD

Heritage Music Trail of Southwest Virginia

ESTIMATED LENGTH: 300 miles

ESTIMATED TIME: A full week, or, better yet, make occasional day or overnight trips to the area

HIGHLIGHTS: Live music—some scheduled, some not—all along the road in theaters, fire halls, and groceries. Places you won't want to miss include: **Floyd Country Store**, in particular, on Friday evenings or Sunday afternoons. The **Galax Fiddlers Convention** in August, or Galax's **Barr's Fiddle Shop** every day. The wild ponies of **Grayson Highlands State Park**. **Virginia Creeper Trail** and **New River Trail State Park**, a pair of rails-to-trails biking and hiking trails. **Southwest Virginia Cultural Center & Marketplace** in Abingdon. **The Birthplace of Country Music Museum** in Bristol. Shows at the **Barter Theatre** in **Abingdon** and **Carter Family Fold** in **Hiltons**. **Ralph Stanley Museum and Traditional Mountain Music Center** in **Clintwood**. The beauty and remoteness of **Breaks Interstate Park**, the so-called Grand Canyon of the South. A visit to **Big Stone Gap**. Breakfast at the **Hillsville Diner**. Dinner at **The Tavern**, an actual tavern constructed in 1779, in Abingdon.

GETTING THERE: The Crooked Road, which for much of its path follows the twists and turns of US 58 through the mountains and valleys of Southwest Virginia, runs roughly between **Rocky Mount** in Franklin County and **Breaks Interstate Park** on the Virginia-Kentucky line. As for getting there, it depends on which end you consider the starting point. To reach Rocky Mount in the east, take US 220 from Roanoke and go south for 25 miles. To reach Breaks Interstate Park in the west, take US 460 west from Bluefield for 65 miles to Vansant, west on VA 83 to Haysi, and north on VA 80 to the park.

LEFT: A SIGN OUTSIDE BREAKS INTERSTATE PARK ALERTS MOTORISTS THAT MUSIC AND CURVY ROADS ARE AHEAD

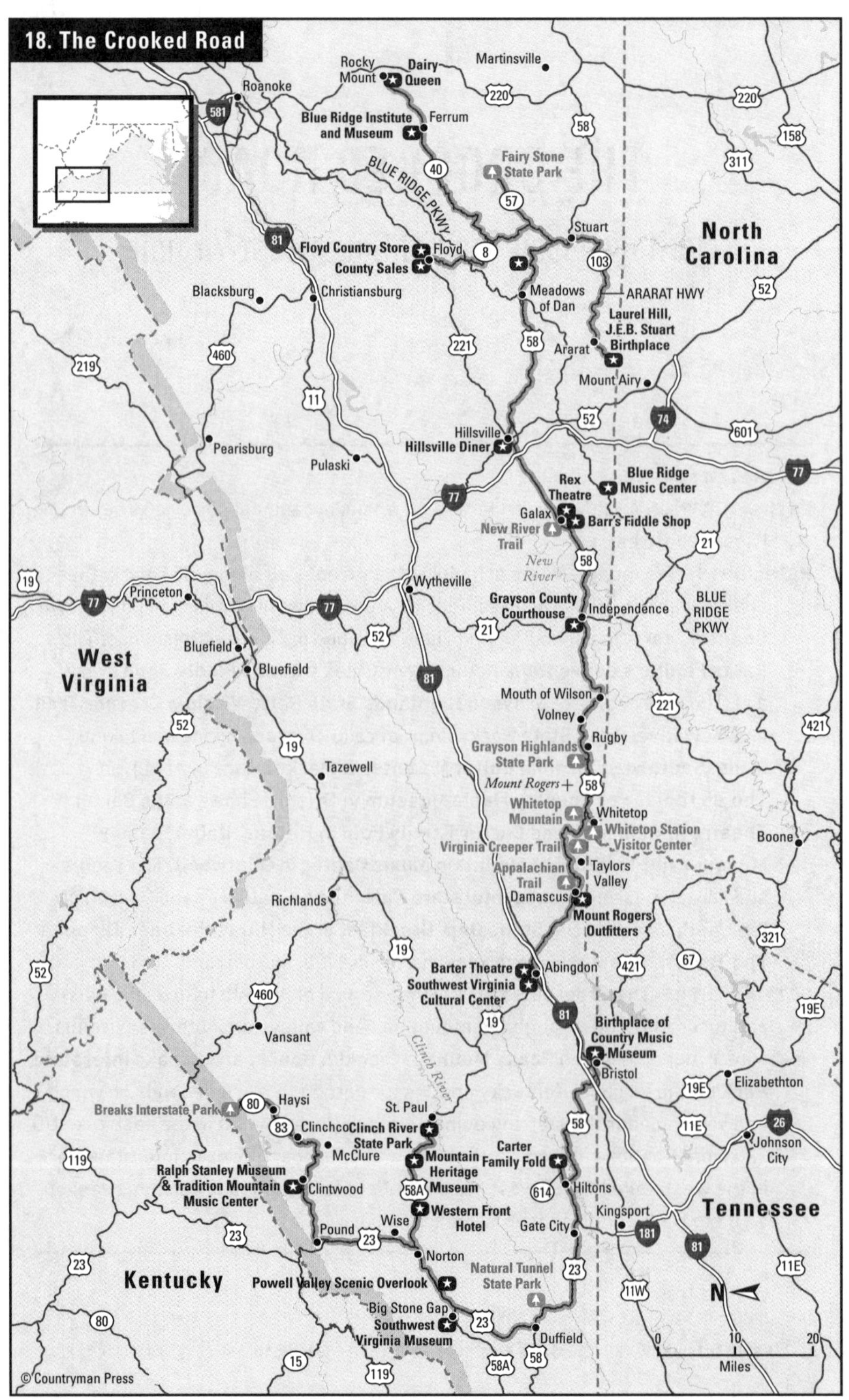
18. The Crooked Road
Rocky Mount
Dairy Queen
Martinsville
Roanoke
Blue Ridge Institute and Museum
Ferrum
Fairy Stone State Park
BLUE RIDGE PKWY
Stuart
North Carolina
Floyd Country Store
Floyd
County Sales
Meadows of Dan
ARARAT HWY
Laurel Hill, J.E.B. Stuart Birthplace
Blacksburg
Christiansburg
Ararat
Mount Airy
Pearisburg
Pulaski
Hillsville
Hillsville Diner
Rex Theatre
Blue Ridge Music Center
Galax
Barr's Fiddle Shop
New River Trail
New River
Princeton
Wytheville
Grayson County Courthouse
Independence
BLUE RIDGE PKWY
Bluefield
Bluefield
West Virginia
Mouth of Wilson
Volney
Rugby
Grayson Highlands State Park
Tazewell
Mount Rogers
Whitetop Mountain
Whitetop
Whitetop Station Visitor Center
Boone
Virginia Creeper Trail
Taylors Valley
Appalachian Trail
Damascus
Richlands
Mount Rogers Outfitters
Barter Theatre
Abingdon
Southwest Virginia Cultural Center
Birthplace of Country Music Museum
Vansant
Clinch River
Bristol
Elizabethton
Breaks Interstate Park
Haysi
St. Paul
Clinchco
Clinch River State Park
McClure
Mountain Heritage Museum
Carter Family Fold
Ralph Stanley Museum & Tradition Mountain Music Center
Clintwood
Hiltons
Johnson City
Western Front Hotel
Tennessee
Gate City
Kingsport
Wise
Pound
Norton
Kentucky
Powell Valley Scenic Overlook
Natural Tunnel State Park
Big Stone Gap
Southwest Virginia Museum
Duffield
N
0
10
20
Miles
© Countryman Press

The Crooked Road isn't an easy drive—it's not The *Straight* Road, after all—but it sure is fun. The banjo and fiddle sound of Appalachian music helps define this region of Virginia, and serves as the soundtrack for the lives of many families for whom music was a great escape and a shared joy in an otherwise isolated existence. Seemingly around every curve of the Crooked Road you'll find something music-related: an annual festival or a weekly jam session, an engaging museum or a luthier's workshop. Wayside kiosks all along the road provide information about the musical contributions of specific areas and, when you tune your radio to the correct frequency, a sampling of picking, singing, and narration that sheds further light on the locality and its story.

Former Virginia State Folklorist Jon Lohman, now executive director of the Center for Cultural Vibrancy, describes the Crooked Road as a "vibrant center for the continuation of these cherished musical traditions."

"While Virginia is home to an abundant number of excellent driving trails passing through important historic sites, the Crooked Road engages the traveler in living, breathing communities, where traditional mountain music is played with buoyant joy and breathtaking artistry," Lohman tells me. "The visitor to the Crooked Road will see the finest players in the most intimate and relaxed of settings—local jam sessions, fiddlers conventions, and cozy, time-worn dance halls. Whether one is a musician or a toe-tapper, the Crooked Road is, simply put, one hell of a good time."

There aren't many traffic lights along the 330-mile route that includes nineteen counties, fifty towns, and four cities, but there are other impediments. Getting behind a rumbling coal truck on a steep, narrow, tortuous stretch of pavement in Dickenson County will challenge your patience and make you adopt an unhurried approach to your driving tour. Which is another way of saying: Don't be too ambitious. A map of the Crooked Road lying on your kitchen table looks like a day's drive, maybe two, but don't be fooled. The Crooked Road, primarily two lanes for much of its length, will never be mistaken for an interstate highway, so dial down your travel expectations. Besides, the joy of driving the road is not *driving* the road; it's in the stopping, looking, and listening. Poking around small towns or hiking mountain trails. Enjoying the hospitality of local residents or pulling up a chair at a local diner. And, of course, hearing the music. That's what it's all about.

The best thing to do before driving the Crooked Road is to check out its website, www.thecrookedroadva.com, and see what's available when and where you're going. There's nothing worse than showing up on a Saturday evening for a weekly music jam that was held the night before. And if you want to spend a little time reading up on what you'll be seeing, try *A Guide to the Crooked Road: Virginia's Heritage Music Trail* by the late, great Joe Wilson, who helped inspire the creation of the trail. The book is informative, enlightening, and fun.

Let's hit the road.

The Crooked Road connects the dots of major musical venues throughout the region, beginning on the eastern edge 10 miles west of Rocky Mount on VA 40 at the Blue Ridge Institute and Museum at Ferrum College, the official center for Blue Ridge folklore. The institute interprets and showcases the region's folk heritage through exhibitions, festivals, and a permanent collection of recordings, photographs, and documents. The museum is open year-round. The Blue Ridge Folklife Festival, a popular event, is held here every October, on the fourth Saturday. The day features music, old-time crafts, and contests involving farm animals, such as herding dogs and jumping mules.

Before you get to Ferrum, though, you might want to check out Rocky Mount, the sort of small town where you can find live music at a place like Dairy Queen (995 Franklin Street), which hosts a music jam every Thursday morning. You can't beat bluegrass and Blizzards.

Floyd, at the intersection of US 221 and VA 8, is the quintessential small town with a single traffic light. But Floyd has something else going for it: a vibrant community of musicians and artists, and a spirit that has enabled a series of local nonprofit thrift shops, Angels in the Attic, to donate hundreds of thousands of dollars to local charitable organizations over the years. Oh, and there's lots of music, mostly bluegrass and old-time mountain music, but also Celtic, jazz, and rock.

The musical hub is the Floyd Country Store, where the Friday night jam-

THE FLOYD COUNTRY STORE IS AN OLD-TIME GENERAL STORE AND A MUSIC HALL WITH ITS LIVE SHOWS AND JAM SESSIONS

THE SUNDAY AFTERNOON JAM SESSIONS AT THE FLOYD COUNTRY STORE BRINGS TOGETHER MUSICIANS OF ALL AGES

borees and Sunday afternoon jams draw big crowds. You also can find live music at places such as Dogtown Roadhouse, where you can dine on wood-fired pizza and listen to live music. But the town's sidewalks seem to be as good a spot as any to find live music. On days or evenings of indoor performances, it's not unusual to find little groups of musicians congregating outside to pick a little and share a tune. You just can't beat wandering around the town most any time or day of the week, poking your head in shops or just enjoying the pleasant, small-town vibe.

If you can time your visit accordingly, the annual outdoor FloydFest in late July, featuring four days of all kinds of music in a spectacular mountain setting, is a must-do event.

Stuart is a 25-mile drive south of Floyd on VA 8. Named for Confederate General J. E. B. Stuart, who was born at nearby Laurel Hill, the town offers musical diversions plus other attractions. Fairy Stone State Park, 20 miles to the northeast of Stuart, off VA 8 and VA 57, is named for the rare mineral crosses you can find in abundance in the park. The legend goes something like this: Fairies who once cavorted in the area wept when they received word of Jesus's death. As their tears fell to earth, they crystallized to form crosses. The crosses are actually stones made of staurolite, a combination of silica, iron, and aluminum that crystallizes at sharp angles, resulting in

We walk into **Floyd Country Store**, past the old-time soda fountain and the old-fashioned barrels of penny candy, all the way to the back, where we find 13 people seated in a circle playing fiddles, banjos, mandolins, dulcimers, and guitars. Maybe twice as many are gathered around them, listening, tapping their toes, and applauding appreciatively.

This is the weekly Sunday afternoon jam, a time for anyone to bring an instrument and join in. The Friday Night Jamborees are a little more formal, with an hour of gospel music and then scheduled old-time bands and dancing. Sundays are casual. We stand and listen for a while. The performers take turns choosing songs and singing. It's democracy with a pick and bow.

The store opened in 1910 as a farmers supply store, and it remained a hardware store, or general store, and a community gathering place for most of the century. During the 1990s, it stopped being a store, although it stayed open one night a week for music: the Friday Night Jamboree. Woody and Jackie Crenshaw bought the store and renovated it, making it a country store once again as well as a vibrant community gathering spot. Current owners Dylan Locke and Heather Krantz enjoy creating unforgettable experiences with the music and dancing and offering all kinds of things that you might have found in such stores long ago: toy tractors, handmade dolls, and rolling pins. I'm not sure about the tradition of the "potted possum," but I once found a can on a shelf for $2.75 if you're interested. They also have an extensive collection of old-time and bluegrass recordings for sale, as well as all kinds of clothes. On Friday nights, they roll out the merchandise and make room for the dance floor.

"We are honored and heartened to have the opportunity to be the next stewards of the Floyd Country Store," Dylan Locke says. "We have a deep respect for the people, the music, and the culture that makes the Floyd Country Store such a vibrant part of this community. Our focus will be to respect and continue the efforts of all of the folks along the way who had the vision for this community jewel, to ensure that the Floyd Country Store is a welcoming place for friends and family to enjoy the music, dance and share the stories of the Blue Ridge Mountains."

The cafe offers a diverse menu dominated by salads, sandwiches, and sides—from hummus to collard greens, from reubens (classic or vegetarian) to the local standby of pintos and cornbread. We eat in a window booth, listening to the music being played in the back of the store and watching people strolling the sidewalk. It's a fine way to spend a Sunday afternoon.

the cross-like shape. Geologists tell us these crystals were formed by very specific geothermal processes.

Laurel Hill, site of Stuart's birthplace, is in Ararat, about 25 miles southwest of Stuart off VA 8 and VA 103, and the property is open for self-guided tours, though the house itself burned down in the 1840s and was never rebuilt.

Leaving Stuart and heading west on US 58, you climb higher into the Blue

Ridge. The first time I ever drove this stretch of road, we motored to the top of a particularly twisty stretch of road to a graffiti-covered overlook known as Lovers Leap, with a small parking lot and a huge view of the surrounding mountains. All of that is changing as part of a major highway expansion project. The 36-mile section between Stuart and Hillsville is the last remaining section of the widening of US 58 from Virginia Beach to Interstate 77.

Head down the mountain, continuing west on US 58, and reach Meadows of Dan, a crossroads with the Blue Ridge Parkway (which we've covered in the chapter on the parkway). From there, it's a 20-mile drive to Hillsville, the seat of Carroll County at US 58's intersection with I-77, and home to the annual Labor Day Gun Show and Flea Market, sponsored by the local Veterans of Foreign Wars post, which typically attracts massive crowds every year.

Food-wise, you ought to stop for a bite at the Hillsville Diner, a true, old-style diner that's been a landmark in town since the 1940s, when it was hauled from its previous location in Mount Airy, North Carolina.

Next up, a dozen miles to the west on US 58, is Galax, an old farming and factory town that's twice the size of Hillsville. You'll find "big box" stores here, as well as a number of attractions, most notably the annual Galax Old Fiddlers Convention, a weeklong event of country and mountain music hosted by the local Moose Lodge in the town's Felts Park. Thousands pitch tents and camp for the entire week; others drive in for a day or two. The stage serves as the focal point as musicians compete for cash prizes, but there's just as much music—even more—in the parking lot and campground where festival-goers bring out their guitars, fiddles, and banjos and sit around in lawn chairs and play old, familiar tunes deep into the night.

When the convention's not going on, you can hear live music on Friday nights at the Rex Theatre, and in the warm-weather months down the road at the Blue Ridge Music Center and Museum, 6 miles south of Galax. (See chapter on Blue Ridge Parkway.)

Stroll through downtown Galax, stopping in one of the antique shops or maybe **Barr's Fiddle Shop**, a gathering spot on Main Street for musicians who want to try out one of the handmade fiddles, banjos, or dulcimers, or just chat music. If music makes you hungry, head over to Tlaquepaque, an excellent Mexican restaurant just before downtown in a nondescript, warehouse-looking building on US 58. I look forward to eating there every time I'm in the area. I also enjoy El Torito, a short drive along US 58 toward downtown.

If you have the time and your bicycle, you might consider pedaling a few miles on the **New River Trail**, a 57-mile-long linear state park whose southern terminus is Galax. A parking area for the multiuse trail is just off US 58 near downtown. The trail follows an old rail bed, paralleling the scenic New River for much of its length. The trail features two tunnels, three major bridges (the longest more than 1,000 feet), and more than two dozen shorter

PEDALING THROUGH A TUNNEL IS PART OF THE EXPERIENCE ON THE NEW RIVER TRAIL, A CONVERTED RAILWAY

bridges and trestles. Camping is available along the trail, as well as several access points for parking or arranging pickups or drop-offs if you don't want to travel the entire trail at once. The trail certainly has some climbs, but you don't need to be a veteran cyclist to do it. How do I know this? My son, when he was 6 years old and had been riding without training wheels for only a few weeks, pedaled the entire trail over a period of a few days.

US 58 surges westward, following along the New River for a time and then leaving behind a brief period of four-lane road for the familiar two lanes as it reaches **Independence**. Fifteen miles from Galax, Independence has a pretty courthouse built in 1908 that doubles as a small museum and visitor center, a Fourth of July parade (of course), and a local newspaper called the *Declaration*.

Now, the Crooked Road starts to get really crooked. The road rises, falls, and bends through lovely countryside and past Christmas tree farms, one of this area's greatest cash crops. It ventures beyond **Mouth of Wilson**—home of Oak Hill Academy, one of the nation's best and best-known high school basketball teams—to Volney, about 17 miles past Independence at the **Corner Market & Cafe**, where US 58 makes a sharp left turn. If you keep straight, you'll be on VA 16, and you'll miss all of the fun.

Grayson Highlands State Park is next, and I cover that in its own chapter.

If you're lucky, you might run into one of the musicians who make this area a hotbed for homegrown music—someone like Wayne Henderson. A first-rate, finger-picking guitarist, Henderson lives in the tiny community of **Rugby**—"population of 7," Henderson likes to tell audiences—and has played on stages all over the world, including Carnegie Hall. He's also a master instrument-maker and a great storyteller. Get him to tell you the one about the elephant that escaped from the zoo and wandered deep into the hills.

If you're in the area in mid-May, make plans to attend the annual **Whitetop Mountain Ramp Festival**. Held the third Sunday of May, the festival celebrates the wild leeks that grow in the surrounding mountains. There's music, arts and crafts, and lots of food. You won't want to miss the ramp eating contest that's always highly competitive and entertaining—the year I attended the festival, bottles of mouthwash were among the prizes—but just don't stand too close.

It's only about 30 miles from Grayson Highlands to the next town, **Damascus**, but it's about an hour ride as the road slinks this way and that through the mountains. Damascus is known as Trail Town for the various trails that intersect here, most notably the **Appalachian Trail**, but also the **Virginia Creeper Trail**, the **Trans-America National Bicycle Trail**, the **Iron Mountain Trail**, the **Daniel Boone Trail**, and, of course, **the Crooked Road.**

Also known as the Friendliest Town on the (Appalachian) Trail, Damascus is a happy sight for hikers who've been in the woods for weeks. They can get a hot meal, a hot shower, and a warm bunk at The Place, a hostel for hikers operated by the local United Methodist Church. If hikers are living high on the hog, they might spring for a night at one of the town's bed-and-breakfast inns. Every May, the town holds Appalachian Trail Days, a weekend festival

NEW RIVER TRAIL CABINS IN GALAX ARE STEPS FROM NEW RIVER TRAIL STATE PARK

ATTORNEY FRANK KILGORE HAS TURNED HIS COLLECTION OF SOUTHWEST VIRGINIA ARTIFACTS INTO MOUNTAIN HERITAGE MUSEUM IN ST. PAUL

celebrating the AT and those who hike it, the timing coinciding with when many thru-hikers heading to the northern terminus of the trail at Mount Katahdin, Maine, come through.

There are a number of bike-rental shops that will provide wheels and a shuttle service to either end of the Creeper Trail, if you'd like to park in Damascus. Likewise, there are several outfitters stores if you need hiking or camping gear or, as in my case on a recent trip, hiking socks. I somehow managed to leave all of mine at home.

An easy 15-mile drive from Damascus, Abingdon is at the crossroads of US 58 and I-81. Abingdon is a great town with a nice combination of mountain friendliness and artistic sensibility. Nothing exemplifies those qualities better than the Barter Theatre, founded in the Great Depression on the concept of offering entertainment to the public in exchange for food from area farms and gardens to feed the actors. The Barter, now the state theater of Virginia, no longer accepts spinach, eggs, or country hams for admission, but the spirit lives on at the theater that has served as a starting ground for numerous actors who've gone on to perform on the national stage. Today, you can see Barter productions in two different venues in Abingdon: the traditional 500-seat theater, Gilliam Stage at Barter Theatre, on US 58, known locally as West Main Street, and Barter's Smith Theatre, a 167-seat setting for more intimate productions.

Artwork is on display and for sale at the Arts Depot (314 Depot Square), in an old freight station, and at Holston Mountain Artisans (214 Park St). Another good stop is Southwest Virginia Cultural Center & Marketplace, a visitor center for tourists that features the work of Southwest Virginia artists. You can get a real good feel for the region through crafts and music. The distinctive building is visible from I-81 at Exit 14.

Every summer, around the beginning of August, Abingdon hosts the Virginia Highlands Festival, a major event featuring performing arts, crafts, antiques, and more. As for lodging, Abingdon offers a variety of possibilities, from the upscale Martha Washington Inn and Spa, a one-time women's college across the street from the Barter, to cabins in the country. Because of Abingdon's location next to I-81, a full range of chain motels and hotels, is available, too.

Take I-81 south for 15 miles to Bristol, the birthplace of country music that sits on the Virginia-Tennessee border. In fact, the state line runs down the middle of State Street. In the music world, Bristol gained its historic standing in 1927 when Ralph Peer of the Victor Talking Machine Co. came to town to arrange the first commercial country music recordings that introduced local

THE BARTER THEATRE REMAINS A FEATURED ATTRACTION IN ABINGDON

The Carter Family Fold is all about promises.

"My mom promised her dad when he was dying that this place would live on," Rita Forrester tells me backstage at the Fold before the weekly Saturday evening show, "and I promised her I'd do everything in my power to maintain what she started."

Forrester's mother was Janette Carter, her grandfather the legendary A.P. Carter, who was involved in the famous 1927 Bristol recordings that put country music on the national map. And what Forrester has kept going is the Carter Family Fold at the **Carter Family Memorial Music Center** on the Carter family's old homeplace at the foot of **Clinch Mountain**. Every Saturday night, February through November, hundreds of enthusiasts park their cars and trucks on the grassy shoulders on the side roads near the Fold, and fill the seats of the semi-outdoor hall to listen to good, down-home music.

We arrive on a warm August night, the sides of the ingeniously designed hall raised to welcome any gentle breeze that happens by. Some people sprawl on the grassy hillside outside the hall, enjoying the night air. We take our seats under cover. Before the show starts, we amble down to the concession stand, manned by a small army of volunteers, where the menu includes hot dogs, popcorn, and such fare, but also a weekly special: this evening, it's soupbeans and homemade cornbread. My son and I order two specials and return to our seats to enjoy supper.

The **Tennessee Mafia Jug Band**, who mix old-time tunes with good-natured humor, headline tonight's show. People leave their seats to flat-foot dance in front of the stage. Audience members come from all over this region and from states across the country and beyond. One is from Russia, evidence of the Fold's draw as a major tourist attraction in this part of Virginia. At intermission, we walk over to A.P. Carter's birthplace, a log cabin, which is on the property and open to visitors. The A.P. Carter Store, now the Carter Family Museum, is next door to the Fold.

The music here is more than just catchy tunes. It's about family, culture, and pride. Forrester says she will get tired and discouraged and then someone comes up and tells her how much the Fold and the music mean to them or how it brings back such happy memories of growing up deep in these mountains. Then she knows what she's doing is worthwhile, a promise kept.

musicians such as Jimmie Rodgers, the Stonemans, and the Carter Family to the world.

Live music abounds in Bristol at places such as the Paramount, a historic theater, and the outdoor stage at the Downtown Center on State Street on summer evenings. If you like country music, you shouldn't miss the Birthplace of Country Music Museum, which tells the story of those 1927 recording sessions and connects it to the big role music plays in the region today.

SATURDAY NIGHTS AT THE CARTER FOLD—A RUSTIC YET INGENIOUS MUSIC HALL IN HILTONS—ARE A TIME TO VISIT WITH FRIENDS AND CELEBRATE THE HERITAGE OF MOUNTAIN MUSIC

The museum, which is an affiliate of the Smithsonian Institution, opened in 2014 in a downtown building that used to house Goodpasture Motors.

Back on US 58, we head west toward the far reaches of Southwest Virginia. Twenty miles west of Bristol, come to Hiltons, home of the Carter Family Fold, a performance hall and shrine to one of the first families of country music.

From Hiltons, follow the Crooked Road through Gate City and past Natural Tunnel State Park (see the chapter on the Wilderness Road) to Duffield, where you'll leave US 58 and take US 58-Alternate toward Big Stone Gap, the town made famous by *The Trail of the Lonesome Pine,* a 1908 romance novel by John Fox Jr., and, more recently, by the *Big Stone Gap* books of Adriana Trigiani and, later, a delightful movie, *Big Stone Gap,* which was filmed on location in the town. Big Stone Gap has the Southwest Virginia Museum, a state park housed in a mansion built in the 1880s that tells the story of a region, settled by pioneers, that later developed around the mining industry. On summer evenings, you can attend the stage version of *The Trail of the Lonesome Pine* in an outdoor theater in town.

Big Stone Gap is a town of about 5,000, founded in the mid-1800s at a time when industrialists were drawn to the area for its mineral and timber resources. It was said the town—then known as Mineral City—was poised to

A TREE-CARVING ALONG THE GREENBELT TRAIL IN BIG STONE GAP

become "the Pittsburgh of the South." Things didn't exactly work out that way, but Big Stone Gap, as it came to be known, has a good story and a rich past.

A good place to start a visit to Big Stone Gap is at the town's tourist information center, a vintage gas station that was spiffed up to be used as a set in the film. You can find the visitor center in the middle of town at 306 Wood Avenue, next door to the historic Mutual's Pharmacy, a landmark that readers of Trigiani's *Big Stone Gap* novel will recognize as being the pharmacy owned and operated by the star of her books, fictional pharmacist Ave Maria Mulligan (Ashley Judd played the role in the movie). The pharmacy, in real life, closed a few years ago, but the building is now occupied by Curklin's, a family-friendly restaurant with a wide-ranging menu. Right across the street is another dining option offering down-home food, Country Kitchen.

We spend a morning strolling along the Greenbelt Trail, a walking and biking path almost 3 miles long that encircles the town. The trail makes for a pleasant walk following the Powell River. There are several parks along the way, including Bullitt Park, which features a small football stadium, a playground, and a "splash pad" open in the summer. There also are benches and picnic tables along the way.

Head back to US 58-Alternate toward Norton. On the way, you will come

SIDE TRACKS

There are any number of small towns in Southwest Virginia, along the Crooked Road or a few miles off it, that are worth a visit. Together, they tell the story of an often overlooked region; individually, they have distinctive personalities, such as that of **St. Paul**, a town on US 58-Alternate and at the crossroads between the region's coalfields and farmland. St. Paul was a rocking place in the early 1900s after it passed an ordinance allowing the sale of alcohol—an oasis, so to speak, in a desert of dry counties. The saloons of St. Paul became a destination for men all over Southwest Virginia, and the results were not always pretty: bootlegging, gambling, fighting, and occasional killings.

"They called it 'the Western Front,'" said Frank Kilgore, an attorney and tireless booster of his hometown. "It was a real tourist draw."

Times have settled down, and St. Paul is making itself into a tourist draw once again. The town of about 1,000, which relied on the mining and railroad industries for years, is now bringing in visitors by way of its natural resources and beauty, specifically the Clinch River that flows through town.

Another of the town's sparkling assets is the "new" **Western Front**, a charming boutique hotel in a century-old building in the heart of town. The rooms and suites feature eclectic décor reflecting early Appalachia, and the room numbers are emblazoned with full-size paddles outside each door. Family friendly? Some rooms are equipped with bunk beds. A "fresh Mex and seafood" restaurant occupies the ground floor.

A prominent attraction is **Clinch River State Park**, open but still in development, which, when complete, will follow the river for 100 miles through a number of small towns in Southwest Virginia. The first segment of the park to open is the so-called Sugar Hill Unit at St. Paul, on land once owned by Kilgore, who developed the earliest trails with his son. St. Paul also is a gateway to the **Spearhead Trails system**, a series of trails for all-terrain vehicles, which bring in ATV enthusiasts. The town allows ATVs on its streets.

Kilgore, whose father was a coal miner, founded the **Mountain Heritage Museum and Gallery**, which features historic railroad, mining, and cultural artifacts he's been collecting for more than 50 years. The small museum, in the same building as his law practice, is open for tours by appointment: www.mountainheritagemuseum.org.

to the Powell Valley Scenic Overlook, which offers a small parking area and an easy, paved walk along the road to a lovely valley view. Back on the road, US 23 peels off to the north to Wise and Pound. Hang a right on VA 83, which will carry you to Clintwood, home of the Ralph Stanley Museum and Traditional Mountain Music Center, a magnificent tribute to one of the most respected figures in old-time music.

Stanley was born and raised in this part of Virginia, and lived in these mountains most of his life. He was a local legend and kept his band's tour bus

SIDE TRACKS

We walk into the **Ralph Stanley Museum and Traditional Mountain Music Center** about 3 p.m. on a Friday afternoon. A sign says the place closes at 4. The genial fellow at the desk—which is the shape of an oversized banjo—says not to worry. "Take your time," he says. "We always say, we'll welcome you in, but we'll never run you off."

We pay our admission and start a self-guided tour of the two-story museum. The building itself is a marvel, a restored, century-old, four-story mansion that in earlier days was a boarding house and a funeral home, though not at the same time. The museum takes you from Stanley's youth in nearby McClure, where he learned to sing a capella in the Primitive Baptist Church, to the present day, including when in his seventies he became a national sensation for his high, lonesome sound in the 2000 film, *O Brother, Where Art Thou?* Plenty of instruments and other artifacts are on display, but there's a lot more listening than looking here. You'll be given a set of headphones to carry around the museum and plug into various listening stations among the interactive exhibits. You easily could spend hours here, enjoying the recorded music and interviews with Stanley. As it was, we stayed past closing time, but, as promised, no one ran us off.

IN CLINTWOOD, THE RALPH STANLEY MUSEUM AND TRADITIONAL MOUNTAIN MUSIC CENTER IS A WELCOMING PLACE AND A FINE WAY TO SPEND AN AFTERNOON

BREAKS INTERSTATE PARK, STRADDLING THE BORDER OF VIRGINIA AND KENTUCKY, IS A PLACE OF UNMATCHED BEAUTY

parked behind a local grocery store. I interviewed Stanley near the end of his life and he gave me a tour of the museum, of which he was mighty proud.

The last 25 miles or so of the Crooked Road include some of its most challenging terrain. We leave Clintwood, continuing along VA 83 toward Clinchco and Haysi, where we will head north on VA 80 for the final stretch to Breaks Interstate Park. The roads through the coalfields are particularly crooked, often framed by a mountain on one side and a creek or small river on the other. There is little wiggle room. Don't go too fast. The aforementioned coal trucks will make sure of that.

Breaks Interstate Park straddles the Virginia-Kentucky border, one of only two "interstate" parks in America, meaning that it's governed by Virginia and Kentucky. About two-thirds of the park is in Virginia. It's been called the Grand Canyon of the South because of the deep gorge cut by the Russell Fork of the Big Sandy River. Breaks has a lot more trees than the Grand Canyon, though, which is something Daniel Boone noticed when he came through in the 1760s, searching for passes through the mountains—or breaks—to the west. The thick forest and the steep gorge, not to mention

TOP: THE BIRTHPLACE OF COUNTRY MUSIC MUSEUM IN BRISTOL REFLECTS ON THE MUSIC THAT MADE THE CITY FAMOUS
BOTTOM: THE LINE SEPARATING VIRGINIA AND TENNESSEE RUNS THROUGH DOWNTOWN BRISTOL

copperheads and rattlesnakes, encouraged Boone to turn around and find another passage.

We find the woods and the gorge, but, thankfully, no snakes on our visit. Ruggedly beautiful with scenic views of the gorge and surrounding countryside, Breaks is another world for those of us from the eastern part of Virginia. It's a long haul that's well worth the time and miles. We hike along a ridge on a well-marked trail that includes several overlooks. A coal train chugs along far below and then disappears into a mountain tunnel.

The park is remote, but not without amenities. We stay in the motel-like lodge, which offers spacious rooms at decent rates with unmatched views. There also are luxury cabins built on the shore of the park's 12-acre lake, rustic cottages, and a campground. On the mornings of our visit, I sit on the porch of our room sipping coffee, listening to the river rushing hundreds of feet below us, and watching the morning fog lift to reveal the sheer rock faces of the mountains across the gorge. Breakfast is served in the Rhododendron Restaurant in the park's visitor center, a wall of windows serving mountain scenes with plates filled with pancakes.

Besides hiking, we rent a pedal boat and tour the park's lake. The park also has a man-made pool and water park and an outdoor amphitheater, cut into the side of a mountain, where a number of music festivals are held annually, including the Labor Day Weekend Gospel Sing that attracts upwards of 20,000 visitors. I've attended one of those, and this much is true: The hills truly are alive with music. What could be more fitting on the Crooked Road?

IN THE AREA

Accommodations

Floyd

HOTEL FLOYD, 300 Rick Lewis Way, Floyd. Call 540-745-6080. Website: www.hotelfloyd.com. Built in 2007 and designated as a "Virginia Green Lodging" establishment for its use of sustainable building materials and furnishings.

PINE TAVERN LODGE, 585 Floyd Highway, Floyd. Call 540-745-4428. Website: www.thepinetavernlodge.com. Renovated, historic hotel.

Damascus and Abingdon

MARTHA WASHINGTON INN AND SPA, 150 W. Main Street, Abingdon. Call 276-628-3161. Website: www.themartha.com. Historic upscale inn across from the Barter Theatre.

MOUNTAIN LAUREL INN, 22750 JEB Stuart Highway, Damascus. Call 276-475-8822. Website: www.mountainlaurelinn.com. Country home built in the early 1900s.

St. Paul

WESTERN FRONT HOTEL, 3025 Fourth Avenue, St. Paul. Call 276-738-3040. Website: www.westernfronthotel.com. Boutique hotel in the heart of town.

Big Stone Gap

QUALITY INN & SUITES, 4609 Aerial Way, Big Stone Gap. Call 276-523-5911. Website: www.choicehotels.com. Lodge-like lobby lends the motel a rustic feel.

Breaks Interstate Park

RHODODENDRON LODGE, Breaks Interstate Park, Breaks. Call 276-865-4413. Website: www.breakspark.com. Motel with a view. Park also has cabins and cottages.

Attractions and Recreation

BARTER THEATRE, 127 W. Main Street, Abingdon. Call 276-628-3991. Website: www.bartertheatre.com. Year-round productions at the State Theatre of Virginia.

BLUE RIDGE INSTITUTE AND MUSEUM, 20 Museum Drive, Ferrum. Call 540-365-4416. Website: www.blueridgeinstitute.org. A repository for documenting, interpreting, and presenting the folk heritage of the Blue Ridge.

CARTER FAMILY FOLD, A. P. Carter Highway, Hiltons. Call 276-594-0676. Website: www.carterfamilyfold.org. Live music every Saturday night, museum, and store.

FLOYD COUNTRY STORE, 206 S. Locust Street, Floyd. Call 540-745-4563. Website: www.floydcountrystore.com. Old-style general store with live music on Friday nights and Sunday afternoons. Soups, sandwiches, homemade baked goods, and old-fashioned milk shakes.

RALPH STANLEY MUSEUM AND TRADITIONAL MOUNTAIN MUSIC CENTER, 249 Main Street, Clintwood. Call 276-926-8550. Website: www.ralphstanleymuseum.com. Tribute to Dickenson County native son and old-time mountain music star.

Dining

CURKLIN'S, 314 Wood Avenue, Big Stone Gap. Call 276-524-4983. Website: www.curklins.com. Family-friendly, casual dining.

HILLSVILLE DINER, 525 N Main Street, Hillsville. Call 276-266-3066. Website: www.facebook.com/p/The-Hillsville-Diner-100063739471368. True-blue diner.

THE TAVERN, 222 E. Main Street, Abingdon. Call 276-628-1118. Website: www.abingdontavern.com. Constructed in 1779, the building is one of the oldest west of the Blue Ridge. Used from the beginning as a tavern and overnight inn, The Tavern serves intercontinental cuisine in a casual setting. Closed Sunday.

TLAQUEPAQUE, 1003 E. Stuart Dr., Galax. Call 540-236-5060. Website: www.facebook.com/TlaquepaqueGalax. Mexican restaurant with good food and fast service.

Other Contacts

SOUTHWEST VIRGINIA CULTURAL CENTER & MARKETPLACE, One Heartwood Circle, Abingdon. Call 276-492-2400. Websites: www.swvaculturalcenter.com or www.visitswva.org.

THE CROOKED ROAD: VIRGINIA'S HERITAGE MUSIC TRAIL, One Heartwood Circle, Abingdon. Call 276-492-2400. Website: thecrookedroadva.com/. Information on maps, accommodations, and attractions along the route.

19

WILDERNESS ROAD

Onward to Cumberland Gap

ESTIMATED LENGTH: 100 miles

ESTIMATED TIME: 8 hours

HIGHLIGHTS: Stopovers at **Natural Tunnel State Park** and **Wilderness Road State Park**, a scenic valley drive through the far southwestern corner of Virginia, and a visit to historic **Cumberland Gap** itself.

GETTING THERE: From Bristol, which is on I-81 and straddles the Virginia–Tennessee line, head west on US 58 to Cumberland Gap.

Daniel Boone, the legendary frontiersman, could be the patron saint for anyone who has done any traveling in unfamiliar settings, not only for blazing trails through the wilderness but for his wry reflection of it.

"I can't say as ever I was lost," he famously said, "but I was bewildered once for three days."

When I see that quotation posted in an exhibit at the visitor center at Natural Tunnel State Park, I do what I do every time I see or hear it: smile. Although I can't say I've been as fortunate as Boone, for I have been lost *and* bewildered, sometimes all at once.

Getting lost is still possible in this rural corner of Virginia, but not likely if you stick to US 58. The road roughly follows the last stretch of the old Wilderness Trail that Boone and his axmen fashioned, hacking through the forests and mountains to reach Cumberland Gap in 1775. Easy to navigate and often four lanes, US 58 presents far less of a challenge than what Boone faced when he was cutting through the steep, rough terrain, creating a gateway to the western frontier.

LEFT: THE ROAD TO CUMBERLAND GAP CARRIES THE TRAVELER THROUGH A GORGEOUS VALLEY OF PASTURES WITH MOUNTAIN BACKDROPS

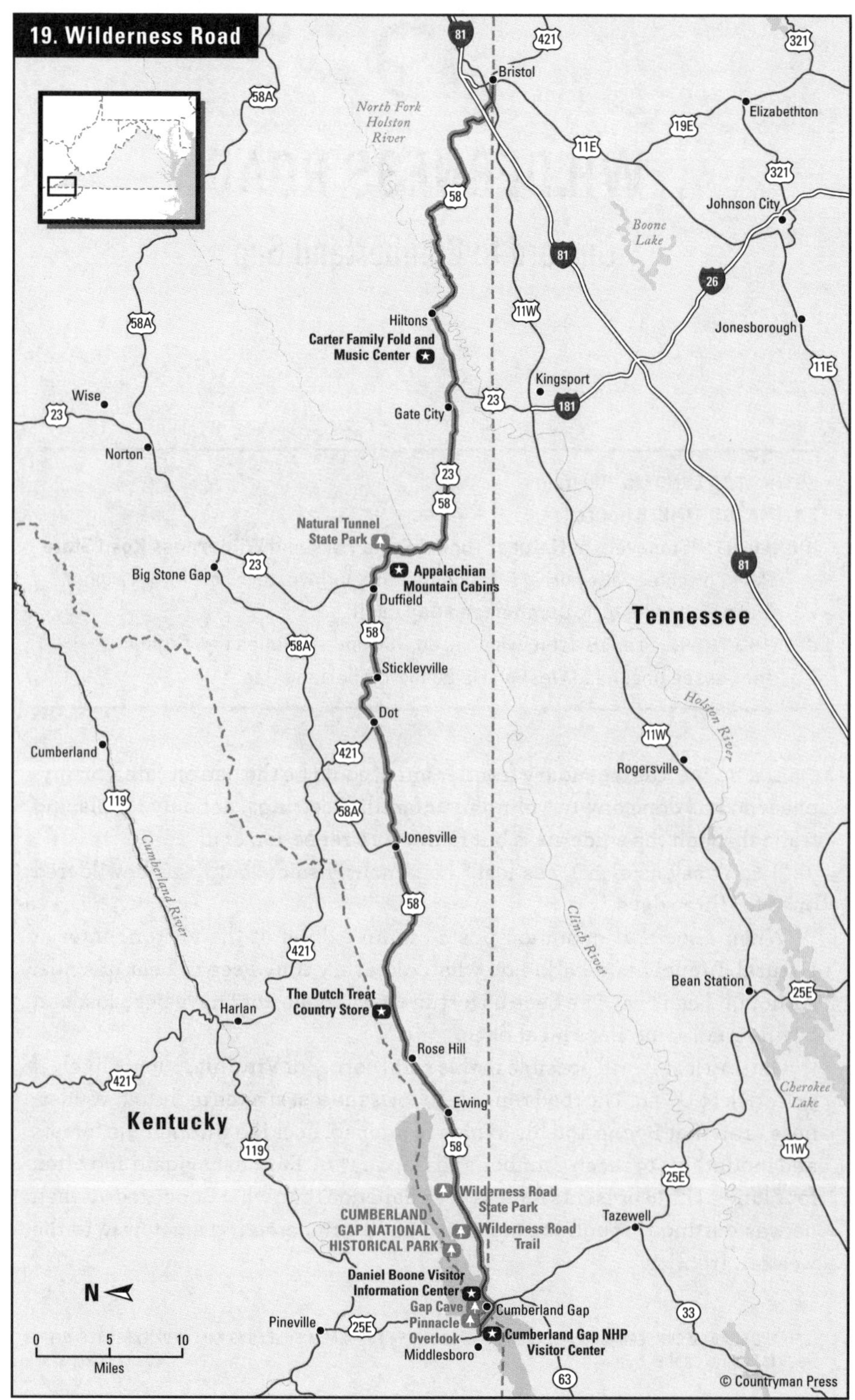
19. Wilderness Road
Bristol
North Fork Holston River
Elizabethton
Johnson City
Boone Lake
Hiltons
Carter Family Fold and Music Center
Jonesborough
Kingsport
Wise
Gate City
Norton
Natural Tunnel State Park
Big Stone Gap
Appalachian Mountain Cabins
Duffield
Tennessee
Stickleyville
Holston River
Dot
Cumberland
Rogersville
Jonesville
Cumberland River
Clinch River
Bean Station
The Dutch Treat Country Store
Harlan
Rose Hill
Cherokee Lake
Ewing
Kentucky
Wilderness Road State Park
CUMBERLAND GAP NATIONAL HISTORICAL PARK
Wilderness Road Trail
Tazewell
Daniel Boone Visitor Information Center
Gap Cave
Cumberland Gap
Pineville
Pinnacle Overlook
Cumberland Gap NHP Visitor Center
Middlesboro
N
0
5
10
Miles
© Countryman Press

We make our way west from Bristol into a part of Virginia that many Virginians never see. We will be more than 400 miles from the Atlantic coast by the time we reach Cumberland Gap, the westernmost point in Virginia that is as far west as Detroit. On previous trips here, I have met residents surprised and pleased to see someone from Richmond, their state capital.

"Most people think the state of Virginia ends at Exit 7," a man in the little community of Stickleyville told me, speaking of one of the I-81 exits in Bristol. "They say we're a suburb of Tennessee and Kentucky."

Indeed, at another stop on an earlier journey, folks living near Cumberland Gap introduced me as being from "Richmond, *Virginia*." It seemed an odd reference until it dawned on me. Richmond, *Kentucky*, is 350 miles closer than Richmond, *Virginia*. In their eyes, we truly were from a faraway region, if not another realm.

The Daniel Boone Wilderness Trail, a self-guided driving tour with suggested stops along the way, stretches from Kingsport, Tennessee, through Cumberland Gap, a natural break in the mountains where Virginia, Kentucky, and Tennessee converge. We pick up the trail at Gate City, on US 58, and make our first stop, 15 miles later, at Natural Tunnel, declared the "eighth wonder of the world" by William Jennings Bryan. He might have moved it into the Top Five had the park's chairlift been around back then. The chairlift, when operating, makes it easy to travel from the visitor center

The **Cumberland Gap**, a rare break in the Appalachian Mountains, fueled the beginning of America's great migration west. In 1750, Dr. Thomas Walker, a surveyor, became the first white man to explore the Gap, which had been known to American Indians for generations as a route to western hunting grounds. However, his name takes a backseat in history—except in Virginia's **Lee County**, where a high school is named in his honor—to Daniel Boone who blazed a road to the Gap in 1775.

Soon, settlers seeking land and fresh starts flooded through this new gateway to the west. From 1780–1810, more than 200,000 people passed through the Gap to Kentucky and beyond. The Gap declined in importance in the later 1800s as canals, railroads, and better wagon roads crossed the Appalachians.

By the mid-1900s, a paved highway, US 25E, passed through the Gap, following the course of the original trail itself. Besides spoiling the historical spirit of the Gap, as well as its natural setting, the winding road was a motorist's nightmare and a frequent scene of accidents. With the completion of the Cumberland Gap Tunnel in 1996 and the removal of the old roadway, the restoration of the Gap is under way. Visitors can once again walk in the footsteps of Boone and see for themselves, up close, the famous V-notch in the mountains that opened the door to westward expansion.

COAL TRAINS STILL RUN THROUGH NATIONAL TUNNEL

down to the "floor" of the park and a 500-foot boardwalk that leads visitors to an up-close view of the tunnel. A walking trail from the visitor center also goes to the tunnel.

Carved from limestone and bedrock by thousands of years of flowing water, the tunnel is 850 feet long and 100 feet high. Stock Creek runs through the tunnel. So does the railroad. Coal-carrying trains rumble through the

SIDE TRACKS

If you have time, sign up for a **cave tour at Cumberland Cap**. Our small group gathers at the **Daniel Boone Visitor Information Center**, a couple of miles east of the main visitor center, just off US 58, near Cumberland Gap, Tennessee. Two knowledgeable and entertaining young park rangers will lead the way.

We walk into the restored Gap to reach the mouth of the cave, where the year-round temperature is 59 degrees. It's also always dark. We carry flashlights provided by the rangers. We spend two hours in the cave, moving from chamber to chamber and level to level. We see bats and salamanders. We duck a lot, passing through places with low clearances the rangers have given names like Tall Man's Misery. One long, steep set of steps is dubbed The Ultimate Thighmaster. Besides knowing what they're talking about, the rangers also are very good-humored.

One also can sing. Lucas Wilder, who grew up in Ewing, breaks into song in the Music Room, a chamber with amazing acoustics. So, there we stand, in the dark, as Wilder sings a capela, a haunting country classic, "Long Black Veil." The cave is stone-silent except for Wilder. Spellbound, no one else even breathes loudly.

We see Cleopatra's Pool, a lovely, still reservoir, as well as quirky formations that look like fried eggs, strips of bacon, and the Pillar of Hercules, all the result of centuries of relentless dripping of mineral-laden water. Near the end of the tour, we find Civil War-era graffiti—soldiers having spent time in the cave, which, perhaps, was used in that era as a temporary hospital.

Walking through the cave is moderately strenuous, tight in spots, abruptly vertical in others, but no belly-crawling is required. The footing is generally quite good, a walkway having been laid when the cave was a privately owned tourist attraction earlier in the twentieth century.

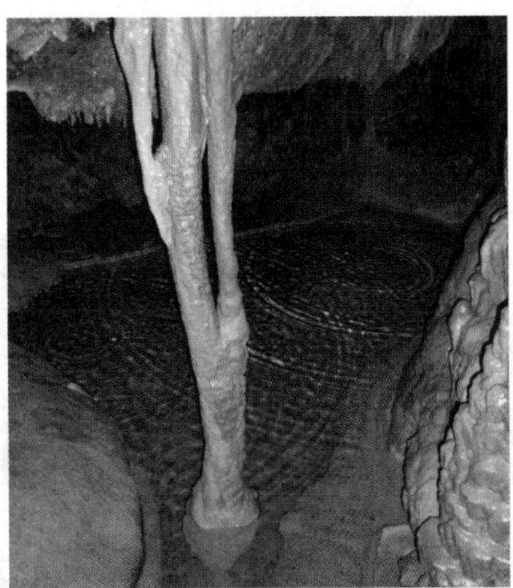

But here's what I really like: the genuine enthusiasm and affection the rangers show for their work. When we're out of the cave, I ask Wilder about growing up in this part of the world. He loves this place, he says, and acknowledged he even sheds "a little tear" whenever he sees the WELCOME TO LEE COUNTY sign.

It means he's home.

A CAVE TOUR AT CUMBERLAND GAP TAKES VISITORS PAST CLEOPATRA'S POOL AND OTHER NATURAL ATTRACTIONS

tunnel several times a day; passenger trains ceased operation years ago. If you like loud noise, you'll love standing on the observation deck near the mouth of the tunnel as a train comes through. And if you like feeling small, you'll love looking up at the 400-foot-high cliff walls, trees perched precariously along the edge.

Elsewhere in the park, find the Wilderness Road Blockhouse, a re-created structure representative of gathering places for pioneers headed to Cumberland Gap. The park also offers hiking trails, a swimming pool, and an amphitheater for live music.

We stay a couple of nights at Appalachian Mountain Cabins, a complex of four cabins on a hillside just a few miles from the park (on a very narrow road, it should be noted). The cabin is great and the setting is terrific. The steep gravel drive to the cabin challenged our old minivan a bit, but it all works out in the end. A nice place to stay in an area without a lot of conventional lodging choices.

Back on US 58, we head to Duffield, a small community with shopping and gas stations, and then on to Stickleyville and Dot. Yes, Dot.

Dot is a dot on the map and little more. My first time here, my companion

FROM PINNACLE OVERLOOK IN CUMBERLAND GAP NATIONAL HISTORICAL PARK, YOU CAN LOOK INTO KENTUCKY, TENNESSEE, AND VIRGINIA

THE BLOCKHOUSE AT NATURAL TUNNEL STATE PARK IS A REPLICA OF THE STRUCTURES THAT SERVED AS ASSEMBLY POINTS FOR THOUSANDS WHO USED THE WILDERNESS TRAIL TO VENTURE WESTWARD INTO KENTUCKY

and I saw the "Dot" sign that signals to motorists they have arrived. We thought we'd drive to the end of town, find the "Dot" sign for eastbound traffic, turn around, and come back. Except we found no town. Just a convenience store, a few scattered homes, and a business or two. We never saw the other "Dot" sign—until we turned around, came back, and found it on the other side of the first signpost. Hello and goodbye, back to back. Great fun. I've liked Dot ever since.

Little more than a crossroads, Dot once had its own post office, but it's long gone. Now Dot is simply a wide spot in the road, a place to stop and get gas or a cold drink on your way to the Gap. A little beyond the Dot intersection, where US 58 and US 421 meet, you will find Axe Handle Distilling, a family-run distillery where bourbon, rye whiskey, gin, and vodka are produced. The porch is open for rocking and bluegrass picking, the bar for samples and mixed drinks.

WAGON WHEELS LEAN AGAINST A WALL IN WILDERNESS ROAD STATE PARK

After Dot, we see a gleaming example of economic revitalization: a $100 million, high-security federal prison that means jobs and revenue in a region that has lost both in recent years. Just the same, we maintain a steady speed and don't stop.

Next up is Jonesville, a town of fewer than 1,000 residents and the county seat of Lee County, named for Light Horse Harry Lee, a Virginia governor and father of General Robert E. Lee. Jonesville has a few shops and a Confederate cemetery. Civil War reenactors gather every June for a reenactment of the 1864 Battle of Jonesville, which the Confederates won.

The road opens up as we head west from Jonesville for the last 30 miles to the Gap. Tobacco fields and rolling, green pastureland set against a dramatic, seamless mountain backdrop make for as pretty a drive as you'll find anywhere.

Part of the appeal of this stretch of road is the bucolic nature of it and its lack of commercialization. The flip side: There aren't a lot of places to eat. An occasional diner in one of the small communities just off the main road could be an option.

But for a slightly different dining experience, check out The Dutch Treat Country Store in Rose Hill, a small family-run grocery and bakery with the best sandwiches in the valley. They have interesting cheeses and Amish butter. The freshly baked breads and pastries are excellent, too. I *highly* recommend the pumpkin roll.

"This is an amazing valley," says Sam Yoder, who operates The Dutch Treat, when I stopped in for the aforementioned pumpkin roll, a rolled-up pumpkin sheet cake filled with cream cheese and dusted with powdered sugar. "There's so much history here."

Down the road, just past Ewing, we come to Wilderness Road State Park, behind a split-rail fence along US 58. Drive the park road behind the visitor center to find Martin's Station, a replica of a frontier fort that serves as a living-history museum. A relatively easy 8-mile multipurpose trail, called the Wilderness Road Trail, bisects the park and connects it with the campground at Cumberland Gap National Historical Park. A small herd of bison roams a nearby pasture.

We didn't have time to walk the entire Wilderness Road Trail but did hike several short trails within the park. I'd like to return and walk or bike all the way to the Gap on the Wilderness Road Trail, which links to more than 50 miles of other trails at the Gap. We snacked at one of the park picnic tables—we like snacking on our hikes—and enjoyed visiting the reconstructed Martin's Station, the outdoor living history museum depicting life on Virginia's frontier in 1775.

Virginia runs out before we get to the Gap, although the road doesn't. Staying on our same path, we cross briefly into Tennessee and then enter the Cumberland Gap Tunnel, which was built in the 1990s to replace the twisting, mountain road that actually followed the original Wilderness Trail along the edge of the mountain. The 4,600-foot tunnel goes through the mountain. When we come out the other end, we are in Kentucky. Take the next exit to reach Cumberland Gap National Historical Park and the main visitor center.

To appreciate the history that came through here, you should spend some time viewing the exhibits and films at the center. You will certainly want to drive the steep, twisting 4-mile-long Skyland Road to the Pinnacle Overlook, which affords a spectacular view of the three states. On the paved walkway leading to the observation deck, you can do something less dazzling but perhaps more satisfying: straddle two states. A painted white stripe marks the spot where Virginia and Kentucky meet. There's even a bench if you'd like to sit and savor the moment. We spend the day at the park, hiking a couple of the other trails, among more than 85 miles of trails within the park.

If you decide to stay the night, the nice little town of Cumberland Gap, Tennessee, just east of the tunnel, has several lodging options and a couple of restaurants, as well as a few shops. A few miles west of the tunnel, you'll find Middlesboro, Kentucky, which seemingly has every motel and restaurant chain known to man, and a Walmart, too.

It's a far cry, of course, from the pioneer days. But before you go, take the time to stand in the restored Gap, gaze off in the distance, and then down at your feet, knowing you're walking in the footsteps of Daniel Boone and hundreds of thousands of others who traveled the same path as they headed west to build America.

"This," a park ranger told me, "is ground zero for history."

IN THE AREA

Accommodations

APPALACHIAN MOUNTAIN CABINS, 126 Appalachian Drive, Duffield. Call 276-940-1155. Website: www.amcabins.com. Complex of four cabins on a scenic hillside, near Natural Tunnel State Park.

CUMBERLAND GAP INN, 630 Brooklyn Street, Cumberland Gap, TN. Call 423-869-3996. Website: cumberlandgaphotel.com. Motel within walking distance of shops and attractions.

OLDE MILL BED & BREAKFAST, 603 Pennlyn Street, Cumberland Gap, TN. Call 423-869-0868. Website: www.oldemillinnbnb.com. An 1889 mill and 1750s cabin make this a historic place to sleep.

Attractions and Recreation

CUMBERLAND GAP NATIONAL HISTORICAL PARK, US25E South, Middlesboro, KY. Call 606-248-2817. Website: www.nps.gov/cuga. History, hiking, camping, cave tours.

NATURAL TUNNEL STATE PARK, 1420 Natural Tunnel Parkway, Duffield. Call 276-940-2674. Website: www.dcr.virginia.gov/state-parks/natural-tunnel. Hiking, chairlift to tunnel, amphitheater, camping, and cabins.

WILDERNESS ROAD STATE PARK, 8051 Wilderness Road, Ewing. Call 276-445-3065. Website: www.dcr.virginia.gov/state-parks/wilderness-road. History, hiking, biking, picnicking. Primitive group camping available.

Dining

CAMPUS DRIVE-IN, 432 Kane Street, Gate City. Call 276-386-3702. Website: www.explorescottcountyva.org/dining/the-campus-drive-in. Burgers, fries, onion rings. Nothing fancy, a local institution.

THE DUTCH TREAT COUNTRY STORE, 133 Deroyal Industries Road, Rose Hill. Website: www.thedutchtreat.biz. Sandwiches, baked goods, hams, and jams.

Other Contacts

DANIEL BOONE WILDERNESS TRAIL. Website: www.danielboonetrail.com. Maps, attractions, links.

MIDDLESBORO, KENTUCKY. Website: bellcountytourism.com.

LEE COUNTY TOURISM, 33640 Main Street, Jonesville. Call 276-346-7766. Website: www.ilovelee.org.

Index

Italics indicate illustrations

LEFT: CHESTNUT CREEK FALLS, NEW RIVER TRAIL STATE PARK

C

M

U

V

W

Y

Z